# BULLS BEARS AND OTHER BEASTS

Santosh Nair is Executive Editor at CNBCTV18.com, with over two decades of experience in business journalism. He began his career at *Business Standard* in 1997 as a stock market reporter, a stint that gave him a ringside view of the structural changes sweeping the Indian financial markets. His daily column 'Street Signs', documenting the major deals of the day, market trends and related chatter, was hugely popular with the investor community. As Markets Editor of *The Economic Times* from 2006 to 2010, he shed light on some of the savvy but highly reclusive investors of that era through well-researched profiles, besides writing on institutions, trends and various shenanigans. As Editor of Moneycontrol.com from 2011 to 2020, Santosh helped build a vibrant newsroom, leading the transition from a largely data- and tools-driven destination to a full-service digital financial publishing platform. Santosh lives in Mumbai with his wife and two daughters.

# BULLS BEARS AND OTHER BEASTS

## A STORY OF THE INDIAN STOCK MARKET

SANTOSH NAIR

PAN

First published 2016 by Pan
This fifth anniversary edition published 2021 by Pan
an imprint of Pan Macmillan Publishing India Private Limited
707 Kailash Building
26 K. G. Marg, New Delhi – 110 001
www.panmacmillan.co.in

Pan Macmillan, The Smithson, 6 Briset Street, London EC1M 5NR
Associated companies throughout the world
www.panmacmillan.com

ISBN 978-93-90742-56-1



7 9 8



Typeset by R. Ajith Kumar, New Delhi
Printed and bound in India by Replika Press Pvt. Ltd.

*To anyone and everyone who thinks that the stock market is a substitute for hard work*

# Contents

# Foreword

The book you are about to read is a remarkable story of bulls, bears and other beasts such as wolves (in sheep's clothing) who devour herds of sheep-like investors.

The protagonist is a 'fictional' character called Lala who is a close witness to much of the circus of the Indian stock markets over twenty-seven years – from the end of 1988 till late 2015. Lala, who comes from a poor family, starts his career in 1998 as a clerk in the back office of a broker at Bombay Stock Exchange, then becomes a stockjobber, and eventually a wealthy broker with a significant net worth.

Over the course of these decades, Lala takes us through a riveting journey – recounting many of India's financial scandals, political and economic upheavals, a war with Pakistan, the growth of India's IT industry, the rise and fall of many companies, their stock market valuations and the reputations of both business owners, managers and 'market men'.

The book also chronicles the modernization of India's stock exchanges – from the days of paper trading, 1.5 per cent brokerage rates, an open outcry system of price setting with very high bid-offer spreads, to the modern paperless trading without the need of a stock exchange 'trading floor', short settlement cycles and wafer-thin bid-offer spreads and brokerage rates.

We also learn a great deal about human nature – how people game systems, how regulators are almost always behind the crooks who keep evolving faster, how the innocent and the foolish are parted from their money by these crooks, and how perverse incentives in the broking business, investment banking and money management often result in clients getting short-changed

Take, for example, this excerpt from the book, which reflects on what happened in the 1994 IPO bubble and which made me wonder about what's happening in India right now:

> *Merchant banker: Sir, would you like to raise Rs 10–15 crore?*
> *Promoter: Not at the moment.*
> *Merchant banker: But markets won't be as hot for long. You must raise money when it is available.*
> *Promoter: What is the rate of interest?*
> *Merchant banker: There is none.*
> *Promoter: Really? But I still have to return the money at some point, right?*
> *Merchant banker: No, and that is the beauty of it.*
> *Promoter (suspiciously): You mean, I get the money, I don't have to pay interest, and I don't have to return it. Is that what you are saying?*
> *Merchant banker: Exactly.*
> *Promoter: You have got me interested.*

As I read this exchange, I was reminded of countless IPO bubbles of the past starting from the South Sea Bubble (chronicled in Charles Mackay's *Extraordinary Popular Delusions and the Madness of Crowds)* right up to the one building up in India as I write this.

Dozens of companies that raised money in the 1994 IPO bubble disappeared and I can say with some confidence that the outcome won't be very different this time either. The outcome is *never* different.

Human nature does not change. Greed and envy, fear and hubris, and overconfidence have all characterized us for millions of years and these innate traits are not going away. That's why we will also have scams and booms, busts and crooks, and sheep-like people and wolf-like people. This is the way it's always been, and this is the way it will always be. A Harshad Mehta will be replaced by a Ketan Parikh and an MS Shoes by some other company. Nothing changes, except the numbers and the characters.

This book provides quite an accurate profile of many such people who were, or are, as real as you and me. You will learn about the mechanisms used by the 'wolves' – front running, insider trading, stock price manipulations and promotional behaviour of promoters (what else can we expect them to do except to 'promote' their stocks?) of many companies who collected money from IPOs and then vanished (SEBI has recognized and investigated these 'vanishing companies'.) As you read Lala's story, you must ask three questions:

1. Will this happen again?
2. What does this remind me of?
3. Why does this remind me of it?

Pattern recognition is a critical component of understanding how the world really works. Historical books like this one provide ample opportunities to recognize the recurring manifestation of hubris and irrationality that lead to the eventual downfall of people and the organizations they run. *Bulls, Bears and Other Beasts* outlines many such patterns.

The key details of the major incidents covered in the book are factually accurate because of a peculiar habit of the author's – peculiar at least for modern times. Santosh, who has spent the last twenty-five years as a career journalist (he is presently Executive Editor at CNBCTV18.com and previously was Markets Editor at *The Economic Times* and Editor of Moneycontrol.com), has been maintaining a daily diary for many years. In this diary, he meticulously records details about important events, interactions and other experiences of his day. (Many years ago, when I first met him over breakfast, he had paused his eating several times during the meal, to make notes in his diary.)

It's a wonderful habit which, I think, enormously contributed towards the creation of this book. It seems that Santosh, the author, created Lala, the protagonist, to make him tell us what the author had been writing in his diaries all these years. In that sense, Lala is not a fictional character at all!

The book conveys what we need to know about the *grim* side of Indian equity markets. But there is a *bright* side too. When the events in this story took place – towards the end of 1998 – Sensex was at the 3,000 mark. By the time the book ends, that is in the last leg of 2015, Sensex had crossed 26,000 points. As I write this foreword, in September 2021, the index has topped 59,000.

The bright side is this: none of those scams, stock price manipulations, the political and economic crisis, war and numerous types of schemes of unethical behaviour by market participants described so well in the book prevented a staggering amount of wealth creation for long-term investors in Indian equity markets. All they had to do was to invest in equities (while exercising adequate caution) and just sit tight and ignore all the circus that takes place inside the stock market. In the aggregate, real wealth was made, not by the crooks, but by long-term investors, who overlooked the cacophony of the stock market and instead focused on the fundamentals of businesses, and that of India.

Perhaps it's time for Santosh to write another book. This time about the bright side of investing in Indian equities; perhaps about all the ingredients required for wealth creation in public markets for long-term investors – entrepreneurship and innovation, growth and profitability, and good governance. But even if he does not write that book, I encourage you to read this one just to be aware of the dangers of being a participant in Indian equity markets and to not become a sheep fated to be devoured by a wolf.

**Sanjay Bakshi**
Distinguished Adjunct Professor
Flame University
September 2021

The bright side is that many of those scams, stock price manipulations, the political and economic crises, war and natural [illegible] or other types of unethical behaviour by market participants described so well in the book, prevented a staggering amount of wealth creation for long term investors in Indian equity markets. All they had to do was to invest in equities (while exercising adequate caution) and just [illegible] ignore all the chaos that takes place around the stock market. In the long run real wealth was made not by the crooks, but by long term investors who rode the compounding of the stock market and focused on the fundamentals of businesses and trust of [illegible].

Perhaps it is time for Sanjiv to write another book. This time it should be a [illegible] investing in India, [illegible] perhaps about all the ingredients required for wealth creation in public markets. The [illegible] the [illegible] and [illegible] growth and [illegible] and good governance. [illegible] book? [illegible] to read this one first to be aware of the dangers of being [illegible] in Indian equity markets and [illegible].

Sanjay Bakshi
[illegible] Adjunct Professor
[illegible] University
September 2021

# 1

# A Troubled Adolescence

My name is Lalchand – Lal to friends who knew me at school and college, and Lala to friends and acquaintances in the stock market. I was born in 1968 in a nondescript nursing home in Bhandup, a suburb of Mumbai. Father, or Bauji, as I called him, worked at the Bhandup factory of the engineering firm Guest Keen Williams as a plant technician till his retirement in 1992.

My parents were originally from Jaipur, and had moved to Mumbai under difficult circumstances, the details of which are not relevant to the story I am about to narrate. At the time of my birth, they were staying in the Shivram Singh chawl, off the arterial Jangal Mangal Road in Bhandup West. Bauji was just about able to make ends meet in those days, and having to provide temporary lodging for job-seeking relatives from Jaipur strained his meagre resources further. His generosity irked Ma at times, as it would fall to her to manage the house on a shoestring monthly budget.

I got into bad company early on – not my fault entirely, when you consider the environment I was exposed to in the chawl, located as it was in one of the crime-infested suburbs of the city. But looking back, I feel I was always inclined to get on the wrong side of the law, despite the decent upbringing my parents provided me.

I studied in National Education Society, among the better schools in Bhandup at the time, and well known for its Hitler-like principal whose very sight had the boys running for cover. Bauji had managed my admission through a well-connected friend of his.

When I was twelve, we moved into a one-room kitchen flat in a newly constructed building not far from our chawl. Bauji had to really stretch himself financially to buy the flat. But he was determined to move out of the chawl, not so much out of any desire to move up the social ladder as much as from the realization that the chawl was not a place where his children should grow up. He was aware that I was moving around in wrong company.

The change of locality made little difference to my delinquent ways. By the time I was in the ninth standard, I had already tasted hard liquor and had taken a liking to the occasional cigarette. My buddies at school were Arthur and Shankar, both a year senior to me, but two years older in age, having flunked the ninth standard. Arthur was a violent boy, always spoiling for a brawl. Shankar was cool-headed, but the strongest of us and also the cruellest.

Shankar used to moonlight for Babu, brother of municipal corporator Kim Bahadur Thapa who was later killed in a gangwar in 1991. I was taller than most boys my age and of decent build too. But more importantly, I had what Shankar used to call 'daring'. Looking back, I shudder at the crazy things I did in those years.

Shankar ran petty errands for Babu, which meant intimidating hawkers who did not pay up, keeping a close watch on or beating up people at Babu's command, buying him groceries and other such things. Arthur and I assisted Shankar in his assignments.

I was an average student but was good at Maths. It was Bauji's cherished desire to see me become an engineer. He had not studied beyond the twelfth standard, but had a good technical bent of mind and was an expert at repairing gadgets, from radios to kitchen taps.

'You know, *beta*, seeing me fix a fault at the factory, trainee engineers often ask which engineering college I am from. I tell them that I am not an engineer, but some day my son will become one,' he said more than once at the dinner table.

But gradually, his hopes faded as word of my exploits slowly got to him. As with every father, there was the initial disbelief when he learnt of my misdeeds.

I was in standard ten when my father smelt alcohol on me. He had long suspected it but the reality unsettled him. Later that night I heard him tell Ma that unless he took some drastic steps, I would ruin my life and theirs too. What probably helped him stay sane through the trouble I was causing him was that my brother Satish and sister Anju were shaping up well academically.

Within a month of the alcohol episode, Bauji sold off the flat in Bhandup, and we moved into a rented house in Dombivli. I was halfway through my last school year, but Bauji had decided that I was not to set foot in Bhandup so long as he could help it. Using some connections, he managed to get me admission in the South Indian Association High School in Dombivli West.

Our moving house caused more inconvenience to my father than to me, since he now had to commute more than half an hour in a crowded local train to reach his factory, whereas previously it took him less than ten minutes by a BEST bus.

The new school was not to my liking, but I had little say in the matter. An overwhelming majority of the students were south Indian, and so were the staff. There was a bully or two in every class, and some *mawaali* types as well, but they were a far cry from the Shankars and Arthurs I had got to know so well.

I was slow when it came to making new friends, and perhaps that helped me focus on my studies. I scored 71 per cent in my SSC, which even in those days was not good enough to ensure admission to the science course in any of the reputed colleges. Not that I was keen on taking up Science, but it had been my father's dream to see me become an engineer. But by now Bauji too had realized he would not be able to pay the hefty donations that almost every decent engineering college – barring the top two or three – demanded. He had some money left from the sale of our Bhandup house, but it was too much of a gamble for him to stake that money on my academic career.

So that Bauji did not nurse any false hopes for me and set himself up for further disappointment, I confessed to him that I lacked the aptitude for science and would be more comfortable studying commerce, or any of the arts subjects.

He did not try to change my mind, and after consulting some friends and relatives, advised me to take up commerce. Truth be told, Bauji's decision to shift to Dombivli was not a sound one. It could have easily backfired on him but for an unexpected twist of events.

Because of massive real estate development in the suburb, Dombivli soon became a thriving ground for thugs and other antisocial elements. Street fights were common, and so was extortion in public view. Disputes over land led to the rise of organized gangs, and rival groups periodically took on each other in broad daylight with crude revolvers, hockey sticks and cycle chains. In many ways, Dombivli was turning out to be worse than Bhandup on the crime graph.

For somebody like me, who could be provoked easily and was not averse to violence, it was a struggle to stay out of trouble and resist the lure of bad company. I had learnt a few things during my association with Shankar and Arthur, and more than once it crossed my mind to moonlight for one of the local dadas of Dombivli.

But the enormous daily inconvenience that Bauji was enduring just to keep me on the straight and narrow somehow stirred my conscience. That Satish and Anju still looked up to me embarrassed me, and yet I was pressured by what I thought was my responsibility towards them. Torn inwardly, I kept to a small group of friends and to my studies in college.

I was in the twelfth standard when Bauji had an accident at the factory that left him physically disabled for a while. It would be ten months before Bauji was able to get back to work. The last two and a half months of his confinement at home were without pay. That period was very tough on all of us, emotionally as well as financially; at one stage, we were not sure if his foot would recover fully to enable him to resume work as before.

This incident snuffed out whatever little temptation I had left for murky adventures. The last thing I wanted to do was add to the problems at home.

I worked as an assistant in a revolving library called Yogayog near Dombivli railway station for some months. The money was not much, but every rupee counted at that time. The best thing about the job was it introduced me to the world of books. Until then, I had not really enjoyed reading. I used to put in four hours daily at the library, and with enough spare time on my hands, gradually took to reading. I began with the thrillers and graduated to the classics. My reading habit that I accidentally picked up grew stronger over the years and was to help me immensely in my career in the stock market.

An attempt to seek my fortune in the Gulf after graduation ended in disappointment. Bauji had paid a recruitment agent Rs 15,000 for a clerical position for me in a trading firm in Dubai, but the agent never delivered on his promise. Left with little choice, I briefly assumed my old avatar to get him to cough up our money. Of course, unknown to Bauji, because I knew he would have severely disapproved.

I then worked as a trainee accountant in a chemicals firm at Fort for a few months, but the job was not to my liking. However, I could hardly afford to be choosy, given that financially our nose was just above water.

Call it coincidence or the hand of destiny at work, I bumped into Pradeep Mohan, my classmate in college, as I was lunching at my regular food stall one day. We had only been casual acquaintances in college, but we got chatting as though we had been thick friends back then.

Pradeep was working in the back office of a stockbroker, and his job was to maintain client records after the trades were done on the floor of the stock exchange. We caught up over lunch regularly after that first meeting, and a good rapport developed between us. He loved to talk, and I was a good listener. He would paint a vivid picture of the happenings in the stock market for me; about how fortunes were made and lost in a matter of hours, about the guile and the ruthless ways of big brokers, and the sway they held over powerful industrialists. But what caught my attention was his remark that one did not need a fancy degree or even formal education to succeed in the stock market. With a bit of skill, perseverance and, most importantly, luck, there was no limit to the money one could make from trading in shares. On my commute back home, I often reflected on my lunchtime conversations with Pradeep.

# 2

# The Road to Dalal Street

When we had known each other for over a month, I asked Pradeep if he could arrange a job for me at a broker's office. My request seemed to have caught him off guard, and I suspect his initial hesitation may have had to do with the fear of losing a willing listener.

From whatever little I had understood about the stock market from Pradeep, I was clear about one thing – I did not want to work in a broker's back office checking share certificates, settling accounts and shuffling paper. I wanted to be in the midst of the action on the trading floor, shouting orders to buy and sell shares.

At the same time, I was aware that my path to the trading ring would have to start from a broker's back office. I prevailed on Pradeep to get me any job in a broker's office. Seeing my determination, he finally gave in. He seemed to have also sensed that I had bigger things in mind despite a willingness to start small.

'I don't know what big plans you may have in mind, Lal, but don't be reckless,' he told me, after he had secured a job for me with one of the lesser-known brokerage firms.

'There are plenty of rags-to-riches stories on Dalal Street that get talked about often. What does not get publicized as much are the riches-to-rags stories, which far outnumber the success stories. People get carried away, thinking it is easy to make money in the stock market, and learn the truth the hard way,' he said.

I knew Pradeep was speaking the truth, but I did not want to be weighed down by fear of failure so early in my career. If a steady job with a steady salary had been my goal, I would have been content with my job in the chemicals firm.

It was in the dying days of 1988 that I began a new chapter in my professional career. Shares had not caught the imagination of retail investors in a big way yet, though awareness about investing in them was steadily on the rise. Easy money had been made by the lucky few who had subscribed to the initial public offerings of some of the best multinational corporations like Colgate, Hindustan Lever, Cadbury, Ponds and the like in the late 1970s and early 1980s. The market was controlled by a group of powerful brokers who mostly speculated on stocks using their own money. Within this group, a smaller subset had the lion's share of whatever institutional business existed in those days. Other than these brokers, the major players in the market were the domestic institutions – Unit Trust of India being the Big Daddy of them all – and the promoters of companies themselves. In terms of the size of investment corpus, the Life Insurance Corporation was bigger than UTI, but it did not invest in equities as aggressively as UTI did. Foreign institutional investors (FIIs) would start flocking to India in a big way only 1993 onwards.

Brokerage rates were a princely 1.5 per cent at that time, which in some ways seemed justified because of the complications with physical shares. Despite the juicy commissions, brokers were careful about whom they would accept as clients as there were many dubious operators who would sell them fake shares. These would be detected only when the buyer sent them to the company to get them transferred to their ownership. The seller's broker would then have to replace the lot or refund the money to the buyer; and if his client did not oblige, he would have to make good the loss himself. That is why you needed somebody to recommend you to a broker before he would accept you as a client.

Investment based on the fundamentals of a company was still in its infancy. A big reason for this was the lack of sufficient publicly available information on companies. Whatever little information was available was from their balance sheets, which were dated by the time they came into the hands of the shareholders. And few brokerages, even when they were shareholders, sent representatives to the annual general meetings of companies, which were probably the only platform available to shareholders to meet up with managements and quiz them on their business. Still, many brokerages would claim they were the first ones to recommend stocks to their clients based on their meticulous research of companies and their sectors.

A lot of what passed off as 'research' in those days would constitute insider trading today. One heavyweight speculator-cum-investor-cum-broker of that era managed to get a job for his relative in an auto-component firm in which he owned shares and traded in them frequently. The relative would pass on details of the firm's monthly production figures to the broker, who in turn used the information to trade in the stock.

More than stock market professionals, company promoters used to speculate heavily in their own shares, All of them had their favoured brokers, known as 'house brokers', who came to be known as proxies for the promoters in the market even if they were not always trading on their behalf. A skilled market player could observe the size and pattern of trades made by these brokers and figure out if they were acting on behalf of company promoters or other clients.

UTI's business was crucial to the prosperity of any brokerage firm worth its salt. Since UTI dealt in large blocks of shares most of the time, there was good money to be earned by way of commission. But for many unscrupulous brokers, the big money did not lie in commissions; it was to be made by front-running UTI's trades.

Unscrupulous brokers who got buy orders for shares from UTI would first buy some of the same shares for themselves. Naturally, the price of these shares would rise in the market when UTI's orders were getting executed in the market. At this point, these brokers would sell the shares they had bought for themselves at a profit.

If it was a sell order from UTI for a stock, the brokers would short-sell the same stock in their personal capacity. Short selling means selling shares without owning them, in the hope that share prices will fall and that you will be able to buy them back cheap and deliver them to the buyer on the trade settlement day. The brokers would later cover their short positions – that is, buy back the same shares they had sold, but at a lower price – as UTI's sell orders in the market weakened the stock price.

For brokers without orders from UTI, the next best thing to do was to find out what UTI was up to and try to copy those trades. Due to UTI's dominant position, brokers were forever queuing up at its office on Marine Lines in Mumbai after market hours. Many brokers were empanelled with UTI, but the cream of the orders went to a select few. Tales abounded of how some brokers were able to consistently get orders from UTI by giving expensive gifts to the officials in the investments department.

Reliance Industries, ACC, Grasim, Bajaj Auto, Century Textiles, ITC, GE Shipping, Century Enka, Castrol, TELCO (Tata Electric Locomotive Company then, and Tata Motors now), TISCO (Tata Iron and Steel Company), Tata Tea and Tata Chemicals were among the most actively traded stocks of those days.

Nemish Shah, Manu Manek and Ajay Kayan were the high rollers, revered by market players for their ability to make or break a stock. Manu Manek was more feared than respected because he could be downright ruthless to further his business interests. It could be safely said that, as the biggest badla financier on the exchange floor, Manubhai was the final arbiter of the interest rate to be paid by the bulls for carrying forward their trades to the next settlement. He had no qualms about hammering down the price of the very stock he had financed for a bull operator. Manubhai, who was considered something of a mini-stock exchange himself, could quickly figure out a bull operator's capacity to support the stock he was operating. If the operator was weak, Manek would short-sell the stock. And once the operator made a distress sale, Manek would buy back the shares cheaper than he had sold them for, making a tidy profit in the process.

He had an uncanny ability to commit hundreds of trades to memory. While in the ring, he rarely noted down his trades in the *sauda* pad (deal sheet), even though he dealt in multiple stocks. At the end of the day, he would get back to his office and dictate the trades to his clerks.

And he had one more strong point – an excellent rapport with the key officials in the Bombay Stock Exchange (BSE) employees' union. Call it a coincidence, but whenever Manek was in a tight spot over a trade, there would be a flash strike by the employees' union, and the settlement would get extended by a few days, helping him buy time.

Manek was fearless enough – or reckless, as the subsequent turn of events would show – to take on Dhirubhai Ambani by leading a bear raid on the shares of Reliance Industries. The bear cartel heavily short-sold Reliance Industries, aiming to break the stock price. There are two versions of the story, and I am not sure which one is true. One has it that it was a planned operation by Manek to assert to Dhirubhai his hold on the stock market. The other has it that Reliance's treasury department (which deploys the funds of the company in various financial instruments to get the best returns) had borrowed money from Manu Manek to make stock market investments. Manek is said to have goaded his associates to target Reliance shares, saying the company was financially vulnerable. He also made some disparaging remarks about Dhirubhai for good measure.

Bears won the initial round as the stock price flagged under their relentless onslaught. But they had not bargained for an equally fierce counter-attack led by Anand Jain, Dhirubhai's key lieutenant. Jain and his associates took over the positions of the brokers and traders who had bought

Reliance Industries shares, and also themselves bought as many shares as they could from the market. On the other side of these trades was the bear cartel, which had short-sold Reliance shares or sold shares they never owned in the first place. As the share price started to climb because of the demand created by Jain and his associates, the bears tried to get out of their positions by buying shares from the market. But the shares were in short supply, as most of them had been bought up by Jain and company, and the bears' attempts to square up their positions only sent the stock price shooting up further.

The bears thought they could buy time by paying an interest charge to the bulls on settlement day to carry forward their trades to the next settlement. They were still convinced that if they hung on to their positions for a bit longer, the price movement would reverse in their favour. But the 'buyers' of Reliance shares refused the offer of interest payment, and insisted that the bears deliver the shares, fully aware that they would not be able to. Frantic buying by the bears to square up their positions further drove up the stock price. The crisis led to the stock exchange itself being closed for a few days as the bears could not deliver the shares and the bulls would not settle for anything else.

A truce was worked out eventually, but not before a few bears were bankrupted and the legendary Manu Manek forced to eat humble pie.

In comparison with Manubhai, Nemish and Kayan kept a far more low profile. Kayan was more active on the Calcutta Stock Exchange than on the BSE. He was also a dominant player in the opaque world of the money market. Before long, Kayan would be locked in a pitched battle with

Harshad Mehta in both the money and stock markets. It was a tussle that would alter the landscape of the Indian financial markets forever.

As for Nemish Shah, he was slowly making a transition from being a speculator and broker to a value investor, and even playing mentor to some budding speculators, at least one of whom would, down the years, become more famous than his guru. Shah's firm Enam Securities was among the reputed brokerages on BSE. Shah himself had been a protégé of Manu Manek at one time, and had learnt the ropes of the trade from him.

All this while, Harshad Mehta's stars were on the ascent. He was an important player, well known in market circles, but not yet a heavyweight in the same league as Kayan, Shah or Manu Manek.

# 3

# Learning the Nuts and Bolts

The brokerage firm for which I was working was not as inconsequential as I had initially thought. It was just that the owner liked to keep a low profile. And, exactly for this reason, some corporations and institutions preferred to deal with him. I worked in the back office, filling the share transfer deeds for buying clients and following up on deliveries to be made by selling clients. This way, I got to learn exactly who was selling or buying what shares. In the shallow market of those days, this information was valuable, since some of our clients were important players in the market.

My salary as a back office clerk was Rs 2,000 a month, about the same that I earned at my previous job. But I had no doubt that I had chosen the right path, even if it did call for a bit of luck to hit the first milestone I had set for myself.

My job was monotonous, but I did it with utmost dedication as I saw it as a stepping stone to the trading ring where the real action lay. After office hours, I would attempt to make friends with my counterparts in some of the other important brokerage firms. Though I was a reserved person,

I began to realize the importance of being well networked, even if I was starting small.

My hard work was not lost on the owner of the firm, and he felt I could be used better than just as a paper sorter at the back office. A broker could have seven of his dealers in the trading ring, apart from himself. Orders placed by clients over the telephone to the broker's office would be conveyed to the dealers on the trading floor, who would then execute the trades. Before the days of the hotline, brokerage firms had runners who would rush to the trading floor to relay orders.

When one of our dealers quit, I was asked if I would be interested in taking his place. I agreed, taking care not to show my excitement. I knew my boss was testing me out. He liked employees who worked hard but was wary of the overenthusiastic types.

Initially, my job on the floor was to answer the hotline and convey the order details to the senior dealers who would be scouting around for good bargains. For one month I was assigned to a senior, and had to observe him as he negotiated deals with brokers and jobbers.

A jobber is a professional speculator, and buys and sells shares for himself. He does not have any clients. His business is to speculate on which way prices are moving and make a quick profit on it. He does not want to buy shares and keep them for the long term as investors do. But, to do business on the floor of the stock exchange, he needs to have a broker as a sponsor. He shares a part of his profit with the broker under a pre-decided agreement.

You could say that in a way he acts as an agent of the broker. If the jobber defaults on a deal, the broker is held responsible by the stock exchange. Brokers, therefore, choose jobbers with care. Jobbers were an important source of liquidity, and brokers would always deal through them.

In those days, there were 'counters' for individual stocks. Jobbers and brokers dealing in Reliance shares would gather at a certain spot, those dealing in Tata Iron and Steel shares at another spot, and so on. 'A' group shares, in which a buyer or seller could carry forward trades to the next settlement by paying an interest charge known as badla, were called *vaida*. 'B' group shares, which were not eligible for carry-forward, were called *rokda* (cash) since they had to be settled at the end of the fortnightly settlement cycle, either with the positions being squared off or with the shares being delivered.

There was a public address system on every floor of the stock exchange building, on which would be broadcast the prices of mostly A group stocks, and sometimes B group stocks if there were big moves on them, corporate results and other important company announcements. For a price, brokers could get an extension of that system so that they could hear the broadcast sitting in their offices. Brokerages wanting to save on costs would usually station one of their employees in the corridor of the exchange so that they could alert their offices about important announcements.

The trading ring was on the first floor. Outside both the first and second floors were huge blackboards on which an employee of the stock exchange would write down the prices of the most actively traded stocks, updating them every thirty minutes. The official would collate the prices by talking to the main brokers and jobbers to find out what prices they had bought or sold for After he had updated the prices on the blackboard, he would trade places with his colleague who had been broadcasting the prices. That official would then head for the ring and update the blackboard after half an hour.

Around half past five in the evening, the stock exchange would publish the '*bhav* copy', a report listing the high, low and closing prices of the stocks traded that day. It was not done very scientifically, but it was broadly reliable. Its compilation was done by means of a stock exchange official collecting the prices by talking to the brokers and jobbers, and checking their *sauda* pads (which were issued by BSE and bore its stamp) if necessary.

The stock exchange issued only a limited number of *bhav* copies, so there was always a scramble to get them. Some ingenious players found a way to profit from this by taking photocopies of the *bhav* copy and selling them outside the stock exchange for a few rupees.

After trading hours there operated an unofficial market for some of the more liquid stocks. This was called the kerb market and, true to its name, the dealings were conducted on the street outside the stock exchange. The prices in the kerb market would be at a premium or discount based on the closing prices on the stock exchange, depending on the sentiment and events. There were players who specialized in kerb market deals and did not trade much in the regular market. When they did deal in the regular market, it was mostly to put through the trades that were struck over the phone or on the kerb the previous day.

The specialist kerb traders had their representatives on the street where the business was transacted, taking orders from clients. Right outside the erstwhile Lalit Restaurant on Ambalal Doshi Marg, parallel to Dalal Street, was where the kerb deals were conducted. Activity on the kerb would rise to a feverish pitch during market-moving events. During such times, it was near impossible to navigate the sea of humanity on that street without being pushed around.

Of all the players in the stock market, it was the jobber whose role fascinated me the most. I would closely observe them as my seniors negotiated trades with them. A jobber helped create liquidity in a stock by offering two-way quotes and also helped in price discovery. He took on the risk, confident that he would be able to sell whatever he bought and buy back whatever he sold. But for this breed of players, it would have been difficult for genuine buyers and sellers to transact with ease.

A jobber would buy from you at a rate lower than what he would sell to you for, and the difference or 'spread' as it was known, would be his profit. The spread quoted by the jobber would depend on the quantity of shares you wanted to buy from him or sell to him – the smaller the quantity, the less the spread, and the bigger the quantity, the wider the spread. A jobber had to ask for a higher spread while dealing in big quantities since the risk he took was higher.

To be a successful jobber, one had to be very good at mental arithmetic. If you were jobbing in more than one or two stocks, then your skills needed to be even sharper. That is because you were carrying an inventory of shares at all times, irrespective of whether you were long (had a buy position) or short (had a sell position) on a stock.

It was not just enough to remember the number of shares you were long or short on; you had to remember the average buying or selling cost of those shares. That in turn would decide the bid-ask spread ('bid' is the price quoted by the buyer and 'ask' by the seller) a jobber quoted.

Jobbers would note down their deals on their *sauda* pads, but sometimes, when there was frenzied trading, a jobber would be doing trades in rapid succession and not get enough time to write all of his deals down. He could also be trading in more than one stock, making his task even more complex. It was in these situations that a jobber's skills were tested to the maximum. I knew of expert jobbers who could memorize their inventory and the average price of trades in nearly two dozen stocks without having to check their deal pads.

A good jobber also had to be a skilled psychologist. It required him to be able to size up a prospective counterparty and gauge whether he was a likely buyer or seller. His profit margin would hinge on his ability at this. No counterparty would reveal whether, and how much, he wanted to buy or sell. All he would do was ask for quotes from the jobber.

A typical conversation between the two would run on these lines:

'What is the quote for Arvind Mills?'

'57-60.' (I will buy from you at 57 and sell to you at 60)

'What quantity is this valid for?'

'500 shares.'

'I want to sell 500 shares.'

'Okay, bought 500 shares from you at 57.'

'Does your quote hold good for another 500?'

'Yes.'

'Okay, I want to sell another 500 shares.'

'Bought 500 from you at 57.'

'I want to sell another 500. What's your quote?'

'56-59.'

'Okay, I am selling 500 more to you.'

'Bought 500 from you at 56.'

'How about 500 more?'

'55-58.'

As the client keeps selling more, the jobber will keep lowering the bid-ask quotes, but not necessarily the spread, which will remain Rs 3. That is because the jobber is now running up a plus-position, and his profit will depend on how cheap he can get the shares.

A good jobber will move in and out of positions as many times as he can for a small profit each time. His aim is to make a decent profit through a series of small profits instead of through one giant trade.

The more heavily traded the stock, the smaller will be the jobber's spread, because there will be plenty of buyers and sellers. For an illiquid stock, the spread would be wider, and at times even outrageous if a jobber enjoyed a near monopoly in that stock. There were different categories of jobbers, depending on the risk they were willing to take.

A jobber also had to have the instinct to figure out who the ultimate buyer or seller of the shares he dealt in was likely to be. Sometimes the counterparty would have information the jobber was not privy to, and the jobber might end up buying or selling a stock, unaware that the die was loaded against him.

A broker transacting with a jobber could be acting on his own behalf, or on behalf of a retail client, an institution or even the promoter of the company whose shares he was trading in. When a promoter is behind a deal, he may not necessarily be capitalizing on some inside information. But if he is, then the jobber would likely be in for trouble.

A jobber was always in demand because brokers preferred to deal with him rather than with each other. Since jobbers played for small profit margins by trading as many times as possible, brokers had the comfort that they would not be overcharged. Most jobbers had to get out of their positions quickly enough, even if it meant taking a smaller profit, since their ability to absorb losses was limited. Rarely did they carry positions to the next day.

There was an unwritten rule that brokers would not try to make a big profit at the expense of the jobber because that could ruin him. At the same time, the jobber too had to respect the confidentiality of the broker dealing with him. If a broker was buying on behalf of a promoter using some inside information or buying a huge block of shares for an institution, he would, after the trade, casually tell the jobber something like, 'Don't keep your position open for too long,' or 'Take your profit and move on quickly.'

This meant that more buying or selling was coming and that the price could see a sharp move. Of course, the broker had to trust the jobber enough to let him in on such information. An honest jobber would then try to close out his position quickly and not take up a position on the same side as the broker so as to profit from the information.

Brokers looking to buy or sell large blocks were often at the mercy of jobbers, and it was to the credit of the jobbing community that a great majority of them did not misuse this power. As mentioned earlier, the quote offered by a jobber was valid only for a certain quantity of shares. Beyond that quantity, a buyer or seller would have to move on to the next jobber or trust the same jobber's ability to source the extra shares or dispose of the remaining shares, as the case may be.

There was a dangerous and hated breed of jobbers called 'robbers'. Though they were in a minority, they were financially strong and had the wherewithal to hold on to large positions. The code of honour and unwritten rules among trading members mattered little to these 'robbers', whose only motive was to earn maximum profit even if it came at the expense of their clients.

Despite knowing the 'robbers' were dishonest, brokers often had to deal with these characters for buying or selling large blocks of shares. If a broker was looking to buy a big chunk of shares, the 'robber' would corner as much of the same stock as he could, to sell to the broker for an exorbitant profit. Similarly, if the broker wanted to sell a big lot of shares, the 'robber' would sell ahead of him at a high price, and then buy the shares cheap from the broker.

Two such 'robbers', AS and PS, had earned notoriety for their practice of exploiting the counterparty at every opportunity. Funnily, AS and PS did not trust each other either. Occasionally, they would buy from and sell shares to each other. I was told that they would peek into each other's *sauda* pads to ensure that the correct details had been entered. And yet, many brokers dealt with them once in a while because AS and PS could procure or dispose of large blocks of shares. And because the duo had deep pockets and were big risk takers too, they could hold on to those positions for a few days or even weeks, till they found another counterparty to square up the trades.

Despite the combined curses of many a client weighing on them, AS and PS have done very well for themselves. Karma is yet to pay them a visit as I write this story.

---

The trades done on the floor of the exchange had to be entered in the *sauda* pad. Every sheet in the *sauda* pad had five columns for five details about the deals – the clearing number of the broker one has dealt with, whether shares were bought or sold, the name of the stock, the quantity of shares, and the price at which the deal was done. Disputes would arise if one broker erred in recording the quantity of shares or the nature of the transaction (buy or sell) in his *sauda* pad. The stock exchange would then issue an objection memo, known as the *vaanda kaapli,* to the two members and ask them to sort out their disagreement. There was a deadline for resolution of the dispute, and the two parties would meet face to face to come to an agreement. In the majority of the cases, the two parties would know each other fairly well, so the resolution was rarely acrimonious. Sometimes you had to give an inch and sometimes you would get an inch.

Looking back, the manner in which disputes were settled in those days appears laughable. Sometimes, the broker who was in the right would produce witnesses who had been standing next to them as the disputed trade was being done. The other broker, if unable to give counter-evidence, would have to accept his mistake.

The colour of the *sauda* pad itself contained information about the traders. Broker-owners had pink *sauda* pads, while their employees and jobbers had blue ones. If the two parties failed to arrive at an agreement, the pink *sauda* pad would prevail, more often than not, since a broker was accorded a higher weightage in the caste system of the stock exchange.

Though none of these methods were foolproof, they worked pretty well most of the time for market players to trust the system.

# 4

# The Tricks of the Trade

I became good friends with Bunty who was managing the treasury operations of a leading non-banking finance company (NBFC) of the time.

One day he came up to me with an unusual request.

'Lala, I want you to find out what jobber M is up to in the Colgate stock.'

'What exactly are you looking for?' I asked him.

'He is accumulating the stock for somebody, and I am keen to know how much he has bought so far. Even better if he can tell you whom he is buying for,' Bunty said.

'M is a seasoned jobber, why would he let me in on the secret?' I asked.

'I am not saying he will tell you straightaway. But there may be a way to get it out of him; I am willing to pay up to Rs 10,000 for the information,' Bunty replied.

'Seems a tough task, because M is quite discreet about his trades, and I have not heard of any underhand dealings by him,' I said.

'Maybe you are right. But figure out a way if you can,' Bunty said.

That he was willing to pay Rs 10,000 for just information told me how crucial the information was to him.

The following day, I hovered around M to sneak a peek at his *sauda* pad. That did not work. I then tried chatting up M when he was a bit free. But M clammed up as soon I casually mentioned Colgate. He rightly suspected that I was up to something. I did not want to play my final card – an outright bribe of Rs 10,000 for revealing his position in Colgate. If the move backfired I would lose face, not just with him, but with his friends and associates too. I again tried to peep into his *sauda* pad, but by now he was certain that I was prying around for information on his Colgate trades. He held his *sauda* pad close to his chest and shot me a dirty look.

The only thing left for me to do was to get back to Bunty and tell him I had been unsuccessful. I knew Bunty would not hold it against me, but I did not want to give up so easily. A stock exchange clerk by the name of Rajesh, with whom I had become friendly of late, travelled most days by the same local as I did after work. I told him about my requirement and promised him money if he could fish out the details. Rajesh promised to do something about it. Two days later he got me the details. I suspect he sourced them from one of the officials who was privy to the scribblings on the jobbers' *sauda* pads. I paid Rajesh Rs 5,000 for the information.

Later that evening I met Bunty over drinks to give him the information he had asked for. He was very pleased and, in fact, surprised that I had managed to get it for him. 'But this is going to cost you, Bunty; I had to pay Rs 20,000 to get this piece of information because I had to tap more than one source,' I told him, after we had downed a couple of pegs.

Bunty took a sip of his drink and gave me a knowing smile. I realized he had caught my bluff. 'No problem, Lala. You shall get the balance,' he said, and then added as an afterthought, 'You are smarter than I thought, you sure will go far.'

It was more a back-handed compliment than a well-meaning one. But I had formed the first of the many rules I would set for myself over the years. Rule number one: if you are dealing straight, you'll get the same from me. And if you are looking to steal . . . I will deal with you likewise.

Bunty came up with similar requests a few more times, and on each occasion Rajesh passed on the required information to me. I did make good money on these deals, but my firm gained too as Bunty routed more of his trades through us.

---

There was an auction system on BSE. When a seller failed to deliver shares on settlement day, his position would be auctioned. BSE would put up the details of the undelivered shares on the notice board, and other brokers could tender shares to the clearing house. Offering brokers would quote a premium to the last traded price, and the lowest offer would be accepted by the clearing house. Sometimes, when a broker or his client defaulted on delivery and the market got wind of it, rivals would push up the price of that stock in the market and then offer shares at the auction at a huge premium.

The AS-PS pair had a near monopoly in this market. The details of the best offers in the auction were not disclosed by the stock exchange. But I learnt from my circle of back office friends that AS-PS managed to put in the winning quotes most of the time, whenever a chunky lot of shares came up for auction. I thought over the possible reasons for this. The straightforward reason could be that they had a robust inventory of shares that allowed them to participate in the auctions more often than other brokers. The other likely reason was that AS and PS got information about rival offers from an insider, allowing them to adjust their offers accordingly.

I had dealt with AS-PS a few times on the floor, and the experience was far from agreeable if not downright unpleasant. Their smugness was annoying, and on a couple of occasions they drove hard bargains, aware that I was trying to get my clients out of a difficult situation.

Once, after having being shortchanged in a deal, I made some nasty remarks about them behind their backs. Word of it got to them somehow, but they seemed more delighted by my discomfiture than offended at my choice of words to describe them.

One day they approached me just as trading for the day ended.

'How was the day, Lala? Made some good money for your clients?' AS greeted me with his usual, oily smile. I found it harder to tolerate AS's fake humility than his partner's brusqueness.

'Could have been better,' I replied, knowing they were getting at something else.

'Still sore with us for the way we got the better of you in the last deal?' AS said, trying to rub it in.

I felt my temper rising but had to keep it in check. After all, they were powerful players.

'You should be a bit more sporting, son, you have a long way to go and lots to learn; more importantly, you should be respectful of your seniors,' AS went on, in as patronizing a tone as he could assume.

'I have the highest respect for you both, in fact you both are my role models. I hope to become like you someday,' I said with a smile, giving as good as I got.

'Arre Lala, you say one thing to our face and something else behind our back. Just because you were not smart enough to get a good price from us for Ambuja, you think we are **###%^ about who will go to the extent of selling our own mothers for an extra profit? Isn't that what you are going around telling people about us?' AS said, still smiling.

'I think somebody is misinforming you. I don't recollect having said anything like that,' I said with a straight face.

It was now PS's turn to needle me.

'If you said that, be man enough to admit it. Even otherwise, it doesn't matter what you think of us. There are too many amateurs like you who don't know the first thing about trading and go around whining when they are beaten,' he said, resting his palm on my shoulder. The tone in which he spoke suggested he would have loved to punch me in the face. I bristled, but tried hard to keep my wits about me.

After that incident, I kept away from them as far as possible. The few times we ran into each other in the ring, it was an effort for us to be mutually civil. PS would glower at me and AS would have a mocking grin ready for me.

But I could not live down the humiliating exchange I had had with them. And when I heard about the domination

AS-PS enjoyed in the delivery auction market, I sensed an opportunity to get under their skin. To cut a long story short, I managed to befriend an official in that department using Rajesh's network.

The offers for the auction were submitted in a sealed envelope to the concerned department of the stock exchange.

I went up to my boss and told him that I had figured out a way for our clients as well as the firm to make good money by tendering shares in the auction. Our clients had been regularly participating in the auction process, but with limited success. I did not tell my boss how I planned to swing things in our favour. All I told him was that it would cost money. He trusted me well now, and instructed the accountant to give me up to Rs 10,000 whenever I asked for it.

My contact in the department would tip me off about the offers. I was smart enough not to be greedy and draw attention to myself. I would select two or three stocks that offered us a good chance to make a neat profit, and would quote offers accordingly. Twice, I quoted 10 paise below offers put in by AS and twice I did that with PS's offers too. On each of these occasions, there was a large chunk of shares involved. My clients and my firm made a killing on those deals while AS and PS were left scratching their heads trying to figure out how they were being undercut and by whom.

I must add here that I was quite inspired by the movie *Trishul* in which Amitabh Bachchan's construction firm undercuts Sanjeev Kumar's firm's quotation by one rupee, leaving the latter fuming.

The financial loss hurt AS-PS, no doubt, but what galled them even more was the challenge to their dominance. They made some inquiries and figured out who was stealing their lunch. Naturally, they were mad enough to want to kill me. They could not confront me on this matter because the exchange did not publish the successful offers, and they did not want to explain how they found me out either.

But they let me know that they were aware of what I was up to.

'Hello Lala,' AS greeted me one day as I passed him in the ring. 'Your clients must be quite happy with you, considering the profits you have helped them earn in TISCO and Century.'

I was caught unawares, and my surprise showed. I had undercut AS on both those stocks – it had been 10 paise, as usual. AS stared at me for a few seconds and then walked off without saying anything more.

PS was less subtle when I bumped into him the following day. I tried to avoid him, but he sidled up to me and put his arm around my shoulder as if we were the best of friends. But what he had to say was anything but friendly.

'I have said this once in the past and I shall repeat it again since you seem to have trouble understanding my message. Don't mess with your fathers in the industry, Lala, you could get hurt,' he said, and moved on. As threats went, it could not get more explicit than this.

A couple of weeks later, the duo accosted me just as I was about to get into the ring for the day.

'Saale ★%#@! you think you are smart, don't you? How the ★^$# can your firm regularly offer ten paise below our quotes?' AS asked menacingly.

'I don't know what the hell you are talking about,' I said, trying to stay calm.

AS and PS looked at each other, and AS spoke again:

'#@!*^$, try your acting skills somewhere else. BSE has started putting out the winning offers for the auctions on the notice board from today. Check it out. And, by the way, we know this is not the first time you have done this. $%%#@, you watch out, we will make you pay for this dearly.'

I was at a loss for words, and that left them in no doubt whatsoever about my culpability. Then PS stepped closer to me. 'Kid, you are from Dombivli, aren't you? I have heard the trains on that route are quite crowded . . . ' and then, his voice dropping to a whisper, he went on, ' . . . and people regularly lose their limbs or lives falling off packed trains.'

This time they had rattled me well and good. I stood rooted there for nearly a minute after the duo had left. My hands were trembling, and I instinctively thrust them into my pockets to not let them show. I reflected on what they, especially PS, had said. Perhaps it was a spontaneous outburst arising from wounded pride at being outsmarted. Yet, knowing their uncouth ways, I was worried that they would go to any extent to settle scores. After all, how much would it cost to hire two goons to fix me in Dombivli itself, and make it look like a street brawl or a mugging attempt gone awry?

I had friends in the market, but none in whom I could confide my inner fears. I had half a mind to complain about the duo to the authorities in the exchange. But I saw little point in doing that since these two rogues were quite influential. More worryingly, I could not complain without running the risk of my misdeeds being exposed. There was a real chance that they would carry out their threat of causing me physical harm. At the same time, I did not want to give them the impression that I was beaten. So, in the following settlement, I undercut them in two stocks, but chose those which did not cause either AS or PS a huge loss. I steered clear of the large offers in which they were involved.

For the next couple of months, I would take a good look around before boarding or getting off the train. I also made it a point to position myself away from the footboard except while boarding or alighting.

---

AS and PS would try to finger me whenever they could. I had become competent at sourcing decent lots of stocks. So if I bought a certain number of shares of company X on the floor, I knew which broker would be interested in buying that lot, and would accordingly strike a deal to sell the shares to him at the earliest. Similarly, if I had sold stock Y, I knew which broker would be looking to sell a similar lot, and I would buy it off him to square up my position.

AS-PS were curious to know whom I was sourcing shares from or selling to, and asked their lackeys to keep track of me in the ring. Owl (I named him so because of his saucer-shaped eyes) was one such jobber who owed his existence to the duo and was forever ready to carry out their bidding.

Most brokers of any significance had hotlines on the trading floor. This helped their office convey clients' orders and also helped other brokers or jobbers reach out to them with a deal. After I struck a large deal – by my standards – on the floor, I would call up the concerned broker on his hotline and ask him if he was interested in trading with me.

Once Owl and I were competing on the same stock. I bought a sizeable chunk at a good price, and then called the office of a broker who I knew was interested in that stock.

The dealer at that broker's office asked me to call back in fifteen minutes while he checked with his boss. When I called back after fifteen minutes, the dealer said he was not interested. I found it a bit odd because I knew for certain that the broker had been scouting around for the stock. But I did not give much thought to the incident. When I casually mentioned this to a fellow jobber, he told me that he had seen Owl call on the same hotline shortly after I had made my call. It was only then that I realized Owl was keeping tabs on the brokers I was talking to. I am sure he would have passed on the details to his masters who then offered a better quote to those brokers and snatched the deal from me.

I had to be careful the next time, but before that I decided to have some fun at Owl's expense. I found a chance a couple of days later. I had bought a block of Dr Reddy's Laboratories and knew a broker who would be interested in it. But I did not call the broker straight away. I first picked up a couple of hotlines at random and got the dealers at the other end worked up by talking some arbitrary stuff. Owl could not hear what I was saying but presumed that I was trying to offload the Dr Reddy's shares to those brokers. I knew that Owl would ring those brokers the moment I hung up on them. But I wanted to know how Owl would react when he realized he had called up the wrong brokers. By then I had become friendly with a jobber named Prakash, a couple of years older than I, who agreed to eavesdrop on Owl for me. Sure enough, when I left after my calls, Owl walked up to the hotline, probably relishing the thought of stealing another deal from me. He did not notice Prakash who was close by, overhearing his end of the conversation.

'If you are looking to buy Dr Reddy's, I have a much better rate for you . . . oh . . . not interested . . . well, okay . . . sorry . . . no, but I thought . . . okay . . . I am really sorry,' said Owl, keeping the receiver down. A similar conversation followed on his next call. It had not occurred to Owl that I had played a trick on him.

Two days later I did something similar. This time, realization dawned on Owl that I could be misleading him. He must have reported everything to his masters, for soon one more person was assigned to tail me. This time I dialled four brokers at random before placing the right call.

Owl and the other spy seemed to have had enough of the abuses that came their way from calling the wrong brokers. The AS-PS clique left me in peace after that.

Or rather, I thought so. But I was mistaken. Outwardly, their hostility towards me ceased somewhat, and once in a while even the usually gruff PS would greet me with a smile in the ring. I felt the past was forgiven and forgotten. Little did I know that the duo was patiently waiting for an opportunity to get back at me. And, one day, I myself gifted them the chance they had been looking for.

It was a fairly busy noon when Owl walked up to me inquiring about the rates I was offering for Apollo Tyres. We had dealt with each other a few times after the hotline snooping affair, and things had gone off smoothly. I had no reason to suspect anything. I quoted my rate; Owl said he wanted to sell 500 shares. I bought them off him. He asked the rate for another 500, and I gave him the same quote. He then said he wanted to sell some more. I instinctively felt Owl was trying to pull a fast one on me. I quoted a lousy rate so that he would walk away, but to my surprise he sold me another 500 shares, and asked for still another quote. I quoted an even lousier rate, increasing the spread sharply so that it looked obvious that I was trying to blatantly overcharge him.

I was expecting him to make some scathing remarks and walk away in a huff. But he again surprised me.

'Arre Lala, you are trying to kill me by quoting such rates,' he whined.

'It is up to you whether you want to take it or not,' I said disdainfully.

'You have become a big man, Lala, but that does not give you the right to treat small jobbers like me with contempt,' he protested.

I wanted to walk away, but the fellow wouldn't let me. Even though I had become a bit more tolerant of him lately, I certainly had no love lost for him.

'My rate stands, take it or leave it,' I said.

'The spread you have quoted is so wide that somebody could sell 50,000 shares of Apollo Tyres at this price,' Owl said.

By now I was really annoyed with him, and decided to insult him outright so that he would not prolong the discussion.

'50,000 shares eh? Well, if you have them on you, sell now. You have a buyer in me,' I said, fully aware that Owl did not deal in big quantities.

'Don't be so arrogant, Lala. I know you don't have the capacity to buy 50,000 shares. And you think you can make fun of me like that?' Owl said angrily.

I was pleased with myself now that I had managed to get him worked up. Somewhere during our conversation I recalled how he had managed to snatch at least two good deals from me. The memory of those losses made me want to inflict pain on him.

'You don't worry about whether I have the capacity to buy 50,000 Apollo Tyres or not; your concern should be whether you have those many shares to sell,' I said smugly.

I did not realize he was playing to a plan.

'Fine, Lala, I accept your offer. Sold to you, 50,000 Apollo Tyres,' he said, and quickly whipped out his *sauda* pad, noting down the deal.

I was stumped. It was true that I did not have the capacity to deal in 50,000 shares. While my boss had not specified any position limits, it was understood that I would not take excessive risks. After all, if the jobber defaults on his obligation, the broker has to make up for it.

I had taken Owl on because I knew that he did not deal in such large quantities either. Besides, it is common on the floor for traders to talk down each other so as to be able to get a competitive rate.

'Hey, wait . . . don't joke with such large numbers,' I said, realizing how perilous the situation could become, and hoping that Owl was just fooling around.

It was now Owl's turn to hurl barbs at me.

'Why, what happened, big man . . . did you just wet your pants at the thought of 50,000 shares? The way you were talking, I felt it was loose change for you,' he said, barely trying to conceal his glee.

The only way out of this mess was to claim the deal never happened, or that Owl had misheard me as having said 50,000 when I had actually said 500. But there were witnesses to our trade; Owl had ensured that. If I backed out of the deal, my reputation would take a knock and others would become less trustful of me.

Another option was to grovel before Owl and request him to cancel the trade. But my pride would not allow that. And even if I did plead with him, he would first savour my discomfort and then still refuse me. If I stood by the deal, there was a high probability of my having to take a loss beyond my capacity. Every one rupee of loss meant I would be out of pocket by Rs 50,000.

I was sure that Owl was fronting for his masters, who seemed determined to force me out of this profession in disgrace. As of now, they had won half the battle.

The settlement was about a week away, and even if I did manage to get out of my position in Apollo Tyres, it was likely to be at a loss. Knowing AS-PS's hatred for me, they would spread the word that I was desperate to offload 50,000 shares of Apollo Tyres. Anybody looking to buy from me would then try to beat me down on the price. I had nobody to blame for this situation but myself.

Later that day I bumped into AS as I was leaving the ring for my office.

'I understand you have a big lot of Apollo Tyres to sell. Can I be of help?' he asked with mock seriousness.

I tried to ignore him, but PS did not give up so easily.

'Well, Lala, we warned you enough times not to play around with us. And I had promised you that I would make you pay. I hope you have already thought of an alternative profession for after next week,' he said as he went away.

My situation appeared to be beyond salvage. I tried to picture various scenarios. The best-case scenario would be my making a fat profit on the trade. The chances of that looked next to impossible, especially since my foes would have spread the word that there was a desperate seller hawking 50,000 shares. The next-best scenario was to get out of the position at no-profit-no-loss, but with a lesson learnt in humility. The chances of that too appeared slim. A loss of even one rupee per share would be painful, but I could still prevail on my boss to keep me in the job and work off my debt. A loss of two rupees, and I could not be sure of my job, though I could still plead for leniency; a loss of more than two rupees, and I would have to look for a job outside the stock market; no broker would be willing to hire me after hearing about my blunder.

I wondered if I should ask Bunty to help me out by buying the block for his fund because I had still got it at a competitive price and would gladly have sold it to him at the same price. The problem here was that Bunty's fund did not have any previous exposure to Apollo Tyres, and Bunty would find it difficult convincing his bosses about his sudden interest in the stock.

My boss was out of town and was not expected till three days later. That gave me some breathing space. I was not sure how he would react if word about my reckless trade got around to him. He was by nature a rather level-headed person, but just like the stock market, people can be irrational at an inopportune moment.

I slept fitfully that night, beset by nightmares of being chased out of the stock exchange building with just my undergarments on.

I had to drag myself to work the following day. I was unsure whether I should be going into the ring at all. With the Apollo trade playing on my mind, I was likely to make more mistakes and aggravate an already bad situation. I thought over it for a while and took a decision: I would try to first trade my way out of Apollo and only then take up other deals. I tried a bit of self-motivation so that I did not betray my desperation and make myself vulnerable to more bad deals. Maybe this was a test by God to make me a better professional, I thought, as I walked into the ring.

I inquired about the rates for Apollo Tyres. To my dismay, the prices on offer were low, and so were the volumes. I tried trading some other stocks, but my mind kept going back to Apollo. I again checked the rates, but they were still not in my favour. I decided to hold on to my position for one more day before making up my mind.

With 10 minutes left for the day's session to end, Sharma casually came up to me. We knew each other by face, but had not interacted before. The outspoken and jovial Sharma was known to be part of Harshad Mehta's inner circle. I was a bit surprised when he approached me, considering we had never spoken before.

'How goes things, Lala?' he asked.

'Surviving,' I said, forcing a smile.

'Hmm . . . we all are, in one way or another,' he said, eyeing me closely.

To what do I owe the honour of your accosting me, I wanted to ask him.

We sized each other up for a few seconds. Then Sharma spoke: 'I would like to buy some stock off you.'

I immediately realized he knew about my Apollo Tyres trade. No client ever reveals his hand before asking for a quote.

'Which one?' I asked, knowing the answer fully well.

'Come off it, Lala, you know which one, else I would have asked for a quote first,' he said.

'Since you know where I stand, it goes without saying that you already have a price in mind,' I said, trying to sound dignified.

'You are right, let's deal straight. What did you buy it for?' he asked.

I told him the right price, aware that he knew it.

'Okay, I will buy it from you at ten paise below your cost price,' he said.

'That's generous on your part, knowing the situation I am in,' I said, and then wondered if I had given myself away.

'Let me put it this way. Some people would like to see you in trouble, and we would like to deny them that satisfaction. Besides, we are buyers in the stock if the price is reasonable,' Sharma said.

'Who is the "we"?' I asked, just to confirm my conclusion about who could be behind this gift from heaven.

'Too clever by half, aren't you, Lala? I take it that you are sufficiently informed about who I work for,' Sharma said.

'Even if it is unintended generosity, why not go the whole way and buy my position at cost?' I asked.

'So that you realize there is a cost to stupidity. Ten paise is no big deal. But if you are let off the hook clean, you could get into bigger trouble next time,' Sharma said, noting down the deal in his *sauda* pad.

'Am I supposed to be grateful for this act of kindness?' I asked.

'Well, that's up to you,' Sharma said, walking away.

The following day, Owl approached me, saying he was willing to buy back the Apollo Tyres position at three rupees below my selling price.

'We all make mistakes, Lala, but I don't want somebody to be out of a job because of his immaturity,' Owl said, perhaps hoping that I would beg him for a better price.

'That's very magnanimous of you,' I said, and leaning forward, whispered into his ear where he could shove up that offer.

But for AS-PS themselves having made a formidable enemy in my unlikely benefactor, I would have been in serious trouble. The loss of Rs 5,000 pinched for about a month, but I kept telling myself that things could have been much worse.

# 5

# The Republic of Dalal Street

The Dalal Street of the 1980s and early 1990s was the financial market equivalent of the Wild West. Insider trading by companies, in collusion with brokers and market operators, was rampant. In fact, it did not even strike the companies that their trading practices were illegal as there was nothing in the law that forbade them from keeping up these practices.

As for the brokers, many were known to regularly front-run their big clients or cheat on the rates at which they would execute orders in the ring. Brokers would confirm their trades only at the end of the day. So they would claim to have sold at prices close to the lowest price of the day and bought at levels close to the highest price of the day. This way, they could pay less money to the client who sold shares through them and take more money from clients who bought shares from them.

With the entry of the National Stock Exchange (NSE) and the introduction of screen-based trading in 1994, this practice ended, as clients could verify what prices their shares were traded for.

In the pre-NSE days too, brokers had to adhere to rules specified by the stock exchanges. But in reality, these rules were frequently violated. Non-payment of margin money to the exchanges, violations of trading restrictions, and reluctance to submit data on prices and volumes in a transparent manner were common. BSE, for instance, was supposed to audit the books of broker members but this was rarely done, and even when it was, it was a peremptory exercise. There was no proper mechanism to address the grievances of investors.

Influential brokers got a free run because the governing board of the stock exchange was packed with broker members. On paper, the stock exchange was answerable to the Ministry of Finance, but the government nominees rarely attended meetings of the governing board. In effect, the exchange was controlled by a clique of influential brokers, to such an extent that many joked that BSE was an abbreviation for Brokers' Stock Exchange and not of Bombay Stock Exchange. Naturally, disciplinary action against erring members was rare. Occasionally a broker would be penalized, but the fines were insignificant.

Cartel wars in a stock were quite common at the time, and usually saw the Marwari brokers arrayed on one side and the Gujarati brokers on the other. One group would take a bullish view on a stock, and the other would try its best to hammer the price of that stock down. Having friends in the stock exchange governing board or in the company helped tilt the balance of power. Bulls could be caught on the wrong foot if the stock exchange suddenly increased the margin on buy trades, and bears could be trapped by a sudden wave of buying, usually by players funded by company promoters.

India was still a closed economy then, and stock market players did not look beyond the stocks whose companies they had an interest (usually vested) in.

My jobbing skills were steadily improving, and in a good month I would take home close to Rs 10,000.

Occasionally I ended up annoying some of the big players of the game. Once Manubhai Manek asked me to buy a block of shares of a certain stock. It so happened that his son-in-law, who sat a few offices away from Manek's, wanted to sell a block of that same lot. I got him the block he wanted, and charged him the usual brokerage of 1.5 per cent.

A few days later Manubhai learnt the identity of the seller and was miffed with me. 'You could have told me that my son-in-law was looking to sell the block,' he told me when we bumped into each other in the ring. I grinned at him, but Manubhai was not amused.

'You should be called *chakku* (knife); you could slit somebody's throat to earn a commission,' he said.

But only a week later he made me an offer when we met in the ring.

'Hey *chakku*, what is your boss paying you?' he asked.

If it had been anybody else I might have asked him to get lost. But this was Manubhai himself, whom I had managed to get on the wrong side of once. Twice would be asking for trouble.

'Rs 5,000 fixed, plus jobbing commissions,' I said.

'You are worth much more. I will pay you Rs 15,000 plus jobbing commissions; join me from next month,' he said.

Perhaps it was the tone of the proposal that put me off. It sounded more like an order than an offer. But then, Manubhai was never really known to charm people. 'I am quite happy with what my boss is paying me right now. Besides, he gave me a job when nobody else was willing to take me on. I can't walk out on him just for some extra money,' I said.

He did not realize that had he been a bit more tactful, I could have easily been persuaded to cross over. After all, who would not want to work with one of the biggest names on Dalal Street? But if he thought he could buy me out with just money, he was mistaken.

Manubhai was a bit taken aback by my answer. I guess he was not used to being rebuffed by a jobber barely a year into the profession.

'Good to hear that you still treasure old-world values like loyalty, otherwise everybody is out here to get rich quick by whatever means possible. If ever you are in need of a job, you can always call on me,' he said, walking away without waiting for my response.

Soon after that he gave me a couple of decent-sized orders, which I managed to execute well. But more important than the commissions they fetched me was the relief I felt in knowing that he still thought sufficiently well of me to give me business.

# 6

# The Rise of Harshad and the Equity Cult

But for the general elections in November, which saw the defeat of the Congress and brought the Janata Dal-led national coalition to power, 1989, as well as the first half of 1990, saw very little activity on Dalal Street.

V. P. Singh had come to power with many a promise, but was caught up in trying to keep the coalition partners happy. Student agitations across the country, and suicide attempts by a few students in the wake of the Mandal Commission report on reservations for the backward classes undermined Singh's position within his own party. By then, the term 'policy paralysis' had not been coined, and the stock market appeared to be existing in a cocoon of its own, unmindful of the economy as a whole. Investors did not concern themselves beyond policies that impacted specific companies or sectors.

All this time, unknown to the stock market at large, action was slowly hotting up in the little-known, murky interbank market for government securities. It was a market in which banks – nationalized as well as private sector banks – bought and sold bonds among each other to meet their liquidity requirements and to make profits too. Before long, the reverberations from the developments in the money market – as it was called – would be felt in the stock market.

The Sensex had been trading between 700 and 850 from January to June 1990, giving little clue as to which end of the range it would break out from. However, starting July, the index broke out of the upper end, and by the close of the month had risen to within sniffing distance of 1,100. Even more strangely, the market rose through August and September, when crude oil prices had begun climbing after Iraq's invasion of Kuwait. Logically, costlier crude meant a higher import bill for the country and a strain on its already measly foreign exchange reserves, and should have been seen as a negative sign by the markets.

Harshad's scale of activity had increased considerably by then, and the big moves in stocks like ACC, Apollo Tyres, Gujarat Ambuja, Tata Tea and SPIC were being attributed entirely to him. It would be some more months before he attained cult status in the stock market and even beyond – on a level that has not been seen since with anybody else on the stock exchange – but he was already well on his way to becoming the first superstar of Dalal Street.

What many in the stock market did not know was that Harshad had by then risen to become a powerful broker in the money market too. In becoming so, he had broken the stranglehold on the business that established players like the Ajay Kayan-owned Smifs Mackertich, the Hemendra Kothari-controlled DS Purbhoodas and Bhupen Dalal's CIFCO.

Harshad had begun his career in the financial market in the early 1980s as a jobber in stocks and had done well enough to acquire a membership on BSE by 1984. Three years later, he ventured into the money market, hoping to replicate his success in the stock market. While one could rise from a lowly jobber to a broker in the stock market, breaking into the money market was a much tougher proposition.

There is an apocryphal tale about what spurred Harshad to dive into the money market. I heard it from Sharma some years later when we were reminiscing about the old times over a drink. Harshad was at the office of a broker friend. A fairly important money market broker happened to be there too. When this broker got talking about the market, Harshad got a bit curious and asked for elaboration on something. The broker apparently turned to Harshad and told him, 'This is way beyond your league, you'd better stick to the stock market,' or something to that effect. That pricked Harshad's ego, enough to set him aching to prove that he could be as good in the money market as he was in the trading ring on Dalal Street.

Harshad's first year as a money market broker was a disaster. It took him almost six months to crack his first deal and that earned him a paltry Rs 5,500 as commission, net of stamp duty. The next six months were nothing to write home about either. Anybody else in his place might have given up and turned his attention back to stocks. But not Harshad, who wanted to prove a point, no matter what.

Just the previous year, Harshad had nearly defaulted on a trade in SPIC. His rivals, led by Manu Manek, had made a near-foolproof plan to bleed him financially. Harshad had big buy positions in shares of SPIC in his personal capacity as well as on behalf of his clients. A listless Union Budget had soured market sentiment in general, and SPIC was among the major casualties. The stock crashed from Rs 180 to Rs 125 within a couple of trading sessions.

Suddenly, rumours began doing the rounds that Harshad would default on his pay-in obligation to the stock exchange. If a broker buys shares, he has an obligation to the stock exchange to pay money (pay-in of funds) for the shares on settlement day. If he sells shares, he has to deliver the shares, or make a pay-in of shares to the exchange on settlement day.

The bears were trying their best to further depress the appetite for SPIC and hammer its price down by unnerving the bulls into liquidating their positions. Had the stock price fallen further, Harshad would have found it difficult to get financiers to carry forward the trade to the next settlement. On the advice of a trusted broker friend, Harshad decided to make the pay-in of funds for SPIC ahead of schedule. He made the pay-in and requested M. R. Mayya, executive director of the BSE, to announce it on the stock exchange notice board. Mayya declined to do that, citing exchange rules. But he assured Harshad that he would confirm the development to anybody who came checking its veracity.

The move helped, but only to the extent that the bears backed off from hammering SPIC shares further. But it was not a clean win for Harshad, who had to stretch himself to pay the funds ahead of schedule. Some of his clients were cooperative and paid up, but there were others who refused. The net result was that Harshad's firm had to absorb a good part of the losses arising from the steep fall in the stock price of SPIC.

In 1987, when Harshad first tried to gain a foothold in the cloistered club of money market brokers, there was not much action in the market. Banks had to keep almost half of their deposits aside to meet the Cash Reserve Ratio (CRR) and Statutory Liquidity Ratio (SLR) norms set by the Reserve Bank of India (RBI).

CRR, which helps RBI control the money flow in the system, is the proportion of deposits that banks must deposit with RBI. A CRR of 4 per cent would mean that for every Rs 100 of their deposits, banks must deposit Rs 4 with RBI. The banks did not earn any interest on CRR. SLR is that portion of their funds that banks have to compulsorily invest in government securities (bonds issued by the government). SLR investments earn interest, but the interest is much lower than the interest banks charge their corporate borrowers. Today CRR is 4 per cent and SLR 21.5 per cent (total: 25.5 per cent). Back then, the two ratios added up to nearly 50 per cent.

What this meant was that banks could only lend Rs 50 out of the Rs 100 they received as deposits. This reduced their ability to earn decent profits. Whenever CRR and SLR limits were raised, some banks had to borrow cash or securities to maintain compliance. Some banks realized that planned purchase of bonds to fetch optimum yields was a good way to boost earnings. But for most banks, buying and selling of bonds was done mostly to meet regulatory requirements.

To get around the stringent CRR/SLR rules, banks came up with a 'buyback' or 'ready forward' arrangement. Bank A, which needed cash, would sell some of the securities in its portfolio to Bank B, and a few days later buy back those securities at a slightly higher price. This difference was, in fact, the interest that Bank A was paying Bank B for the short-term loan. For Bank B, the difference in the buying and selling price was the interest it charged for lending the money for those few days.

There also existed a call money market in which banks, mutual funds and corporations could borrow funds from each other for short durations. But RBI had capped the interest rate chargeable in this market at 10 per cent. As a result, banks were not keen to lend in the call market, the rates they were charging through ready forward deals being much higher.

As the number of ready forward deals increased, so did the use of an instrument called bank receipt (BR). When Bank A sold securities to Bank B, often the securities – which were held in physical form, and not electronically – could not immediately be delivered to the buyer. So Bank A would issue a BR to Bank B that was valid until the time the securities were physically delivered to Bank B. Once the securities were delivered, the BR would expire. A BR was valid for 90 days or until delivery of the securities it represented, whichever was earlier. At least, that was the way it was meant to be under the rules for BRs.

Before long, BRs began to be misused on a large scale. In many transactions, the physical securities never changed hands; only the BRs did. Issue of BRs was meant to be an 'exceptional method' of delivery of securities under special circumstances. But soon it became the norm.

Banks started issuing BRs against BRs, which was forbidden. This meant that Bank B could trade the BR it was handed by Bank A with a third bank, as though it already had delivery of the underlying securities. The third bank in turn would trade that BR with a fourth bank, as though it now owned the securities.

If Bank A, for whatever reason, were to default on delivery of the securities, there would be a series of defaults along the chain. It was also very much possible that Bank A never had the underlying securities to back the BR it had issued to Bank B. It probably issued the BR thinking it would reverse the transaction before the 90-day validity period for BRs. Bank A would then not have to deliver the physical securities at all to Bank B. What it would not have bargained for was Bank B trading that BR with another bank.

And that was exactly what happened. Some banks started issuing BRs that had no underlying securities. They were confident that the purchasing banks would not bother to ascertain the selling banks' ability to deliver the securities. Cooperative banks like Bank of Karad and Metropolitan Co-operative Bank, which eventually went bust, issued securities that were 'worth' many times the value of the banks' entire investment portfolio.

To make matters worse, some brokers like Harshad Mehta started taking huge positions on their own instead of simply acting as brokers to the buying and selling banks. If Bank A wanted to sell a certain government bond and Bank B wanted to buy it, Harshad, who should ideally only have connected the two and earned a commission, was now big enough to buy the bond from Bank A and sell it to Bank B for a profit.

Banks were allowed to trade securities only with other banks. But Harshad rewrote the rules of the game when he decided to become a counterparty, and not just a broker, in trades among banks. This would see him strike a deal with Bank A to buy securities at a certain rate, confident that he would be able to offload those to Bank B at a higher rate. Or, he might even short-sell securities to Bank A, hoping to deliver the securities by buying them cheaper from Bank B.

Actually, it was even more complicated than this, as neither Bank A nor Bank B could directly deal with a broker, according to the rules. Harshad got around this by enlisting the help of Bank C, which would lend its name to the transaction. On paper, it would appear that both Bank A and Bank B were dealing with Bank C, though both banks were aware that they were directly dealing with Harshad.

The payment cheque would be received in the name of Bank C, which would then immediately credit the funds to Harshad's account after deducting a fee. Similarly, Bank C would also deliver securities from its portfolio to the buying bank, and receive securities later from the buying broker.

It was this facility that helped Harshad rapidly scale up the size of his transactions. The jobbing skills he had learnt the hard way in the trading ring of BSE would be put to good use in the money market. Depending on which side of the trade he was on, he would make a security liquid or illiquid to get the best deal for himself. In addition to acting as counterparty, Harshad would also broker trades for banks. On paper he would not be charging banks any brokerage on some of the transactions. But here too, Harshad was benefiting from the wide spread between the rates at which one bank sold and the other bank bought.

Soon, the banks that Harshad did business for trusted him so unquestioningly that they would credit large sums into his account on his instructions. In theory, they were paying him for the securities he was supposed to buy for them. In practice, Harshad would use the money for his own stock market investments. He would buy huge quantities of his favourite stocks using the money from the banks, sending share prices skyward in the process. He would keep the profits from playing the stocks and pass the funds on to the selling bank, or return the funds to the buying bank, depending on the arrangement. Nobody knows when he hit upon the idea of diverting banks' funds into the stock market; it began to get talked about only in 1991 when the size of his bets grew very large. In 1990, however, Dalal Street was yet to catch the imagination of the masses, most of whom had only a vague idea about shares and the stock market.

A couple of months after his generous gesture, Sharma asked me if I wanted to meet Harshad in person. I was very keen, having heard so much about him. A few days later, when we met in the ring, he told me that Harshad was meeting up with a few friends over dinner at the Grasshopper restaurant in Vile Parle that evening.

'Bhai will be happy to have you with us,' Sharma said.

I was a little tense about the meeting. I had heard that Harshad was quite voluble, the exact opposite of somebody like me who had trouble making conversation. I worried my reticence would make me appear unimpressive to Harshad.

Sharma and I went together to the Grasshopper. We were ten minutes late. Harshad was already there with seven others, all of them stock market friends. I knew all of them by name, and I guess they too were aware of my existence. As usual, Sharma was to the point while introducing me.

He placed his hand on my shoulder and said to Harshad, 'This is Lalchand, better known as Lala.'

I managed to mutter a feeble hello to Harshad, but was so awestruck that I involuntarily bowed while greeting him.

Harshad eyed me for a couple of seconds, and I could sense that he was sizing me up.

'I am Harshad, how do you do, Lala?' he responded with a warm smile.

I was a bit taken aback at the humility with which he introduced himself. Of course I knew his name. But then, that was part of Harshad's charm, and as I would learn later, he had a knack of putting people at ease in his company.

'*Arre* Sharma, when you mentioned a jobber who loved to finger those robbers, I certainly did not imagine a college kid,' Harshad said, and turned towards me. 'You seem to have got the hang of the game early on; that's important if you are to survive the first couple of years, always the toughest. Reminds me of my initial days in the ring.'

I would be lying if I said the remarks did not swell my head. And that's exactly the effect Harshad must have intended. But it made me all the more tongue-tied, and I did not know what to say.

But one of Harshad's friends saved me the trouble by butting into the conversation. Being a Friday, there was a fairly long waiting list of diners. From the look of it, I felt we would have to wait for anywhere between half an hour to an hour.

'. . . that's why I was saying, Harshadbhai, we should have booked in advance. It is going to be a long wait,' the friend, Viren, told Harshad.

'But why take the trouble of booking in advance when you can get a table without much difficulty?' Harshad said.

I wondered if Harshad had thought he would be recognized by the restaurant staff and promptly ushered to a table. He might be well known in stock market circles, but out here, he was just another patron looking to have a good time over good food.

'If it is so easy, why don't you get us a table?' Viren said.

'Are you challenging me?' Harshad asked.

'Yes.'

To cut a long story short, Harshad managed to get us a seat without much delay. He did that by posing as a tour operator to the steward at the door allotting the tables. Harshad first told the steward to take good care of a group of twelve in the waiting list (he figured that by peeping into the steward's notepad). He said they were wealthy diamond merchants from Gujarat and that he had specifically recommended this place to them. A little later, he again walked up to the steward and said he had another group of guests more important that the first group and that they be given priority. I was quite impressed with Harshad's street smartness, but at the same time I suspected that he would not be averse to pulling off something similar at a bigger level if it helped him get ahead.

I do not have much recollection of that dinner, except that I chose a seat as far away from Harshad as possible. I was worried that he would pop me some questions on the market, and that I would say something silly in reply.

Still, he sought me out and asked me something about a company. I was self-conscious, and mumbled something. He heard me out attentively and then asked a counter-question.

'True, Lala, but what if you were to look at it in a different way. Assume that . . . '

I responded with some more drivel, anxious that he should not question me further because I now had nothing more to say.

'Hmm . . . you may have a point,' he said, with a thoughtful look, as though I had presented him with an entirely new perspective.

As we parted after dinner, Harshad put his arm around my shoulder and said. 'You seem to be an interesting fellow, Lala. Let's keep in touch.'

He gave me his visiting card and asked me to ring him whenever I had interesting ideas.

A couple of weeks after that dinner meeting I started doing trades for Harshad. Sharma was my link to him, and all the orders would be relayed through him. It was mostly to buy shares; sometimes with a price-limit instruction, and at other times being allowed a free hand. I was doing all these deals in my capacity as a jobber and not as a dealer for my firm. Still, a share of the profits went to my firm, under the arrangement I had with the owner.

The trades were small to begin with, but I guess they were testing me out for efficiency and integrity. Once they were satisfied, the orders slowly started getting bigger and more regular. My commissions were growing steadily, and I was confident that in another couple of years I would be able to realize my dream of owning a house in Ghatkopar.

# 7

# Dalal Street Gets a New Big Bull

The Bharatiya Janata Party withdrew support to the V. P. Singh government in the last week of October after Bihar chief minister Laloo Prasad Yadav had L. K. Advani arrested during his *rath yatra* in that state. Although the market moved in a contrary direction, gaining a bit, the Sensex crashed the following January as a war in the Gulf appeared imminent after all diplomatic efforts to persuade Iraq to withdraw from Kuwait had failed.

However, one stock was steadily and mysteriously rising through all these market swings – that of Associated Cement Companies. The sudden fancy for it stemmed from Harshad's heavy purchases in the stock. I had sourced a sizeable chunk of it myself for him, and knew that he was buying whatever ACC shares he could lay his hands on. The stock had more than doubled over the last six months, and the bears had lost a packet short-selling it on the hunch that it was overvalued.

I was among those who had sold the shares short at Rs 1,000, thinking they were unlikely to rise further. I was wrong, and ended up squaring my position at Rs 1,100, losing more than half the jobbing commission I had made that month. I would try this again a few months later, and the results would be no different.

The Gulf war ended in a decisive victory for the allied forces led by the US, but that did not really perk up the stock market. The crisis had aggravated India's already precarious foreign exchange situation and there was a risk of the country defaulting on payment obligations. Inflation had climbed to a record 13.6 per cent, and there was a sense of despondency everywhere. The dismal state of finances was public knowledge, and it did not disappoint the market when the Congress party withdrew support to the stopgap Chandrashekhar government in March and called for fresh elections.

The market remained comatose in the run-up to the general elections to be held in May 1991 as the prospect of another hung parliament loomed. Rajiv Gandhi's assassination on 21 May was a shock for the market, as it had been betting on his return to power and continuing the reforms he had initiated during his stint in power. The market was closed the following day, but held up well when trading resumed on 23 May, with the Sensex closing flat, any panic having been averted by support from the domestic financial institutions.

The market remained in a tight range till the end of May. Most players were expecting the political uncertainty to continue even after the elections as no party was expected to win a clear majority. Then followed more bad news. Left with barely enough forex reserves to pay for three weeks of imports, the Chandrashekhar government had to borrow from the International Monetary Fund by pledging its gold reserves. The public was outraged, but this development fully revealed the mess the country was in.

Once again, the market did not crack as was widely expected. I learnt from the market that Harshad and brokers close to him were buying in a big way. I asked Sharma about it.

'Bhai feels the government's decision to pledge gold shows it will go to any length, to avoid a default,' Sharma said. I remained bearish, certain that it would be some time before the new government could get the economy out of the hole it had sunk into.

To everybody's surprise, the Congress did well in the second phase of the polls because of a sympathy wave following Rajiv Gandhi's assassination. It managed to form a government with support from some of the smaller parties. The Sensex climbed around 100 points, but the market reaction was still guarded.

The party on Dalal Street began after Manmohan Singh's path-breaking Budget of 24 July, which signalled India's willingness to open up its economy to the world by lowering import barriers and scrapping the licence system for industries. Among other things the stock market will remember that budget for was the government's promise to allow FIIs to invest in India. Private players were allowed to set up mutual funds. And the Controller of Capital Issues was proposed to be replaced by the Securities and Exchange Board of India (SEBI) to regulate the stock market and stock exchanges.

Over the next month, rampaging bulls lifted the Sensex by over 300 points. The leader of the herd was none other than Harshad himself, who was now known by the nickname Big Bull, a title that had previously belonged to the UTI boss M. J. Pherwani.

To justify the absurd valuations that many of his favourite stocks were quoting at, Harshad advocated the 'replacement cost' theory, which held that a stock should not be valued on the company's earnings potential, but on the basis of what it would cost to create a similar company. The concept caught on like wildfire in the stock market, sending the prices of even the most inefficient and mismanaged companies shooting through the roof.

Even today, Harshad is credited with having come up with the 'replacement cost' theory, but that is not true. He may have propagated it, but it was not his original idea in any way. As I mentioned earlier, my brief stint as a library assistant helped me develop a lifelong love for reading. Many years later, when I read the full 1956 debate in the Rajya Sabha over the Securities and Contracts Regulations Act, I came across a passage in which P. D. Himatsingka, a member of parliament from West Bengal, had made an interesting argument. He justified the steep rise in the share price of the Indian Iron and Steel Company, saying it was cheaper for a buyer to purchase shares from the open market and take control of the company rather than to incur a much heavier expense setting up a new steel plant.

ACC shares had by then climbed to Rs 3,000, having almost doubled since the beginning of the year. The moment Harshad or his associate brokers simply made inquiries about a stock, its price would start rising, even without a single share having been actually purchased. The sixfold rise in ACC over the previous year was proof to the market of what Harshad could do to the fortunes of a stock.

Promoters began to seek him out, and he, in turn, would seek out promoters of the companies he was interested in.

Not all these meetings were fruitful, but sometimes the promoters would leak news of the meeting to the market, hoping to fire up their stock. At other times, Harshad's associates would spread the word, creating the same effect.

By now, Harshad's flashy lifestyle was making headlines. With his 15,000 square-foot apartment in Worli overlooking the sea, his designer suits and fleet of imported cars, the Big Bull had become a role model for almost every player on Dalal Street.

While the bulls were celebrating, there were subtle policy changes underway in the money market, which would have major implications for the stock market too. In August, RBI removed the ceiling on interest rates on bonds and debentures issued by public sector companies. With the new securities offering higher interest rates, the older securities declined in value, causing losses to the banks that held them. When new bonds were offering, say, 11 per cent on maturity, who would want to buy the old bonds in a bank's portfolio that were offering 10 per cent on maturity, unless they were sold at a discount to their face value?

Trading volumes in the money market surged as banks tried to minimize their losses by getting out of the older securities. Brokers were only too glad to help stricken banks, and banks returned the favour through cosy arrangements benefiting the brokers.

Back in the stock market, Harshad continued to drive the prices of his favourite stocks even higher by continuing to peddle the 'replacement cost' theory. The market was curious about Harshad's source of funds, and there was much speculation about it, including rumours that the Big Bull was being financed by politicians and the underworld.

As Sharma would later tell me, Harshad's foes knew exactly where the money was coming from. The only trouble was that they too were guilty of misdemeanours similar to Harshad's, albeit on a much smaller scale. Many – if not all of them – played around with bank funds, but were careful to deploy them in less risky short-term instruments, including badla financing. This allowed them to get extra returns on their deals but kept them in a position to return the funds at short notice.

Harshad was now threatening this second income of theirs by recklessly investing the money in stocks and drawing public attention with his glamorous lifestyle. His foes were now eager to trap him but lay low, knowing their own source of funds would be cut off once the authorities got to know about the loopholes. It must have caused them immense frustration to be outsmarted by Harshad in both the money and stock markets, and be able to do nothing about it.

Harshad's initial bets were companies with sound fundamentals, but I guess he gradually got carried away by his success and the following he had. He started buying shares of mediocre companies, and his purchases soon extended to outright dubious ones. Perhaps Harshad started to have delusions about his power – that companies' performance would improve because *he* had invested in them!

The post-Budget excitement in the market lifted the Sensex to 1,900 by mid-September. In less than two and a half months of the Congress government's coming to power, the index had rallied an astounding 50 per cent.

July and August had been bumper months for me. I netted Rs 41,000 in jobbing commissions in July and Rs

46,000 in August. And yet, I was disappointed for not having been able to hit the Rs 50,000 mark. Each month I took Rs 25,000 out of these profits home, depositing the rest with my employer, with the intention of taking bigger bets when the opportunity arose.

Bauji and Ma were awestruck when I handed them my earnings. Bauji had some idea about the stock market and its fickle ways, but he found it hard to believe that a 23-year-old could make Rs 25,000 two months in a row.

'I hope you are not doing something wrong, Lalchand,' he told me one evening after dinner.

'No Bauji, every rupee has been earned the hard way. And this is just the beginning. With my efforts and God's grace, we should be able to move to Ghatkopar in two years' time,' I said. I could understand his concern; my wayward ways during our days in Bhandup were still fresh in his memory. I could see that he was not entirely convinced by my answer, and that he did not want to voice his doubts either.

'Bauji, I know I have caused you grief in the past, but that's a closed chapter. I give you my word that I will never do anything that will cause you to hang your head in shame,' I said, clasping his hand. That put him at ease somewhat.

'But tell me, Lala, if you can make Rs 25,000 two months in a row, you could also lose that much, isn't it?' he asked.

'True, that's why I pre-decide the quantum of loss I can bear and stay within that limit. If I exceed that, I am likely to get fired from my job,' I said.

Unlike me, moving into a bigger house was not Bauji's priority. Satish had enrolled for a B.Sc. that year as his Higher Secondary score was not high enough to get him a seat in a good engineering college purely on merit. And we lacked the resources to pay for a seat in the management quota. We could have just about managed that, but Bauji was not certain if the investment would be worth the money. But now that I was making decent money, Bauji saw a chance to realize his cherished dream to see at least one of his children become an engineer.

'Lala, would it be asking for too much from you to set some money aside so that we can get admission for Satish in a decent engineering college next year?' he asked with some hesitation.

'For all the trouble I have caused you, that is the least I can do to make up for it,' I told him.

He was so moved that he embraced me. I had never felt so close to him as I did in that moment.

# 8

# Swimming against the Tide

However bullish the overall sentiment, the market could not keep on rising indefinitely. And for all its logic, even the replacement cost theory had its limitations. The bulls were beginning to tire after a nearly one-sided rally that began in July and lasted up to mid-September, taking the Sensex up from around 1,275 to a new peak of 1,916.

The market then began to flag, and over the next one month shed around 200 points. I saw this as a good opportunity to have another go at ACC and recoup my losses of the previous year from short-selling the stock. The entire market had been baffled by the spectacular rise in ACC shares, and the short-sellers who tried to predict its peak price had to pay dearly. That, however, did not deter the more adventurous from taking up the challenge, but only to meet with a similar fate.

The stock had come close to hitting Rs 4,000 in early September, and even the most diehard supporters of ACC felt it was unlikely to go much higher.

Except Harshad.

Nemish Shah, a close friend of Harshad's and as much of a bull on the stock as he, sold out at around Rs 3,500 a share. This was a clear signal that the stock was now overvalued. What else could it mean, when one of the finest investors on Dalal Street decides to sell out in the face of strong demand for the stock? I told Prakash that there was good money to be made by short-selling ACC.

'A player of Nemishbhai's stature feels the stock is overvalued. What more do you want?' I told Prakash excitedly. But he did not share my enthusiasm.

'Having seen two more Diwalis than you in this trading ring, I can tell you one thing confidently. No matter how big or accomplished a player, nobody can correctly predict the top or bottom of a stock,' he said.

I still went ahead, and short-sold the stock at around Rs 3,150. Over the next week, the stock gained Rs 100 as the market as a whole started rising again. I met up with Sharma over tea a few days after I had short-sold ACC. We discussed many stocks, and towards the end of our conversation I casually asked him about ACC.

The seasoned trader that he was, Sharma could deduce which side of the trade a market player was on from his very tone.

'You are trying too hard to be indifferent about ACC, which tells me that you are in a spot of bother. In case you have been stupid enough to short-sell ACC, my advice to you would be to square immediately,' he said with a wry smile.

'Okay, I will be upfront. I am short on the stock. How high can it go from here?' I asked.

'Bhai says it can go to a level beyond anybody's imagination,' Sharma said.

'And what is that level likely to be?' I asked.

'You seem to be a bit hard of hearing. I just said beyond anybody's imagination, and that holds for me as well. Honestly, Lala, I don't think even Bhai would have expected ACC to come so close to hitting Rs 4,000; and it is very likely he does not know how high it can go from here either,' Sharma said.

My chat with Sharma made me a bit nervous about my trade, and I regretted having spoken to him. With the stock price showing no signs of weakness, I decided to wait for one more day before squaring up my position. That evening I went over to Prakash's place at his invitation for dinner. There I met an elderly relative of his, a gentleman in his mid-seventies who had been working at a broker's office till five years ago. Though not a trader himself, he had many interesting tales to tell.

Soon the conversation veered to the bull run in ACC. I asked him if he recollected having seen anything like this during his career in the stock market. 'Crazy things used to happen in the market even then,' he said, after mulling over my question. 'I remember a similar bull run in the shares of Tata deferred ('deferred' being a class of shares back then) sometime in the late 1960s. The stock went from Rs 30 to Rs 2,500 in a matter of months. A few players were made for life but far more were bankrupted trying to short-sell the stock,' he said. The next morning I covered my ACC position at a loss. But I was still lucky, considering the stock rallied by Rs 300 over the next three days after my exit. While the bulls paused for a breather in October, there came another important development in the money market. New government bonds with higher interest rates took the sheen off the older bonds, whose prices started to drop. The government bond portfolios of state-owned banks diminished in value. This triggered another round of frenzied trading in government securities by banks, as they tried to tide over the losses that ensued. Again, this passed unnoticed by the stock market, a wide section of which viewed the rise and fall in share prices in isolation.

The bull market in shares resumed in January, with Harshad's purchases believed to be the driving force. Harshad may have been the biggest buyer in the market, but to say that he was single-handedly forcing the market up was to exaggerate his influence. Again, I am making this observation with the benefit of hindsight. Back then, even I was a believer in Harshad's powers to make the market dance to his tune.

Shallow as the market may have been back then, the daily traded turnover had risen to around Rs 400 crore towards the end of 1991-92. Harshad may have had the charisma to drive the market, but it was impossible for him – or for anybody else, for that matter – to have enough money to dictate the market day after day. Even the most powerful of market operators can influence the market for at most a day or two, and that too only when they are on the same side as the majority. It may appear that the market operators are driving prices, when in reality they are just riding the wave. Stock market history is replete with players who went bankrupt after having made the error of thinking they had become bigger than the market.

Somewhere along the way, Harshad seemed to have lost his sense of proportion. He was becoming dangerously overconfident. The bear cartel repeatedly attempted to fell him by short-selling the stocks he was long on. Not only did they fail, but they also suffered huge losses in the bargain as those stocks continued to spiral skywards.

I doubt if there will ever be another bull run like the one in the market between 1 January and 2 April of 1992. During that period, the Sensex more than doubled, from 1,957 to a high of 4,546. Harshad's prophecy about ACC did come true – the stock touched Rs 10,500 on the day the Sensex peaked. It was indeed a price beyond anybody's imagination.

Harshad celebrated his triumph over the bear cartel by actually feeding peanuts to a bear in the city zoo, and getting that recorded by the video magazine *Newstrack*. Some of the old-timers felt he had overreached himself by publicly humiliating his rivals in this way.

Over the three months of the bull run, I made close to Rs 3.5 lakh. In the meantime, my relationship with Harshad had frayed. After that somewhat tentative start with him, we had begun to get closer. On a few occasions, I had got good deals for him, which he appreciated. He also trusted me enough to give me open-ended orders to buy shares for him, certain that I would not betray him.

A couple of people in his inner circle resented my growing proximity to him. Sharma hinted about them to me but did not name them, but I had a fair idea who he was referring to. Once in a while I would go short on some of the Big Bull's favourites. This was faithfully relayed to him. I do not think he would have taken offence to that, though it did mean I was challenging his judgement in taking an opposite position. But he was informed that my loyalty lay with the bear cartel. Since I got along well with Manubhai and did some trades for him as well, some thought of it as more than just a business relationship.

Then, on one occasion, I got a really poor price for a block of shares he had asked me to sell for him, despite my best efforts. His cronies told him that I was regularly ripping him off on deals. Earlier, I could pick up the phone and speak to him directly whenever I had a block of shares he was interested in. But now a wall seemed to be gradually growing between us. He was either too caught up with bigger things to spare time on small fry like me, or he had begun to suspect me because of the tales he was being fed. Once I had a good block on offer and called his office to inform him about it. His dealer came on the line and told me that they would get back. They never did. Two days later, I learnt that they had done the deal through somebody else. This happened once again, and by now I was really mad at the shoddy manner in which I was being treated. It would be a long time before I would speak to Harshad again.

The reckless manner in which Harshad was ramping up his stocks meant that he was pushing his luck too far. People say that had he slowed down a bit, he could have walked away a rich man without anybody the wiser, and perhaps the game could have gone on for longer. I think he fell into a trap of his own making. Once stock prices rise to a certain level, you need increasingly bigger purchases to maintain the stock price. Else, the price will simply collapse and trigger further selling as more people exit the stock in panic. I feel that even if the game had been prolonged, the end result would not have been any different, knowing Harshad and his eternally bullish world view.

The Big Bull eventually ran out of luck in April. The starting point of his trouble was the government's decision to establish SEBI to supervise the stock exchanges in the country. The first major decision by SEBI was to ask brokers to re-register themselves by paying a higher registration fee. The powerful broker lobby, which until then used to set its own rules, did not take to the SEBI diktat kindly. In protest, many exchanges across the country went on strike from 16 April to 24 April. All trading activity came to a standstill.

This made matters difficult for Harshad as he was counting on the pay-out from BSE to repay the funds he had 'borrowed' from the State Bank of India (SBI), promising to buy them securities. While reconciling its books, SBI found that Harshad had not delivered the securities he had taken money for. The bank pressured Harshad to either deliver the securities or repay the money, and before Harshad could reach a settlement with the bank, the matter found its way to the press.

That effectively blew the lid off the scam, and it was found that many banks and financial institutions were not holding the securities they had paid for, or were holding fake or forged bank receipts instead of the actual securities. News of the scam sent the market into a tailspin, and the Sensex crashed to below 3,000 by the end of May. The size of the scam was initially estimated at a little over Rs 4,000 crore. Later, the Central Bureau of Investigation (CBI) put the figure at over Rs 8,300 crore, based on the cases registered.

Harshad was not the only one in trouble. The scam tarnished many reputations on Dalal Street, ended many promising careers at the banks involved in the scam, and also ruined the lives of many junior employees who were only following orders.

Later, a report by the Joint Parliamentary Committee probing the scam would say that irregularities in bank receipts had been going on since 1986, and that the matter had been brought to RBI's notice but nothing was done about it. The report would also say that foreign banks in the country had not only been the major players in the scam, but had also initiated the entire process of the scam. And, in exactly the same way that Harshad had become the face of the biggest rally in the stock market, he was now made out to be the kingpin of the biggest scam to have hit the stock market.

# 9

# A Fresh Start, a New Mentor

Harshad's arrest in the first week of June took the battle out of the bulls. Later, it emerged that the bear cartel had managed to escape by the skin of their teeth. Harshad's reckless purchases and the resultant surge in share prices had pushed some of the smartest stock market bears to the brink. But it also emerged that most of them – if not all of them – had managed to somehow obtain funds to be able to stay in the fight longer than otherwise seemed possible. Had the scam not been exposed they would have been in serious trouble. I would not go so far as to use the word 'bankruptcy'. But the bears would certainly suffer wounds that would take long to heal.

I made over Rs 1 lakh from my trades in April. What saved me was my decision to put aside some money for the donation to get Satish into an engineering college. A good chunk of my winnings since the start of the year was in the bank by the time stock prices began their prolonged slide. I took a hit on most of my trading positions though. But looking at the losses most of my friends and acquaintances had suffered, I had reason to be thankful to the Almighty.

Despite having been in the stock market for nearly a year and a half now, I had still not made a single investment myself. I owned no shares in my name. I had taken delivery of shares a few times, but would sell them off in the very next settlement. The main reason for this was my lack of understanding of companies' businesses; I only understood prices. Another reason was my lack of conviction about the merits of investing for the long term. I had heard plenty of stories about retail investors subscribing to the initial public offerings of MNCs in the late 1970s and early 1980s to become millionaires. But I had also heard about quite a few Indian blue chip firms that had become history after being overrun by competitors.

And lastly, I had heard too many horror stories about fake shares. The perils of delivery-based investment – in which the buyer takes delivery of the physical shares – were once again manifest in the wake of the securities scam.

The special court appointed to try the scam-related cases had 'notified' entities suspected of involvement in the scam and against whom criminal charges had been filed. These entities included Harshad Mehta, his associate firms and some others. Any share certificate that bore the name of any of the notified entities was seized by the custodian entrusted with recovering the dues owed to the banks and the taxes owed to the government. It did not matter that in many cases the shares had been bought before the entities had been notified. In other cases, the shares had changed hands a few times after the notified entities had sold them. Often, investors who were the buyers of shares sold by the notified entities did not send the shares for transfer to their own names. They would hold on to the shares for a while before selling them, and the shares would change hands several times until the investor at the end of the chain sent them for transfer to his name. This further hardened my resolve against buying shares for delivery.

Barring one or two, all our firm's clients lost heavily when the market tanked. They had all invested heavily in Harshad's favourite stocks. A few of them defaulted on huge payments, and the losses had to be borne by the firm. My owner himself had taken some big positions on which he took hefty hits. Our firm was now poised on the brink of a shutdown.

By July, my employer decided to get out of the broking business and try his hand at something else. He owed me around Rs 50,000, including my commissions. He added another Rs 50,000 to it. 'Lala, I would have liked to be even more generous, but I am really stretched at this point,' he said apologetically.

I believed him. He never haggled while sharing profits from the deals I made, and never questioned me on the deals that went wrong. I really respected the man. And, while he may not have been able to give me a handsome severance package, he recommended me to one of the masters of the trade, Govindbhai, who happened to be a good friend of his.

I had heard about Govindbhai though I did not know him personally. He was what they called the broker's broker. His speciality was execution of trades for the big boys of Dalal Street across rival groups. He was not a regular in the ring; he usually worked the phone to source and offload large blocks. At other times, his dealers would be seen bargaining in the ring. His clients trusted him on two counts: one, he would not front-run their trades (take advantage of their orders by putting in his own buy/sell orders, as used to often happen in the case of UTI ), and two, he would not discuss their trades with anybody. Govindbhai's business model was clear: he chose to make his money from plain vanilla broking, which did not entail any risk other than clients defaulting. He had multiple broking memberships and an office in Calcutta (now Kolkata). It was a rainy morning in late July when I walked into his office in one of the nondescript buildings on Nagindas Master Road, which sits at a right angle to the famed Dalal Street.

Govindbhai was of medium height, square-jawed, and had a broad forehead with hair slicked back, but what struck me were his unfriendly eyes. He was in his late thirties or early forties, and I had heard that he had been around for over fifteen years. I do not know if it had to do with his eyes, but there appeared to be a permanent scowl on his face. As I would learn later, it was just a facade. Govindbhai wanted to create an impression of being unapproachable. But he was a genial person once you got to know him, and he trusted you well enough. He had a wry sense of humour too, which I enjoyed a lot.

He greeted me with what I thought was a forced smile. Smiling did not come naturally to him. My first impression of him was of a man mistrustful of the world at large. We discussed the market for a few minutes, and that put me at ease somewhat.

'My friend has a good opinion of you, and I have heard about some of your exploits,' he said, smiling. This time the smile looked natural.

It was now my turn to force a weak smile. I did not know what to say.

'I know you are good at your work, Lala, because I rarely go by recommendations, even if they happen to come from some of my best friends,' he said. The smile had gone, to be replaced by the scowl. 'But let me also tell you that I prize integrity more than smartness. The nature of any broker's business demands that, as you know,' he said, now in a slightly more friendly tone.

'My staff is small, as you can see. I had two dealers, one of whom quit last month. I have two dealers in Calcutta too. I prefer a small team so that secrecy is maintained as far as possible. That is crucial for me if I am to get the best price for my clients,' he said.

I felt a twinge of irritation. Of course I knew the importance of secrecy in this business. After all, I had now been in the market for nearly eighteen months. As though he was reading my thoughts from my expression, Govindbhai suddenly said, 'Lala, I am aware that you know all this. Still, I thought it would be worth your while to know how particular I am about the confidentiality of my clients' trades. They pay me the best brokerage, and I owe it to them to get the best possible rates. I do not tolerate indiscretion. If I hear you have been indiscreet about my trades, I will not demand any explanation. I have enough friends who keep me informed about what is happening in the market. Dealers who betray me find it hard to get another job with a decent broker. I hope you get the drift.'

I nodded.

'What were you getting paid?'

'10,000 plus a share of my jobbing profits.'

'I will match that. Just ensure that your jobbing trades are not based on the orders we get.'

'I will keep that in mind. Do I start today?'

'No. Go back and think over what I have said. Take my offer only if you feel you can abide by my terms. Let me be frank, I can be a very demanding boss.'

'You will find me equal to the task.'

'I like your confidence. Still, I insist you give it a thought.'

I did not have much to think about. I was quite impressed with Govindbhai. I joined him the following day, and it was to be the beginning of an enduring protégé-mentor relationship. Until this time I had been a self-taught trader. But there were plenty of gaps in my learning and I sorely lacked a good tutor. My association with Govindbhai would gradually fill those gaps.

I soon got to know that one of the reasons for Govindbhai's success was the strength of the relationships he had forged over the years, even though he was very choosy about them.

'It is easy to initiate a relationship, but the challenge is to sustain it, and you can never say which one will turn out to be helpful in a crisis,' he once told me.

I learnt a lot watching Govindbhai at work. He would do his best to ensure that the market did not get the full picture of what his clients were up to. He would do that by executing half the trades on the BSE and the other half on the CSE. He would also keep shifting his positions between exchanges before smart traders could get wind of what was happening. Since he was dealing in large quantities, it was not always possible to camouflage the orders beyond a point. But he had a good strike rate, and that was what mattered most.

The Harshad Mehta-inspired rally may have petered out, but a couple of developments helped the market stabilize after the initial burst of selling. The first was the government's decision to abolish the Controller of Capital Issues, which allowed companies to price their issues as they chose; the second was SEBI's notification of guidelines for FIIs to invest in India.

With the wisdom of hindsight, one could say it was a mistake on the government's part to swing from one extreme to the other. The new regulator had no infrastructure to vet the companies that were rushing headlong into the stock market to raise money. Rules were yet to be formed, and the regulator was still learning. The premium asked by companies for the shares they were issuing to the public were not justified by their fundamentals at all. In fact, there was competition among companies to ask for the highest premium.

In the first place, many of the companies themselves were not sure what they were raising money for. Self-proclaimed merchant bankers offered to help companies raise equity capital for fat commissions.

Meanwhile, with the decks cleared for foreign investment in the stock market, FIIs started sending out reconnaissance teams to check out its potential. The representatives of these firms were put up at the Taj, Oberoi and other plush hotels. I was told a horde of brokers could be found in their lobbies on any day, waiting to make a pitch to these officials – derogatorily referred to as *goras* (white-skinned).

One Friday, post trading hours, I decided to check out for myself the stories about brokers falling over each other to curry favour with the foreign investors in the hope of getting business from them. I visited one of the five-star hotels where officials from one of the FIIs were cocooned. Sure enough, many of the high and mighty of Dalal Street were milling about in the lobby, awaiting their turn for an audience with the foreign officials. This ritual was to continue for many more months, till the FIIs were convinced that they had to have a full-fledged office in India.

Foreign investors began cautiously, despite all the talk about India being a reforms story. While the FII guidelines were notified in October 1992, FIIs invested less than Rs 15 crore during the period up to March the following year.

Meanwhile, the revelry in the primary market continued unbridled. Nearly 550 companies raised close to Rs 11,000 crore through IPOs in that financial year. This was almost twice the amount raised in the preceding year. Some were worried that another bubble was building up. Who was to know that the bull market in IPOs was just warming up?

The Mumbai serial bomb blasts in March 1993 – one of them right in the basement of the stock exchange building – had market players worried for a while. The main concern was that FIIs would turn their backs on India if they did not see it as a safe place to do business.

I was in the trading ring when the blast shook the building at around 1.30 p.m. I was chatting with a couple of jobber friends who specialized in trading debentures. Those dealing in debentures gather away from the centre of the ring, whose hemispherical roof made for a lower ceiling height at the sides. The blast was so powerful that the plaster of paris ceiling developed deep cracks, spraying us with the powder from it. There was panic all around; people were screaming and stampeding for the exit. There were no casualties inside the stock exchange building, but we could see that the windowpanes of offices even on the twenty-fifth floor of the exchange were shattered by the impact. The glass shards from them killed a few passers-by and some of the food hawkers plying their trade near the entrance of PJ Tower.

I recall broker Mohan Vijan gathering a few of us together and heading for the basement where the explosion had happened, to check for people trapped there. Some of the drivers who hung around in the basement next to their cars were killed in the blast, and I can still recollect the horrible smell of burnt flesh and blood that made me retch.

The blast happened on a Friday The entire staff of BSE slogged through that weekend to ensure that its systems and infrastructure were in place for regular trading to resume on Monday. By keeping the market open, the government wanted to send a signal to the world at large that India was not to be intimidated by terrorists.

I did not go to the market on Monday; Bauji and Ma insisted that I take the day off and be with them that day. I tried talking them out of it, but later yielded to their request, seeing that my presence at home would calm them down a little. They were more shaken by the incident than I was.

The Sensex rose around 100 points in the first two trading sessions of the week. In all likelihood, the government had directed domestic institutions to buffer any panic selling. But the rally fizzled out, and by the end of he March the Sensex was slightly below where it stood before the blasts happened. Still, the market took the blasts in its stride and chose to focus on the positive developments in the economy resulting from policy reforms.

As for me, I preferred to play the IPOs through the thriving grey market in these issues. The grey market, as it was called, was an illegal market for trading in IPOs before they were listed on the stock exchanges. Back then, it took nearly two to two and a half months for an issue to get listed on the stock exchange after the subscription period. In the intervening period, there was money to be made . . . or lost.

# 10

# Not Black, but Grey

By the end of my second month with Govindbhai – or GB, as he was popularly known – he had taken a liking to me. During trading hours, he was a taskmaster, a boss very hard to please. But once work for the day was done, he would become a different person. Sometimes he would chat with me and the other dealer Dilip and talk about his experiences on the stock exchange. They were fun as well as insightful, considering that GB had been in the market since 1975.

'Have you ever given a thought as to how the grey market in IPOs came about?' he asked us one evening as we were sipping tea.

Both Dilip and I shook our heads.

'It is one of the many consequences of the licence raj and quota raj that used to prevail in the 1970s and 80s. Demand invariably exceeded supply, resulting in a black market for just about everything. You could say that the grey market for IPOs was actually a black market where you could get extra shares if you were willing to pay a higher price for them.

'There was another reason for the emergence of the grey market. Most issues in those days just about got subscribed.

I am talking about the days when IPOs of MNCs had not yet made the share market popular. To ensure that their issues sold, promoters would create a premium on their shares to get investors interested. If an issue priced at Rs 10 was quoting for Rs 11 in the grey market, the public would naturally develop an interest in those shares. The operator willing to buy the shares for Rs 11 in the grey market was backed by the promoter or the investment banker to the issue. After the initial bids for a few thousand shares that helped set a price, market forces usually took over. If that did not happen, the operator would keep buying some more shares till sufficient interest was generated.'

'In a way, the premium created by the promoter was a kind of promotional expense,' I remarked.

'Absolutely. And the grey market was quite active because of the staggered payment structure too. Investors subscribing to an IPO or rights issue had to pay 25 per cent at the time of application, 25 per cent on allotment and the balance 50 per cent when the company would call for it, which would usually be a month or two after listing.

'Retail investors were usually assured of allotment of the full quantity they had applied for. So they could sell an equivalent quantity in the grey market at a premium and deliver the shares once they got allotment. In absolute terms, the gains may not have been huge since the premium itself was not very big. But if you converted the profits into annualized returns, it was as high as 40-50 per cent,' GB said.

Memorable among the many stories he told us was a funny one about the grey market, and another which illustrated how the public issue market functioned.

'There used to be a frail chap called Kamani, who always sported a bowler cap. He was well known in market circles as the agent of operators who were active in the grey market. If ever you wanted to buy shares of IPOs in the grey market, Kamani was the man to go to. He always had a quote ready. I had just joined the stock market and was working with a broker named Shroff.

'Once, Shroff was chatting to a friend on the pavement outside his office, and Kamani happened to be having tea across the road.

'"This Kamani fellow, I tell you, he will sell you anything, even if he hasn't heard the name of the company. Tell him you want to buy tetrapods (the concrete structures along Marine Drive that shield the wall of the promenade from the tides) and he will sell you that too" Shroff told his friend.

'The friend found this hard to believe, and so Shroff decided to prove it. He called Kamani over.

'"Kamani, I want a quote for Tetrapod, which is coming out with an issue shortly," Shroff told him confidently.

'At this, Kamani took out his pocket diary which had the grey market rates. He flipped through a few pages, but did not find any company by the name of Tetrapod. In those days most of the shares were priced at Rs 10. So Kamani ventured a quote, even though he had no idea what the company was about.

'"One rupee," he told Shroff.

'"Is that your best rate?" Shroff asked.

'"Yes, Mr Shroff, I am sure you know that nobody offers better rates than I do," he said.

'"Of course I do, Kamani, I would like to buy 5,000 shares," saying which Shroff shook hands on the deal and

Kamani noted it in his diary.

'Five days later, Kamani came to Shroff's office one evening.

'"Mr Shroff, is this Tetraford a joint venture with the Ford Company of the US?" he wanted to know.

'Even I was amused that Kamani could offer a quote for a company whose very spelling he was not sure about.

'"Yes, of course," Shroff said, sounding serious.

'"In that case, is there some prospectus available?" asked Kamani.

'"Why, what happened??" Shroff asked in return.

'"I told my clients about the company and there is strong demand for it. One of my clients said it could possibly be a JV with Ford. If that is the case, I want to quote a proper premium so that I don't end up on the losing side," he said.

'Shroff promised to get the prospectus for him in a couple of days, and then two days later told him about the joke. Such was the booming grey market that some of the leading newspapers carried the grey market rates for the Tetraford issue alongside the regular stock quotations issued by the exchange,' GB recalled.

'This almost made the quotes appear as authentic as the official quotes for the regular market. The rates were diligently faxed to the newspaper offices by Kamani and his group. Worried that this could invite trouble from the government, BSE president Phiroze Jeejeebhoy called the grey market players to his office and warned them against providing quotes to the newspapers in the manner that they had.'

GB's other story was about a Delhi-based company called Milk Food Products, which was looking to raise money through a public issue.

'The company had hired a top foreign bank to market the issue, but response to the issue was lukewarm. A senior official by the name of Ahuja at the foreign bank was a good friend of Shroff's. He came over to discuss his predicament with Shroff.

'Ahuja told Shroff about the company's strengths and bemoaned the lack of interest in the issue.

'"The company may be good, but the market is not confident about it," Shroff told him.

'"What is to be done for that?" Ahuja asked.

'"I will tell you," Shroff told him, calling out to me, "Just ask Kamani to come to my office and tell him there is a new issue I want to know his views on." He then turned to Ahuja and said: "While I am talking to Kamani, you will not utter a single word."

'Ahuja agreed.

'A few minutes later, I returned with Kamani in tow.

'After some small talk, Shroff asked Kamani what he thought of the Milk Food Products issue.

'"*Kuch dum nahin hain issue mein*. Firstly, you can never trust Delhi-based companies. Six months later, there will be no milk, no food and no products," Kamani remarked casually.

'I could see that Ahuja was trying hard to restrain himself from having a go at Kamani. But having given his word to Shroff, there was nothing he could do. After Kamani left, Shroff told Ahuja: "There is a perception problem. The only way you can fix it is by creating a buzz in the grey market. Unless you are able to do that, the issue is doomed."

'Ahuja agreed, and gave Shroff the mandate to buy as many shares of Milk Food from the grey market as he could.

Shroff did that, and as a result the premium for Milk Food shares in the grey market shot up dramatically. Players who had short-sold the shares realized they could be in for trouble on the day of listing and tried to cover up their positions. This frantic buying only fired up the prices even more.

'Staring at a huge loss, the gang of short-sellers approached the BSE president asking him to put a cap on the price of the stock on listing day. Since it was not possible to do that without being accused of bias, the president decided to do the next best thing. He called for a meeting with Shroff and a couple of other brokers to whom the short-sellers owed big money.

'The president requested that Shroff and the issue manager reach a settlement with the bear syndicate. Shroff was a bit miffed since it would mean having to forgo a chunk of what he felt were his rightfully earned profits. He expressed his displeasure to the president, who in turn felt that matters of the exchange should be settled amicably among the members.

'Shroff relented, as he did not want to hurt his long-standing relationship with the president, who was a highly respected figure of his time,' GB said.

Our evening conversations would sometimes stretch to over an hour. GB also told us how it was the success of share issues by MNCs that got retail investors interested in the stock market.

'Under the FERA Act of 1974, MNCs were forced to reduce their stake to 40–74 per cent by offering shares to Indian investors. The companies that could prove they had special technology were required to dilute only 26 per cent of their stake; export-oriented firms had to dilute 49 per cent of their stake; and the rest, 60 per cent. Conservation of scarce foreign exchange and getting foreign companies to invest more in India were the main reasons for the Indira Gandhi government to initiate that proposal.

'By the time of its implementation, the Janata Party had come to power. The companies that agreed to dilute their stake and get listed on the stock exchange could continue with their business in India while the rest had to pack up and leave the country. IBM and Coca-Cola were among those that chose to withdraw from India. The industries minister George Fernandes has been credited with having thrown both the companies out of India. But the truth is far simpler – the companies left of their own accord.

'Being forced to dilute their holding was bad enough. Worse still, MNCs were not given the freedom to fix the price at which they could sell their shares to the Indian public. That was decided by the Controller of Capital Issues, based on a formula linked to their book value and earnings track record.

'This led to the companies having to offer shares at prices far below what they were actually worth. The CCI rule, though a blessing for Indian shareholders, was hard on the companies, as share valuation is based on perception about future earnings and not the past performance of companies. In fact, nearly every share issue was offered to financial institutions and retail investors for a song. The MNCs' loss was the gain of financial institutions and retail investors. I would go so far as to say that the share offerings helped strengthen institutions like UTI and LIC as they got the lion's share of the issues. This helped them build a first-class portfolio of shares at bargain prices. How else would they have been able to build the portfolios they had?

'There may be plenty of fundamentally sound companies. But you can't make big money by investing in their shares unless you are able to buy them cheap. The equity cult in the country got a big boost in 1977 when Hindustan Lever and Reliance Industries brought out their IPOs within a few weeks of each other. Brokers doubted whether there was enough liquidity in the market to absorb both issues. To everyone's surprise, both issues got a decent response. Those two issues alone would have caused a massive expansion of the shareholder base in the country.

'Through the late 1970s and till the early 1980s, there was easy money to be made from public issues. Colgate, HLL, Castrol, Ciba, Ponds, Pfizer, Glaxo, Bata, Cadbury, Richardson Hindustan (now Procter & Gamble), numerous tea plantation companies and others gave handsome returns to investors who risked their money on the shares.

'Gradually, word got around and more investors began to apply, resulting in issues getting oversubscribed. Once that started to happen, allotments were no longer assured. Still, investors applying for small lots got preference over those who applied for big lots. The offshoot of this was multiple applications by small investors, as this boosted their chances of getting an allotment. Every investor would make at least four to five applications in the names of his kith and kin in addition to his own, hoping at least one would hit the target.

'Other than MNCs names, some quality Indian companies too came to the market in the 1980s. Hero Honda, TVS, Apollo Hospitals, and Dr Reddy's were among the notable names.

'A typical prospectus consisted of a full page in a broadsheet newspaper. Most of the details in the prospectus were statutory information. The small table on profit and loss was sketchy. I guess the volume of information was just right, but the quality of information was suspect. Companies could make any claim, and there was nobody to vet it.

'Right now, people are worried about a possible bubble in the public issue market waiting to burst. If you ask me, what we are seeing right now is nothing compared with the mania old-timers like me have seen in the mid-1980s. There was a boom in leasing companies soon after Rajiv Gandhi came to power. Many sectors were partly opened up, and this led to a huge requirement for working capital. Since bank finance was limited and not all companies could go public, it was expected that leasing companies would fill that gap. That became a sort of self-fulfilling prophecy. Many leasing companies flocked to the market to raise capital. The sums raised were in the range of Rs 60 lakh to Rs 1 crore. The boom in leasing companies soon spread to other segments too. On 11 February 1986, there were 110 issues launched in a single day. I don't think I will see anything like that in my lifetime again. A handful of issues gave good returns, but an overwhelming majority of them bombed.

'Public memory being short, caution was once again thrown to the winds when mini-steel and mini-cement companies started hitting the market to raise capital in the late 1980s. And now there is some new fad going on. This will keep happening every few years no matter what history has to show. This short-lived public memory is what has kept the stock market going all these years.'

Our discussions with GB did put things in perspective, but one could really learn things only from first-hand experience.

FII activity in the Indian market kept rising steadily. There were more foreign fund managers now staying at five-star hotels. They were inundated with calls and visits from brokers seeking business from them.

Prakash was quite clued in about the gossip on Dalal Street, and would let me in on some of the lurid details.

'Mr X is quite thick with some of the fund managers. Do you know why, Lala?' he would ask me with a wicked smile. I had heard some stories too, and the cast in every story would usually be different even if the plot was the same.

'Go ahead, Prakash, enlighten me,' I would egg him on.

'Well, Mr X goes to the fund managers armed with two lists: one has investment ideas and the other has the names of high-society call girls and B-grade actresses. No prizes for guessing which list helps clinch the business,' Prakash would say with a chuckle.

'But in all fairness,' he continued, 'Mr X is far more professional compared with Mr Y, who goes to meet fund managers with just one list.' More laughter would follow.

In 1993-94, around 770 companies raised over Rs 13,000 crore through IPOs. Investors were lapping up everything on offer, never mind the credentials of the promoters or the business models. There was one high-profile fiasco, though: Morgan Stanley's maiden mutual fund scheme launch in India. The US-based investment bank was the first foreign player to start a mutual fund company in India. Its maiden offer in January 1994 was the Morgan Stanley Growth Fund, a fifteen-year close-ended equity scheme. Those who invested would have their money locked in the scheme till it matured fifteen years later. The units were priced at Rs 10 each, and retail investors thought this was no different from a regular IPO, which could double or even treble on listing. Few knew the difference between open-ended and close-ended schemes, and even fewer understood the concept of net asset value (NAV) and units. Soon there were long queues of eager investors to buy application forms to subscribe to the scheme.

Morgan Stanley grandly announced that units would be allotted on a first-come-first-served basis. Nobody asked it how the firm would be able to ascertain which investors had applied first when the application forms were going to be collected from all over the country. I guess even the fund would not have anticipated the kind of response it would get from ill-informed investors looking to make a fast buck.

The fund had aimed to raise Rs 300 crore, but ended up raising Rs 1,000 crore.

Unfortunately for all the enthusiastic investors, the Morgan Stanley fund ended up buying too many wrong stocks and at such terrible prices that when the first NAV was announced, unitholders were poorer by 10 per cent. Worse was their realization that they could not exit their investment for the next fifteen years. The mutual fund units could be traded on the stock exchange, however, but they were quoting lower than the fund's NAV. That experience left a bad taste in the mouth, and for the next few years Indian investors would shudder at the very mention of the term 'mutual fund'.

In the meantime, FIIs were slowly warming up to Indian equities. In 1993-94, FIIs pumped in a little over Rs 5,000 crore into Indian equities, with nearly half of it coming through in the last fiscal quarter. Foreign fund managers finally seemed to have tasted blood on Dalal Street and were thirsting for more.

This spelt a hugely profitable business for many brokers who had managed to build a rapport with the important players. In the beginning, many brokers profited at the expense of the foreign funds. I knew two street-smart dealers – broking firm employees who execute buy and sell orders – at two different, reputed broking firms, who were masters at this game.

Their modus operandi was simple. FIIs dealt in large blocks of shares. These two dealers were expert at sourcing big blocks because of their connections in financial institutions. The shares would be bought cheap from the domestic institution by a broker fronting for the dealers. The dealers would then buy the shares for the FII client from this broker at an inflated price. The difference would usually be settled in cash between the dealers and the front broker. At times, these trades happened with the full knowledge of the officials at both the domestic institutions and the foreign fund houses, since they too got a share of the spoils.

It was not just the institutional brokers who were fattening themselves at the expense of their foreign clients; jobbers too had a field day quoting outrageous spreads. Because it was an open outcry system, FIIs wanting to buy stocks beyond the top ten most actively traded ones were forced to accept the terms of the jobbers in those stocks. Electronic screen-based trading, introduced by NSE towards the end of 1994, would end some of the malpractices, but not all of them.

As for the two sharp-witted dealers, they endeared

themselves to dance girls in the Topaz bar by generously lavishing crisp tenners on them. Each of them is known to have at times blown up as much as Rs 5 lakh in a single night on their favourite girls. Back in the early 1990s, Rs 5 lakh went a really long way. News of their extravagance soon reached the ears of their employers, and the duo had to tone down their wild ways. In another six years, Rs 5 lakh would look like loose change when a few brokers from Calcutta went berserk over the girls.

# 11

# Winds of Change

Foreign fund houses may have been ripped off in the initial days, but the unscrupulous fund managers among them had a fabulous time personally, being wined, dined and fawned upon by brokers eager for business. Some of the big brokerages regularly hosted barge parties off the Gateway of India for their FII clients, and even organized striptease shows.

NSE's arrival on the scene as a competitor to the BSE dramatically changed the way business was transacted. There was no dearth of stock exchanges across the country at that point, but BSE was by far the biggest and most important of them all. It had the maximum number of companies listed on it, and was more liquid compared with its peers. CSE came within respectable distance of matching it in terms of liquidity, while the Delhi Stock Exchange was a distant third.

While many retail investors in far-flung towns preferred to transact on BSE, they invariably ended up getting poor prices because their orders would be routed through a chain of sub-brokers to the main broker in Mumbai. Each sub-broker in the chain would charge his commission, with the result that brokerage charges alone would amount to 3-4 per cent or even higher. Finally, whether the investor got a good deal or not depended on how efficient and scrupulous the main broker was. More often than not, the purchase price was marked up closer to the highest price of the day and the selling price closer to the lowest level of the day. Brokers could afford a 'take-it-or-leave-it' policy with their retail clients, fully aware they could not be assured of reliable prices or good service even if they were to take their business elsewhere.

This is not to say that BSE did not have any progressive-minded members. Mahendra Kampani, when he was president of the exchange, tried hard to computerize the trading process and convert the open outcry system into a screen-based one. With screen-based trading, brokers could put in their orders on a trading terminal from the comfort of their offices. The advantages of electronic trading were twofold. One, liquidity would increase as more investors could simultaneously access the system. This would shrink the spreads (difference between the buy and sell quotes) dramatically. More importantly, there would be greater transparency about the prices at which shares were actually sold or bought.

The move would have been beneficial for investors, but it would have also dented the profitable businesses of many jobbers and brokers who thrived on the wide spreads and opaque prices resulting from low liquidity. In fact, the majority of the jobbers would have been rendered redundant. Not surprisingly, Kampani faced huge opposition from the broking community, and the proposal was put in cold storage.

What the broker-jobber lobby did not realize was that in blocking computerization, they had dealt a crippling blow to BSE, a blow from which the institution would never really recover. Had BSE opted for computerization at that stage, NSE would have had to work harder to snatch market share from it. I cannot say for sure if BSE would have been ahead of NSE had it computerized its systems earlier, because the BSE continued to score self-goals even after the NSE had started nibbling away at its lunch.

Years later, when I met up with a veteran BSE broker who had once been a president of the bourse, he told me how the exchange's electronic trading plan never got the backing it should have from the government. In fact, it appeared as though some influential people in the government had resolved to marginalize BSE.

My own view, which many old-timers also agree with, is that somewhere along the way, the BSE brokers' lobby had become too powerful for its own good and was beginning to be seen as a challenge to the government. In the late 1980s, when former UTI chairman Manohar Pherwani – the original Big Bull of the Indian stock market – tried to get a broking card for a UTI subsidiary, he was denied it. UTI did huge business with the brokers and was aware that it was being regularly fleeced on quite a few transactions. Large deals would be leaked and the prices it got on many trades were far from satisfactory. To get around the problem, UTI decided to have its own broking card. But the big boys of Dalal Street would have none of it. One, the brokers who made a living off UTI's deals would lose a big share of the business. Two, giving membership to UTI would lead to similar requests from other institutions too. It is said that

Pherwani was incensed, but there was little he could do. Some other institutions too tried requesting for membership, but they too were snubbed.

When the newly established SEBI tried to get brokers to register with it for a fee, the proposal was stoutly opposed by brokers and jobbers. They refused to carry out transactions, with the result that BSE had to be shut for a week in April 1992.

Finance Minister Manmohan Singh, who visited Bombay during that time, came down to BSE to meet the agitating brokers. I was told by friends that the brokers behaved badly with the finance minister, shouting slogans and booing him. This must have piqued the government, which was in the midst of rolling out the red carpet to foreign investors to get them to invest in the stock market. The leading exchange of the country holding the government to ransom would have only served to drive the investors away.

Thus it was that NSE, set up with financial institutions as its principal shareholders, and originally meant to be a trading platform for wholesale debt, was given permission to start an exchange for trading in shares too. It commenced operations in November 1994, overnight changing the rules of the game. Incumbents like BSE had no choice but to follow suit or risk becoming obsolete.

While their core business was the same – bringing together buyers and sellers of shares – there was a marked difference between the business models of NSE and BSE. From the first day of its operations, NSE started operations with an electronic trading system. It would take a few more months for BSE's computerized system to become operational. NSE followed a weekly settlement cycle, just like BSE, but unlike on BSE, trades on NSE could not be carried forward. On settlement day, trades had to be either squared up or settled.

The ever-ingenious brokers found a way to circumvent this hurdle too. The NSE followed a Wednesday-to-Tuesday settlement cycle while the BSE followed a Monday-to-Friday settlement cycle. Towards the close of trading hours on Monday, or early on in the session on Tuesday, brokers would 'shift' their positions from the NSE to the BSE. They would do this by closing their outstanding positions on the NSE, and taking up similars position on the BSE. On Wednesday morning, they would shift their positions back to the NSE by closing out their positions on the BSE and taking fresh positions on the NSE. In this way, they could keep carrying forward their trades on the NSE even though it did not have a formal carry-forward mechanism.

The NSE was run by professionals and did not have even a single broker member on its board. In comparison, the BSE's governing board was packed with brokers, and the officials in charge of operations complained of frequent interference by influential brokers. Above all, the NSE's big advantage over the BSE was its pan-India reach, offering services across the country. The BSE had to wait for some months before it could expand beyond Bombay. That head start made quite a difference, as the NSE had already made a mark for itself in many of the smaller towns by the time the BSE came calling.

NSE's biggest contribution to the stockbroking industry was the vast new breed of brokers it spawned. Anybody could become an NSE member by paying a deposit fee and clearing an exam. The day the member wanted to opt out, his deposit would be returned. The closed club culture of the BSE only worked to the advantage of the NSE. The number of membership seats, or cards, as they were called, on BSE was limited. Anybody aspiring to become a member had to buy a card from an existing member. This arrangement helped keep the price of the membership card very high because there were very few sellers. At the peak of the rush for BSE membership, ING Barings bought a seat for a whopping Rs 4 crore. Never was a BSE card sold for anywhere close to that price ever again.

The BSE brokers found the deposit concept of membership laughable, as did the brokers on the Calcutta and Delhi bourses. For the many aspiring brokers who were kept out by the powerful broker lobbies of the Bombay, Calcutta and Delhi Stock Exchanges, the NSE was the answer to their dreams. As for investors, they had been at the mercy of the whims of the brokers in the big city, and stood to benefit hugely.

As much as they derided the NSE in public, many of the large the BSE brokers privately applied for membership on the NSE. They wanted to hedge their positions. They were convinced that the NSE would flop, but just in case it did well they did not want to lose out on clients.

Electronic trading was a grand concept, but there were plenty of operational issues. For instance, if the broker was located in Mumbai, it was easy to have a leased line connecting him to the exchange's trading system. But it was not possible to drag leased line cables to other parts of the country. The NSE solved this by offering a satellite network to help brokers in other states and the far-flung corners of Mumbai city to connect to its trading system. In effect, the

NSE had to start as a telecom company, hooking a stock trading platform to its telecom network!

The NSE's debt market segment went live in June 1994, before its equity segment did. By November that year, the equity segment was operational too. The introduction of electronic trading rapidly shrank the spreads and dramatically improved liquidity. Liquidity, in turn, attracted more players, making the market even more liquid. No longer could brokers fleece investors as the prices were out there for all to see. Collection of daily margins and limits on positions that brokers could take up, helped in risk management.

Before the NSE's arrival, the BSE used to be closed for trading from Christmas day up to the day after New Year's day. Not wanting to risk losing business to its rival, BSE decided to do away with the week-long break.

The screen-based system made the whole trading process faceless. Buyers and sellers no longer knew who was on the opposite side of their trades. When trading used to take place in the stock exchange ring, brokers and jobbers could choose whom they wanted to deal with. The community being a small one, everybody knew everybody else by face and name, even if not personally. Brokers would avoid counterparties whom they suspected of bad faith or of not being financially sound to be able to honour commitments. In the ring, I would avoid AS and PS like the plague. But on the screen, there was no way of saying if I was buying from or selling to them.

With BSE too going electronic, many jobbers saw their income drop sharply. Once the kings of certain counters, quite a few of them had to hire themselves out as arbitrage dealers to brokers. Seated in front of two trading terminals

– one of the BSE and the other of the NSE – these jobbers would try to profit from the brief price differentials on scrips on the two exchanges. They would buy on the exchange where a stock was quoting cheap and promptly sell on the exchange where it was quoting a few paise higher. This called for lightning reflexes and for constantly prowling the screens for opportunities. One advantage with the trading terminals over jobbing in the ring was the ease with which one could keep track of one's positions. At one tap of a key or a click of the mouse, you could know your trading positions down to the last share. But the new format was unexciting in other ways. No longer could you look into the eyes of the counterparty and give a quote based on what you thought he was likely to do. Worse still, you could be beaten by somebody who lacked a genuine understanding of the market, but who simply knew how to work the keyboard faster.

While many jobbers were marginalized in the new system, there were also those who adapted and thrived. Needless to say, yours truly was one among them. And, while electronic trading did make many stocks much more liquid, there were limitations. Large orders could still not be put on the screen because it would drive the prices sharply higher or lower, as the entire market could see them. A large buy order would instantly send the stock price soaring as sellers would seek a higher rate; and if there was a large sell order, buyers would quote very low.

The skill lay in negotiating deals for large blocks beforehand with a potential buyer or seller, and then putting the deal through on the screen. That was where people like GB and, in all humility, I, had an edge over those who only knew how to work the keyboard of their trading terminals.

While electronic trading did away with certain malpractices, it created a few others in the bargain. A group of brokers would get together and trade in a stock among themselves to give an impression of heavy volumes. If five brokers traded 10,000 shares between themselves five times, it would appear that 2.5 lakh shares had been traded. Just creating volumes would not help; the price would have to be pushed up too. So each member of the cartel would sell to the next member of the chain at a slightly higher price.

A member of the syndicate would then spread the word that some big investors had taken a liking for the stock. Within no time, retail investors and day traders would rush in to make a quick buck, and the next 2.5 lakh shares would constitute genuine trading volumes. In the mêlée, the members of the syndicate would quietly unload their positions for a tidy profit and head to the next counter.

In barely eleven months of going live, the NSE nosed past BSE in terms of daily traded turnover, becoming the top exchange in the country. Even the NSE was surprised at the speed with which this happened. As for the veteran brokers on BSE, this was a mighty blow to their egos, especially for those who kept ridiculing the NSE even as it was narrowing the gap with BSE. But it hurt their pockets little, since many of them had already bought memberships on the NSE.

From 1994 till mid-1995, the price of the the BSE membership card kept rising, thanks to demand from foreign investment banks that wanted to start broking operations in India. While membership on the NSE was far cheaper, foreign firms were keen on being members on both exchanges.

The arrival of foreign brokerages also led to a huge demand for analysts tracking equities and the economy. By

1994, quite a few domestic brokerages catering to institutional investors had begun hiring analysts to offer research services in addition to executing transactions. Most of the analysts had been roped in from the term-lending institutions, where they used to make project analysis reports.

The domestic brokerages were paying them a good salary, considering most of them were chartered accountants and MBAs. But overnight, foreign broking firms upended the wage structure of the industry by offering these analysts three to four times their existing salaries. It was a typical *Godfather* kind of offer that most analysts found hard to refuse.

Domestic brokerages were furious, but could not afford to compete with their foreign rivals on salaries. From 1994 onwards, Morgan Stanley, Merrill Lynch, Barclays De Zoete Wedd (BZW), National Westminster (NatWest), Indo Suez WI Carr, Hoare Govett, Credit Lyonnais (later CLSA) ABN Amro, Peregrine, Jardine Fleming, Socgen Crosby, HSBC (in partnership with Batlivala & Karani for a long time), ING Barings, UBS, Credit Suisse First Boston, Caspian, Cazenove, were among the firms that went on to set up shop in India. The aftermath of the Asian currency crisis of 1997 would see many of them retreat from India, and the dotcom bust of 2001 would claim some more casualties.

Some of the big names chose to dip their toes in the perilous waters of Indian stock broking, hand-held by some of the leading domestic names. Merrill Lynch chose DS Purbhoodas as its partner, Morgan Stanley allied with JM Financial, and Goldman Sachs teamed up with Kotak Securities. All the marriages would dissolve over the next decade or so.

The arrival of FIIs improved India's standing in the global markets. It was way down in the pecking order, but had finally got noticed. However, while trading volumes had improved considerably, thanks to electronic trading, there was still not enough liquidity for FIIs to trade in large lots.

The market hierarchy also changed with the entry of FIIs. Once the undisputed king of the Indian stock market, the Unit Trust of India could no longer impact prices or sentiment the way it used to. The same brokers who would queue up for hours at the UTI headquarters were now trying hard to ingratiate themselves with the new masters of the game – the FIIs. Brokers and jobbers were obsessed with what the FIIs were up to, just as they had been trying to sniff out UTI's deals till a few months ago.

## 12

# Money for Jam

With FIIs scaling up their operations in India, the frenzy in the primary market showed no signs of abating. Retail investors regained their love for the stock market, but the quality of companies seeking to raise money was rapidly going from bad to worse. Fly-by-night merchant bankers helped shady promoters raise money for projects that existed only on paper. Eventually, many of the companies and their promoters would simply vanish, never to be heard of again.

Self-proclaimed merchant bankers would cold-call promoters asking if they wanted to raise money. A typical conversation between the merchant banker and the promoter would go something like this:

Merchant banker: Sir, would you like to raise Rs 10–15 crore?

Promoter: Not at the moment.

Merchant banker: But markets won't be as hot for long. You must raise money when it is available.

Promoter: What is the rate of interest?

Merchant banker: There is none.

Promoter: Really? But I still have to return the money at some point, right?

Merchant banker: No, and that is the beauty of it.

Promoter (suspiciously): You mean, I get the money, I don't have to pay interest, and I don't have to return it. Is that what you are saying?

Merchant banker: Exactly.

Promoter: You have got me interested.

In less than a week, a flaky prospectus with ambitious projects and projections would be ready and the company would be all set to go public. The merchant banker would get to keep anywhere between 15 and 20 per cent of the capital raised.

GB once told me about a promoter of an electronic goods trading firm who happened to be a good friend of his. 'Seeing everybody around him make a beeline for the capital market, this friend of mine too decided to try his luck. Sure enough, he managed to get a merchant banker who assured him that his company would find plenty of takers. When I met him at a party, he told me he was planning to price his issue at Rs 50. I told him he would be out of his mind to do so. "On what basis can you price it at Rs 50, and who would want to pay that much when you do not have the earnings to support such a valuation? It is much safer to price your issue at one-third of that," I told him. He promised to think over it.

'I happened to bump into him a week later. He came up to me and said: "Govindbhai, I thought about what you told me at the party the other day. And I kept asking myself about the logic of pricing my issue at Rs 50. Two days back, as I was having a shower, a thought struck me. Why can't my issue price be Rs 75; why should it be just Rs 50? So I have decided to price my issue at Rs 75."'

GB's friend was successful in raising Rs 10 crore. That may sound like chicken feed today, but it was a significant sum at the time. More so for GB's friend, who made less than one-tenth of that sum annually as net profit. It was certainly good enough for some people who would never need to work again for the rest of their lives if they invested it wisely.

I asked GB what happened to his friend.

'I guess he would never have dreamed of coming across such a huge sum in so short a time. He did not know what to do with it. Or maybe he figured it out. One fine day he simply vanished,' GB said.

Aware of the crazy things happening in the market, SEBI stepped in to keep the merchant bankers as well as promoters on a leash. Regulations were laid down for merchant bankers, and those seeking business from companies had to have a licence from SEBI. Merchant bankers were classified as grade I, II, III or IV, depending on their resources and pedigree.

There were other regulations to make the market a safer place for retail investors, such as the requirement of companies to disclose all material facts, follow a code of advertisement, vetting of offer documents by SEBI and furnishing of annual statements. The minimum percentage of the issue to be reserved for the public was reduced to 25 per cent from 60 per cent. When the rule was first introduced in 1993, FIIs and mutual funds had not yet begun to invest in a big way. But as their domination increased over the years, retail investors would gradually be marginalized in the public issue market.

On paper at least, SEBI had put in sufficient checks and balances to avoid a Wild West setting in the primary market. In reality, it was not too difficult for unscrupulous promoters and their merchant bankers to get around the rules, as the MS Shoes fiasco in early 1995 would show.

Usually, when a company received an acknowledgement card from SEBI clearing its prospectus, the promoter would take a bridge loan – a short-term loan – from banks against the expected IPO proceeds. The money borrowed from the bank would be used to ramp up the price in the grey market to ensure the stock quoted at a big premium on listing day. If the company was already listed and doing a follow-on public offering, the bank loan would be used to boost the stock price in the secondary market.

It was not just the promoters and merchant bankers who were greedy. An ex-sheriff of Mumbai and a respected name in social circles was known to charge Rs 5 lakh in shares and Rs 5 lakh in cash to allow his name to be listed as a director on the board of some of the IPO-bound companies. This gentleman would stay on the board for a few months post-listing, and then head for the next company that was looking for credible names.

In 1994-95, over 1,300 companies raised Rs 21,000 crore through public issues. That figure would not be surpassed for some years to come. Some quality companies were part of the procession too, though investors would realize their true worth only many years later.

The boom in the primary market fired up the secondary market, and for players like me, there was money to be made in the secondary market and in the booming grey market for public issues. By mid-September 1994, the Sensex had climbed to a high of 4,643. From then onwards it would be downhill for a long time to come, even though most brokers had taken it for granted that a 5,000 for the Sensex was less than a couple of months away.

That year, I got married to Bina, a match arranged by my parents. I was reluctant to take time off for my honeymoon because of the action in the stock market. But it was GB who prevailed on me to take a break.

'The market isn't going anywhere, Lala. Also, don't make it obvious to Bina that the stock market will always be your first love,' he said in one of his rare jovial moods.

After a two-week holiday, during which we toured Delhi and Himachal Pradesh, I was back at work. Screen-based trading had begun to pick up, despite the misgivings of the older generation of brokers. Initially, like most other traders, I was not happy at having to punch in trades on the screen. It made me feel more like a computer operator than a stock market player. Slowly, I overcame my reservations and warmed to the concept.

Watching the screen and the constant flickering of prices was an education in itself. I would look for patterns and try to guess which way prices were headed. Over the years, I could, with a reasonable degree of accuracy, figure out which operator was manipulating the prices too. In the initial days it had been hard to make out what was happening, as circular trading by cartels often presented a misleading picture of what was going on.

The trading bug slowly spread to retail investors too, now that they could get quotes in real time. Earlier, they were getting the quotes only at the end of the day. Easy access to prices led to many retail investors buying and selling more often than they otherwise had during the days of the trading ring.

Being with GB too made for education of a different kind. I admired his ability to keep cool in the most trying situations and liked the earthy wisdom he dispensed to people seeking his advice.

The promoter of a mid-sized pharma company (which would later grow to become one of the largest firms in the sector) once approached him with a problem.

'Operator X is short-selling my shares almost on a daily basis,' he told GB.

'Is there something about the company that he knows but the market doesn't?' GB asked him.

'There is nothing wrong with the business or the books, if that is what you mean,' the promoter said.

'If you want me to help you, be upfront. Only then can I give you the right solution. Have you pledged a big chunk of your shares with somebody?' GB asked the promoter.

'Trust me, there is nothing wrong. I want you to help me boost the price so that I can teach him a lesson,' the promoter said.

'If there is nothing wrong with the company, my advice to you is to not do anything. Be patient,' GB advised.

'But my stock price will end up getting hammered for no reason. I can't let that happen. I have money to support the price, so why shouldn't I?' he argued.

'You shouldn't, because that is exactly what he wants you to do. Once you start to support the price by buying through friendly brokers, he will see that you are panicking and start hammering the price even more. At some point, when you stop supporting the stock, it will be seen as a sign of weakness on your part and the other bears too will be emboldened to take you on. Let the fundamentals prevail; he will not be able to beat down your stock below a certain level because other informed buyers will find it attractive and start buying. The operator will then be forced to cover his positions,' GB said.

The promoter was not very convinced with this argument. But out of respect for GB he did as he was told. The stock price weakened for a week, but things turned out exactly the way GB had predicted. In less than a month, the price stabilized, and then started inching up as the operator decided to cover up his short positions.

Among GB's clients, I found Radhakishan Damani to be the most disciplined when it came to trading, and most patient when it came to investing. Radhakishan had made a killing in the market crash of 1992 following the securities scam, but had managed to keep a low profile. I got to know from the market that he had come perilously close to bankruptcy and had pledged a sizeable chunk of his blue chip holdings to be able to stay in the game for a few more days. His gamble paid off, and never in his career after that was he revisited by a similar situation.

Radhakishan, at 32, was a relatively late entrant to the stock market, though his father and brother had already been in the stockbroking business for a while when he joined them. He began his working life dealing in ball bearings before he decided to try his hand at share trading. The family's broking card was in the name of his brother Gopikishan S. Damani, and the firm was known in market circles simply as GS. Many years later, even after he had made a name for himself, Radhakishan Damani would still be known in market circles as GS.

The soft-spoken and extremely reclusive Radhakishan found an unlikely partner in the outspoken and high-strung Rakesh Jhunjhunwala, a few years his junior. The duo were like chalk and cheese in many respects but shared a common ideology of value investing, even if they did not always bet on the same stocks. In fact, there were occasions when they took opposite calls on the same stock without their strategies affecting their camaraderie.

Almost everybody on Dalal Street starts his career as a speculator, and the smart few manage to grow their initial profits into a fortune by evolving into long-term investors. By the mid-1990s, the Radhakishan Damani-Rakesh Jhunjhunwala duo (GS-Rakesh, as the market knew the pair) were in the process of that transition after having made a fortune as traders.

Radhakishan had built a sizeable portfolio dominated by MNC blue chips, with Indian Shaving Products Limited (ISPL, later renamed as Gillette India) being one of his big bets. Rakesh was not as big a fan of MNCs as his trading partner, and while his portfolio did have MNC names, it was dominated by domestic companies. I tried to study the strategies of the masters of the game like GS and Rakesh, and improvised on them with some techniques of my own.

Meanwhile, the party in the primary market carried on. Junk companies and their dubious promoters were having a free run, with the underlying strength in the economy giving investors the confidence that the best was yet to come. Then, in February 1995, investors got their first reality check as to the quality of companies and promoters that were raising money from the market. The botched MS Shoes public issue revealed how easy it was for promoters and merchant bankers to hoodwink the regulator. Worse still, the episode also exposed the lax oversight by SEBI in this particular case, and the corruption within its ranks.

The Pavan Sachdeva-promoted company wanted to raise Rs 700 crore to fund a hotel project and a yarn project. It decided to make a composite public issue-cum-rights share offering. The public issue was for fully convertible debentures – bonds that could be converted to equity later on.

MS Shoes was already listed, and the promoter, in collusion with associate brokers, ramped up the stock price to charge a hefty premium for the issue. Shares of MS Shoes climbed from Rs 268 in July 1994 to a record high of Rs 505 by January 1995, thanks to rampant manipulation by brokers backed by Sachdeva. When the stock price of MS Shoes collapsed, the brokers who were buying on behalf of the company could not meet their pay-in obligation to the stock exchange. The BSE had to be closed for three days as the exchange officials sorted out the mess caused by the defaulting brokers. Sachdeva was raided by the taxmen, and soon after, arrested by the CBI. FIRs were filed against two officials of SBI Caps, the merchant banker to the issue and three senior SEBI officials. The government was keen to send out the message that promoters could not take the investing community for granted.

There was some good news for BSE brokers in July that year when SEBI revived badla trading, although the system was revised and was applicable only to A Group stocks on the BSE. The banning of badla had impacted trading volumes on the BSE, though the frenzy in the primary market had compensated for it to a large extent. In 1995-96, industrial output grew a record 11.7 per cent and GDP by 7.1 per cent. The seeds of reform sown in 1991 were beginning to reap a rich harvest and, as it always happens during good times, investors expected the run to continue forever.

But the primary market was slowly beginning to lose steam even as the economy appeared to be in good health.

## 13

# Another Bubble Bursts

The first sign of trouble was a rise in interest rates. In absolute terms, interest rates were quite high at 15–16 per cent in the mid-1990s. Still, companies were able to make good returns on their business even after borrowing at those rates, and continued to expand capacities. Eventually, there came a point when supply exceeded demand and the economy started slowing. Heavy borrowing by the government to balance its books also served to push up interest rates. In addition, the RBI tightened monetary policy, partly to discipline the government and partly to prevent the economy from overheating.

'I think the party is nearing an end; rising interest rates is bad news for the stock market,' GB remarked to me one day as we were having tea after the day's trading.

Seeing the quizzical look on my face, GB explained the link to me: 'Higher interest rates means companies have to pay more on their loans, and this squeezes their profit margins. That itself will cause stock prices to fall in anticipation of reduced corporate earnings. But more importantly, when people can earn 12 per cent on their fixed deposits without breaking a sweat, why would they lose sleep to make 20-25 per cent from equities where the risk is much higher?'

In 1995-96, over 1,400 companies raised a little over Rs 14,000 crore. The year before they had raised around Rs 21,000 crore. The primary market was floundering by now, and the secondary market was doing worse. As long as the primary market did well, a good chunk of the profits would find their way into the secondary market. And while the Sensex remained in a narrow range, there were enough non-index stocks making money for investors. But once the public issue market began to dry up, the secondary market soon began to show withdrawal symptoms.

Towards the end of this phase, my bets in the grey market for IPOs fared badly and I lost a handsome sum. But by then trading was not my only source of income. My ability to find counterparties for investors looking to buy or sell large blocks of shares helped me carve out a niche for myself. As I said earlier, despite the improved transparency and liquidity, it was not easy to buy or sell big quantities of shares through the screen at the punch of a button. These trades would have to be first negotiated over the telephone and then put through the screen.

Soon I grew into something of an inter-institutional broker – or a broker's broker, a more apt term to describe my activity – of whom there were not many on Dalal Street. All I had to do was to point out the interested buyer or seller, and I would get a small fee for my effort. The role required me to be well networked with financial institutions, big brokers and high net worth individuals (HNIs). There were occasions when the temptation to make unethical profits from the information I was privy to tested my willpower. I was on good terms with the dealers at most of the foreign broking firms because of my regular interactions with them. A few of them did proposition me with the lure of a share in the profits. I politely declined, not knowing who might be making a genuine offer and who was simply checking me out.

One of those who made me a proposition, a Punjabi whom I shall call Lucky, persisted in dangling the bait at me. I had to be careful not to offend him because he worked for one of the top broking firms and regularly did business with me.

'What are you trying to prove, Lala? One can't take this high-stress job for long. Make money when you get the opportunity so that you can be out of this game by forty,' he once told me. Like mine, Lucky's too was a rags-to-riches story. He started his working career as an insurance salesman, straying into the broking industry by a quirk of fate and doing well for himself. He lacked refinement, but his street-smart ways and good relationships with people who mattered helped him land a job as a dealer at a foreign brokerage that was among the early entrants in the Indian market.

I had heard many stories about Lucky, one of them about his being on very good terms with a market operator who had got him the job at the foreign brokerage. Lucky repaid his debt to him by occasionally leaking to him information about big trades.

Burly and jovial, Lucky adopted a philosophy that was as earthy as his mannerisms.

'It is God's wish that I should make good money and enjoy life; that is why he put me in the stock market though I had no intention of coming to this industry,' he once told me.

I found Lucky's Pinglish (English with an unmistakable Punjabi accent) quite amusing, and more so when he ranted in English after downing a couple of pegs.

'Everybody here is robbing in some way or the other; the only difference is that some do it in a sophisticated manner,' he would say.

Lucky was aware of his limitations, perhaps the reason why he was so focused in the way he went about things. He was a good storyteller and I enjoyed the tales from his days as a struggler in the industry.

' . . . so there was this elderly fund manager in one of the PSU insurance firms. For some reason he took a liking to me and gave me orders occasionally. That helped me survive in my first job. But there was a price to pay for this kindness even though this gentleman was a much better person than some of his peers at other fund houses. As a token of gratitude, I decided to buy him a fancy bedcover from a friend who dealt in them. It was a beautiful piece – lovely embroidery on fine material – and every bit worth the Rs 1,500 I paid for it. The fund manager initially turned down my present, citing company rules. But when I opened it to show him the design and the feel, he was impressed.

'Still, he maintained that his principles would not allow him to accept expensive gifts from brokers. I lied to him that it was not expensive at all. "I got a very good deal from my friend who deals in export seconds; only Rs 600, sir. That is not very expensive." He accepted the gift and I was happy he liked it. But my happiness evaporated the following day when he called up saying his wife liked the piece so much she now wanted to present similar pieces to her parents and relatives who were coming down the following week.

'He asked me, "Can you arrange for three of them for me, Lucky? I will pay you tomorrow itself." I was caught in a web of my own making. I could not tell him the true price of that piece. I arranged for three more pieces; the fund manager never paid the Rs 1,800 he had promised. I consoled myself that it was a good investment to make. I thought I could expect more orders from him later, but that did not happen either. The following year, he told me that his nephew, an LIC salesman, was falling short of his annual target. "Are you insured?" he asked me. When I told him I was not, he suggested that I buy a policy. And without even asking me, he dialled his nephew saying he had a customer for him. It was obvious that I had to buy a policy from his nephew, whether I liked it or not. Those two episodes taught me the truth in the saying that there are no free lunches; and even if there are, they are not served on Dalal Street, for sure.'

It was not that I was completely disinterested in what the big foreign funds were doing in the market. But I considered it an act of betrayal to front-run trades that were disclosed to me in confidence. I was well networked with dealers at the foreign broking houses, and I had a fairly good idea of the trades the foreign funds were doing. Occasionally, dealers would tell me about their big orders as it boosted their ego.

Because of their large size, buy and sell orders of FIIs influenced share prices. The operators had by then cosied up to the important fund managers, and also had friends among dealers and sales people at foreign brokerages. It was crucial for operators to know what the foreign funds were up to, as their large trades could swing prices either way. Usually, the predators got wind of the big trades and made a killing on them.

Although regular contact with dealers at foreign brokerages afforded you a fair idea of the important deals in the market, you still did not have the complete picture. You might know about a big sell order for a stock at one of the brokerage firms. But there could be a bigger buy order in the same stock at another firm. So, if you only had knowledge of one sell order and short-sold the stock, you could be forced to cover at a loss when the other broking firm punched in its buy order.

As a rule, I never tried to make profits on deals where I had been approached to find a buyer or seller. I remember GB's reply when I asked him what it took to make a lot of money in this market:

'Skill, common sense, patience, inside information and, most importantly . . . ,' he paused to trace out an imaginary circle at the centre of his forehead with his finger, 'kismat . . . it must be in your destiny to make money.

'It is something like this . . . you could be sitting in the lap of the most powerful operator, and he may well punch in your trades before his. But if some disaster were to hit the market at that very moment, you would still end up losing money despite the operator's generosity.'

Broking houses had tried to introduce checks and balances to ensure that client orders were not leaked. All phone lines in dealing rooms were recorded since crores of rupees' worth of shares were bought and sold on verbal communication. The use of mobile phones in the dealing room is banned. Yet, even the best of systems is vulnerable to the ingenuity of the human mind.

Big brokers and market operators had multiple landline connections, even during the pre-electronic trading era. The arrival of mobile phones did not do away with the need for so many lines. In fact, the multiple lines came in quite handy for trading based on confidential information.

Much of the institutional activity happened in a dozen odd pivotal stocks like RIL, SBI, Tata Motors, Tata Steel, ITC and a few others, since these scrips were quite liquid. Each telephone line corresponded to a particular stock. If a dealer wanted to pass on information about an order in a particular stock he would dial a particular number, wait for the phone to ring a few times and then disconnect the call. There would be no conversation. Two rings meant a buy order and four rings a sell order – or the other way round. After a pre-decided interval, there would be another round of rings on the same phone to indicate the quantum of shares that were to be bought or sold.

But this arrangement was not reliable beyond a point. So operators and dealers/fund managers devised code words to share information through what appeared to be innocuous conversation.

There was this trader who was known to friends and associates in the market as Tyson, as he resembled the champion boxer in looks and physique. Tyson was well networked with most of the dealers at the foreign broking houses. They would pass on details of their trades to him before executing them. Tyson would then take positions in those stocks, for himself and for his informants. He would give them their share of the profits in cash. The code language was quite ingenious and even if the dealer was suspected of leaking information, it would be hard to prove the charges in a court of law.

Tyson was thick with Prakash, at whose place Tyson used to trade. Because he was so close to Prakash, I too got along well with Tyson. One day I was at Prakash's office when Tyson walked in saying he wanted to buy a big block of shares. Prakash asked him which stock he intended to buy.

'I will know in ten minutes,' he said.

After ten minutes, his cellphone rang. The conversation lasted barely a couple of minutes.

'Between 3.30 and 4.00, is it? Okay, tell Michael I will be there at the appointed time to collect the papers. Just in case I miss him, when can he make it next? Okay, tomorrow five o'clock, is it? Fine then.'

As soon as the telephone conversation was over, Tyson placed an order for 50,000 shares of Satyam Computer Services. In less than half an hour, Satyam shares rose by Rs 10. Tyson promptly sold out his position. I had no doubt that Tyson had received the tip during the course of the conversation he had on his mobile phone just before he had placed the order.

'So, what is it with Michael and the papers?' I asked, not really expecting an answer. I knew him well enough to take the odd liberty with him. Tyson winked but said nothing. A couple of days later, over a drink, he told me about the code.

'The time I mentioned represented the last three digits of the BSE code for the scrip, Satyam Computer in this case. The exact code is 376, a number between 350 and 400. The dealer friend of mine had told me the previous evening that he was likely to get a big order for Satyam.

'When he got the order, he confirmed it to me over the phone, saying that Michael would come over with the papers.

Michael here refers to a foreign fund house. If the buyer were a domestic mutual fund, the code word would have been Gopal. I then inquired about the order size indirectly, by asking when he would next make it in case I missed him today. My contact mentioned five o'clock, meaning 5 lakh shares. If we had been discussing a sell order, he would have asked me to come over and collect the papers from Michael.

'Obviously, we cannot use the same message every time. At other times, we discuss common friends during the conversation, with each name corresponding to a certain stock. The order size is mentioned in terms of the day of the week or month of the calendar. "I will meet Rohan next Wednesday" means the dealer has a buy order of 4 lakh shares in a particular stock. If he says he won't be able to meet Rohan next Wednesday, it means he has a sell order of 4 lakh shares.

'On other days, the code could be the name of a movie, with the names of the actors corresponding to certain stocks. If the dealer says he liked the role of a certain actor, it meant a buy order. If he says the actor was disappointing, it means a sell order. We could be discussing the timings of local trains, or even a game of cricket. A person overhearing the conversation would not have the faintest clue that we were actually discussing stocks and the orders of clients,' Tyson explained.

It was not too difficult to know which dealers or fund managers were on the take. It was a small world, and word soon got around. Besides, it also showed up in their lifestyle at some point. On a good day, you could easily make a few lakh rupees in an hour. And if you had a few good months in a year, you could make enough to maintain a comfortable lifestyle for the rest of your life.

The information channel I wanted to create was different. If anything, it was quite ambitious. If I spoke to, say, a dozen dealers at big broking firms, I would get to know of most of the important deals. Sometimes dealers would suppress information if they had pending orders to be executed the following day. And rarely would you get to know the name of the client, which to me was important, because the pedigree of the buyer also influenced the short-term trend in a stock. Big fund houses held their shares for longer than lesser-known funds, which were happy to sell out for a small profit.

My quest was for a system by which I got the maximum information by speaking to as few people as possible. I soon found the solution.

Every institutional investor had a custodian that handled shares and payments for them. At the end of the day's trade, the brokerage would send the contract notes containing the details of trades made by their clients to the client's custodian. If it was a buy order, the custodian would then release funds to the clearing house of the stock exchange, and if it was a sell order, it would deliver the shares.

The contract notes were hand-delivered by the broking firm's peon to the custodian. Some traders had already managed to bribe the peons at the big brokerage firms to show them the contract notes before handing them over to the custodian. At times the peons would make copies of the contract notes and pass them over to the traders. But this system had its complications. The broking firms did not always send their contract notes through the same peon. It was not possible to manage all the peons in broking firms.

There was a solution to this problem too. The FII activity data from all custodians had to be finally filed with SEBI. If

I could manage to befriend somebody in the FII department, all the important deals would be at my fingertips. It took me nearly three months, but using my friends-of-friends networks, I finally managed to crack a low-ranking official in that all-important department. I was now set for the big league, or so I thought, since nobody could have the kind of data I would have access to.

The SEBI records did not mention whether the trade was a 'buy' or a 'sell'; instead, it mentioned '1' against a buy trade and '2' against a sell trade. The 1-2 data, as it would be known in market parlance after some months, was the most sacrosanct of all data on FII activity.

I used to pay that official Rs 5,000 every month for the information. I mentally named him 'Mouse' because he would dig out information whenever I requested him to. Our deal was that he would pass me information on a few important trades every day and on certain deals that I would specifically ask for. I never told anybody where I was getting my information from, not even GB or Prakash, the two people I trusted most.

One day, Lucky offered to take me out for a drink in the evening. He suggested White House at Tardeo. I agreed, more out of curiosity than anything else, having heard about that place from so many fellow traders.

The place was dimly lit, but not too crowded for that hour of the evening. We took a table very close to the dance floor where a bunch of overdressed and over-made-up girls were swaying to a 1980s hit number. Lucky called for drinks, and changed a couple of hundreds for crisp tenners to be fired away at the dancers. A few patrons glanced at me, perhaps trying to size me up. Call it my imagination or nerves, but I felt everybody was staring at me. I had been to many bars, but this was the first time I had set foot in a dance bar.

One person looking my way struck me as a market operator Lucky had been pestering me to meet, but whom I wanted to keep away from (it turned out he was not that operator, it was only my imagination). I don't know why, but I was suddenly seized with the fear that Lucky had got me to this place to blackmail me later on. I recalled his persistent offers to me to join the syndicate he was part of, despite my repeated refusals.

Some months before, after he had downed a few pegs, he had put his arm around my shoulder and said: 'You are my true friend, Lala . . . if anybody ever tries to fuck around with you, just let me know. I shall fix him.'

'How? By getting him beaten up?' I had asked.

'No, that will only inflict momentary pain. I have something more lasting. I know people who will have that fellow photgraphed nude alongside some whores; after that he will be at your mercy forever,' he said, laughing. It was a sinister laugh and made my stomach churn a little. I was not sure if he meant what he had said but I could not dismiss his claim outright. After all, he was known to be well connected to the high and mighty in the market.

Sitting with him now, I suspected that Lucky may have a similar plan for me. He was a friend all right, but a pretty ruthless person, as I had realized in these months that I got to know him better.

'Let's leave and go to some other place,' I told Lucky.

'So soon? We have just come,' he said.

I persisted.

He was amused. 'Okay . . . but let's have some fun before that,' he said.

I shifted in my seat uneasily.

He then gave me a rundown on some of the girls on the floor.

'That one in pink there, she is the favourite of a respected businessman who has trouble getting his thing up. His fondness is for money more than women. But somebody introduced him to that girl, and since then he is a regular in this place,' Lucky said, winking ' . . . but I am not going to reveal who that businessman is.'

I didn't even want to know. All I wanted was to get out of that place.

Sensing my indifference, Lucky then said: 'I shall show you somebody who will just blow you over,' and beckoned to a very attractive girl, who would not have been more than twenty-two or twenty-three.

'Payal, I want you to meet my friend Lala,' Lucky said.

'Hello,' she greeted me with a warm smile. I could sense that this girl had some class about her; she was definitely not the run-of-the-mill type.

'Our friend is a bit shy, why don't you liven him up a bit,' Lucky told her.

'Sure,' saying which she moved to the dance floor and began swaying to the number that was playing. I tried hard not to look in her direction, but when I stole a glance I saw that she was casting seductive glances at me.

Lucky handed me a bundle of notes. 'Here, hold this in your palm and fire it away with your finger in the direction of the girl you like. If you want to, you can go right on to the floor and shower it on your favourite,' he said.

'I am fine, why don't you throw it on my behalf?' I suggested.

Our drinks had come by then. I took a couple of sips, trying to look away from the dance floor.

'Look there,' Lucky tugged at my elbow a couple of minutes later, 'Payal is now wearing a different dress. She has taken the trouble to change . . . all for you . . . some effect you must have had on her . . . she is looking at you seductively from time to time . . . what is wrong with you? You are simply ignoring her,' he said.

'Look, Lucky, I just want to leave this place,' I told him firmly.

He stared at me momentarily and said: 'Okay, I give in. But let's at least finish this drink.'

'Promise?' I asked.

'Of course,' he said.

I took my glass and drained it in a few gulps.

'There, I have finished my drink. Come, let's leave,' I said.

Lucky was dumbfounded.

'You are in some hurry, I must say . . . but be a little patient and let me finish my drink,' Lucky said. He took ten minutes to finish it.

As we rose to leave, a waitress (no doubt a retired dance girl now past her prime) asked Lucky for a tip. He reluctantly gave her Rs 50. I thought that was rather cheap. The waitress stood there, looked at the money in her palm and then at Lucky, expecting him to be a bit more generous. Lucky ignored her and had begun to walk away when the lady told him that the tip was too low. This infuriated him. He looked at me and said, '*Saali* . . . she says the tip is too low.' Then, turning to her, he told her in a slightly raised voice: 'I keep telling my boss that my salary is too low . . . but that bastard refuses me, saying he pays his employees only what they are worth. Why the hell should I pay you anything more than you are worth?' I was surprised at Lucky's needless outburst, and had never seen this side of him. It made me all the more wary of him. He need not have paid her more, but neither did he have to insult her.

I was glad that we were finally leaving the place. But Lucky was in no hurry.

'Let me show you the mujra hall before we leave. It is quite a sight, and you may be surprised by some of the faces in the audience,' Lucky said.

I protested, saying I had seen enough for the evening. But Lucky was insistent.

'Don't be such a sissy. You have been quite irritating as it is. I introduced you to one of the girls who has turned down some of the big stars of the market, and you, like an idiot . . . never mind. Come along now!' he almost ordered me in.

This is it, I thought, as we made our way through a narrow passage towards the *mujra* hall. He might just push me into one of the adjoining rooms, get some whores to strip me and pin me down on the bed, have all of us photographed and then blackmail me using those pictures for the rest of my life.

Finally we reached the *mujra* hall. The doorman said there would be no show that day. 'Everybody is busy watching the match (there was a World Cup match that evening), business has been slack for the past few days,' he said.

I was relieved.

At last, we stepped out into the sultry night.

'You surprise me,' Lucky said, as we took a stroll. 'I thought you were like any other normal trader who has his indulgences.'

'I am no saint, Lucky, but in matters of women I have stuck to one rule from the first time I had sex: I only eat what I kill; whores do not excite me,' I told him.

I then asked Lucky if he enjoyed visiting dance bars.

'Not really, but I have become a regular at some of these places without wanting to. When we have overseas fund managers visiting us, my boss asks me to show them some of the "happening places" in Mumbai. Of course, most of the fund managers are eager for such action. To get business from foreign fund houses, we have to keep the fund managers happy. After all, why should they place orders with any one particular broking firm in a trade where none of the firms have anything unique to offer?' Lucky said.

I swore never to visit that place again, and certainly not with Lucky. But a few weeks later, when he again suggested that we meet over a drink at White House, I agreed without the slightest reluctance.

'But don't create a scene like the last time,' he told me with some irritation. 'And I must tell you this – Payal seems to have taken a shine to you. Last week, when I went there, she was asking me about you. I promised to bring you along the next time. But be a good boy and don't insult her again,' he said.

'Don't try your cock-and-bull story on me. Keep it for the fund managers,' I said. But deep in my heart I was hoping what he said was true. Much as I hated to admit it to Lucky, I was smitten by Payal in that single meeting. I kept thinking of the seductive glances she had thrown me, nearly to the point of distraction. In fact, I was looking for an excuse to go back to White House, and was delighted at Lucky's invitation.

To cut a long story short, I went there a few more times. Payal was the hottest item in White House at the time, and she had many suitors vying for her attention. And yet she chose me as the object of her attention, much to the annoyance of aspirants far wealthier and powerful than me. Among them happened to be an uncouth businessman in his mid-forties who ran a chain of Udipi hotels and a diamond trader rumoured to have underworld connections. They showered her with all kinds of expensive gifts, and yet she would have eyes only for me whenever I was there.

The hotelier was so mad at me that on one occasion he threatened me in public.

Once I was at the White House and it happened to be Payal's birthday. After her performance, she sent word that I join her in her room with some of her colleagues for the customary cake-cutting ritual. Of all the patrons present that evening, I was the only one she chose to invite. And it was done in such a manner that everybody around got to know of it.

I thought I was in love with Payal and felt that she too had a soft corner for me. But that delusion was shattered a couple of months later when I learnt from Lucky that she was having a good time with both the hotelier and the diamond trader. The only reason she chose to indulge me in public was to get the other two worked up and lavish more money on her. In market parlance, she was using me as a bait to get them to up their bids.

The experience drained me emotionally and affected my trading too. Even otherwise, 1996 was a terrible year for the stock market. The economy was slowing, companies were struggling after having embarked on ambitious capacity expansions, and the primary market had slipped into a coma.

# 14

# Storms of Change

The introduction of dematerialization of shares would change the character of the Indian market forever, and for the better, much in the way electronic trading had. It would give another leg-up to the Indian market in its quest to rub shoulders with its global counterparts, eliminate frauds by companies and brokers, improve the efficiency of stock exchange clearing houses, reduce brokerage rates and attract more FIIs.

Many FIIs were reluctant to invest in India because of the problem of fake shares. Companies were as guilty of forging share certificates as the brokers and other market players. Physical share certificates had distinctive numbers. Companies would pledge one set of shares with lenders, borrowing money against them. They would then print another bunch of certificates with the same distinctive numbers, and introduce them in the market through a friendly broker or through one of their own privately owned companies. They could do so, safe in the knowledge that the original set of shares would be in the custody of the lenders so long as there was no default on the interest payments to the lender.

Much to the dismay of those who played the market with forged shares, dematerialized shares were fungible; they did not have any distinctive numbers or specific identification. In fact, it was during the process of dematerialization of shares that many instances of fake shares came to light, which otherwise would have gone unnoticed for a very long time. Many companies had more shares in circulation than were legitimately issued by them. Dematerialization immensely helped reduce the settlement risk and shortened settlement cycles, both of which were critical for upgrading the clearing and settlement system.

Another major market reform undertaken by SEBI in 1996 was getting stock exchanges to set up clearing corporations and trade guarantee funds. With this, investors no longer had to worry about counterparty risk. The clearing corporation would ensure pay-out even when a party to a deal defaulted on an obligation, and would later recover the dues from the defaulter.

Trading volumes continued to soar because of the ease with which shares could now be bought and sold. On the flip side, retail investors increasingly started speculating instead of buying and holding shares for the long term as they used to earlier. They would buy and sell within the weekly settlement, happy to make a small profit. Of course, they would lose money as well. Speculation was addictive, and even though most retail investors rarely made consistent profits, the memory of their winning trades would raise hopes of bigger gains and keep them going.

As a result, the percentage of shares that resulted in delivery or actually changed hands fell steeply. To deter overtrading, SEBI introduced daily margins and fixed intra-day trading limits for brokers. There were limits to the positions brokers could take in individual stocks. This was done to make it difficult for any one broker to manipulate an illiquid stock.

Despite having made it mandatory for brokers to collect margins from clients, the authorities rarely enforced this rule. Brokers knew that if they insisted on margins their clients would shift business to rivals willing to overlook margin requirements. Many brokers had suffered huge losses in 1992 because of client defaults. Yet, the fear of losing clients would see brokers repeating the mistake and suffering the consequences when the market crashed in 2001, and later, in 2008.

With computerization, it became easier for stock exchanges to monitor brokers' positions and pull up members who were stepping out of line. The broking community chafed at some of these restrictions, but there was little they could do. The Indian market had no choice but to adopt global best practices if it wanted to be counted among the best international markets. And the government steadily empowered SEBI to ensure safety and integrity in the marketplace, increasing India's appeal to global investors.

SEBI tightened the rules for the primary market too, alarmed at the ease with which dubious companies raised money and then duped investors. This led to a fall in the amount of money raised by companies from the primary market.

On the whole, 1996 was a tough year for making money. In addition to a slowing economy, the political uncertainty following the general elections in April-May further dampened the mood. The Congress party lost the elections, winning only 140 seats – its lowest tally ever. The BJP emerged the single largest party, with 161 seats, and was sworn into office. Within thirteen days, the Atal Bihari Vajpayee-led government quit as it failed to muster a simple majority to win the vote of confidence.

I had a fair idea of what FIIs were doing, thanks to data supplied by Mouse. But that was not of much help, as prices often moved counter to my calculations. On a couple of occasions, I made good money but promptly lost much more the following week.

'It is time you both started building long-term portfolios for yourselves,' GB told me and Dilip one afternoon after we were done for the day. 'Speculation is a good way to build your initial capital, but you cannot make your retirement money through trading alone.'

'Investment too is speculation after all, isn't it? Only that your time frame is longer,' I said.

GB grinned. 'You are right, Lala. But the odds of making money are higher; you won't be under pressure to cut your positions just because the price has moved against you by a few rupees. More often than not, long-term investments work out well,' he said.

'But this is turning out to be a terrible market, and it looks like things will only get worse. Does it make sense to buy now? Why not wait for some more time?' Dilip asked.

'Some rules in the market never change. And one of them is that nobody can ever catch the top or bottom. Besides, to make a good profit, you need to buy cheap. And when can you do that? Only when there is despair all around. Is this the best time to buy stocks for the long term? I really don't know. Maybe the market could fall some more. But what is the probability of making a good profit by buying at these prices? I would say, quite high,' GB replied.

I found merit in GB's argument. But I was not good at understanding business models or reading balance sheets. Frankly speaking, I don't think anybody could claim to be an expert in identifying potential winners. People took calculated bets and some of them paid off. I took GB's advice on the stocks to buy for the long term. He too was no expert and had no pretensions of being one. But from doing trades for the big boys, he had a reasonable understanding of companies.

Once in a while, he would try to pass off some theory of theirs as his own. He would not say that it was his original thought, but he would not attribute it to anybody either. And I would try to needle him while keeping a straight face.

'Does Nemishbhai think it can happen?' I asked at the end of one such spiel.

'Who said Nemishbhai said that?' GB snapped.

'I thought . . . '

'Don't always assume things . . . I have some ideas of my own too,' he said, somewhat testily.

The year 1997 began on a promising note.

The market steadily rose in the run-up to the Budget.

Finance Minister Palaniappan Chidambaram's first full-year Budget surpassed market expectations. Peak personal income tax and corporate tax for domestic companies were slashed.

In a major boost for the IT sector, export profits were exempt from Minimum Alternate Tax. The FII investment limit in listed companies was raised, and dividends were made tax-free for the shareholder. The Budget also laid the foundation for the first round of disinvestment in PSUs, and announced in-principle approval of buyback of shares, subject to certain conditions. The peak customs duty rate was lowered, and so were duty rates on a wide range of imports. The media, industry and stock market were simply bowled over by what was dubbed as a 'Dream Budget'.

But the celebrations were premature. On 30 March, a Sunday, the Congress party, without any warning, pulled the rug from under the United Front (UF) government. Tension between the Congress and the UF had been building for a while, but nobody saw matters reaching a flashpoint so very soon.

The phone lines of the kerb dealers – those who dealt in the illegal market – were ringing off the hook in Mumbai and Kolkata as panicky traders rushed to offload their outstanding buy positions. You could negotiate deals with them after market hours and then legitimize that trade by feeding the details into the stock exchange terminal the following morning. Most operators had been bullish on the market following the upbeat Budget and had huge buy positions. As for me, this was the second time within a month that I was caught on the wrong side.

The bears were plain lucky, though just for a day. The Sensex crashed nearly 300 points when markets opened for trading on Monday, but bounced back over the next couple of weeks as the Congress offered to support the UF government with the soft-spoken Inder Kumar Gujral as prime minister.

The index may have recovered quickly, but traders who lost money in that crazy session on Monday had to wait much longer to make up their losses.

15

# Caught in a Global Whirlpool

Trouble in Southeast Asia had started brewing in May as Thailand tried to defend its currency against speculative attacks. Thai companies had borrowed heavily in dollars and were struggling to pay interest on it because of a slowdown in the economy. The contagion spread to Malaysia, Philippines and Indonesia within a week, and all three countries had to devalue their currencies. There was mayhem in currency and stock markets across Southeast Asia.

Despite the storm raging next door, the Indian market, strangely, was an oasis of calm. The Sensex, in fact, rose a little in July when Thailand, Malaysia, Philippines and Indonesia were battling to save their currencies. It helped that capital controls in India did not allow our companies to borrow in foreign currency at will, and also restricted foreign investments in the country.

Amid all this turmoil, the bull and bear cartels continued to snipe at each other at every opportunity. One of the Sensex companies announced a bonus issue of one share for every one held (a 1:1 issue, in industry parlance), which exceeded market expectations. There had been talk of the company announcing the bonus issue at its annual general meeting. Similar chatter in the past had mostly resulted in disappointment, and some of the seasoned players had felt the bonus issue, even if announced, would not be a generous one. But many in the market had high expectations from the company.

The bears short-sold their shares, betting that the bonus share issue would disappoint the market. The bulls thought otherwise, and loaded up on the stock. I suspect they had some definite information. The bonus share announcement came on a Thursday, and the price of the stock surged. Friday being the last day of settlement on BSE, the stock was expected to rise further as the weaker bears rushed to cover their positions.

The stronger of the bears chose to shift their short positions to NSE, where the settlement was on Tuesday. The bears were confident that one of the domestic financial institutions, which was also a big shareholder in that company, would sell some of its holdings on Monday. What they did not count on was the bull cartel sending two envoys to the house of a senior fund manager of that institution on Sunday and convincing him not to sell on Monday at any cost. In return, the duo assured the fund manager that he would be able to get a much better price for his unitholders on Tuesday as the bears would have to cover in desperation.

The fund manager was convinced, and agreed to hold fire on Monday. By Monday noon the bears were sweating. They had learnt that the institution would not be selling that day, and there was no guarantee that it would sell on Tuesday either. Frantic short-sellers began buying back what they had sold, pushing the stock price higher. The institution finally sold in the last hour of trade on Tuesday. But it was too late for the bears, who had already got out of their positions at a loss.

A week later, over drinks, Lucky told me how the bulls managed to turn the screws on the bears. I was curious to know about the two envoys who had met the fund manager.

'I can tell you about only one of them,' he said.

'Do you know him personally?' I asked.

'Very well; that was me. Don't ask me who the other person was, I can't tell,' he said.

In the last week of October, Hong Kong became the latest casualty of the financial crisis sweeping the region. The US market, which was until then unaffected by the chaos in Asia, capitulated a couple of days later. The Dow Jones Industrial Average crashed a record 554 points, and trading had to be suspended.

Bad news was pouring in from every corner. Despite its economy being in a much better shape, India seemed as vulnerable as any other market. Foreign investors, who had so far shown faith in the India story, had to make up for the losses suffered in other markets, particularly in Southeast Asia, by selling their profitable investments in India. Over the next one year, some of the foreign investors would withdraw altogether from India.

Until that time, mass layoffs were unheard of in the Indian broking industry. Particularly cruel was the manner in which Peregrine Securities fired its employees. Two officials from the Hong Kong office landed up at the Mumbai office for a review meeting. After the usual PowerPoint presentations, the entire staff was taken out to lunch. The officials from

Hong Kong left immediately after lunch, saying they had a flight to take. When the analyst, sales and dealing teams got back to the office, they were barred entry and their ID cards were taken away. The agitated employees demanded an explanation but got none from the security people, whose only instructions were to prevent the employees from entering the office and to collect their IDs. Their possessions would be packed in boxes and handed to them the following day, the staff was told.

For the employees at foreign brokerages that downed shutters or fired staff, the downfall was hard to come to terms with. For one, they were earning twice or thrice more their counterparts at the local brokerage firms. And even if they were willing to take a hefty pay cut, there were not enough jobs going because of the market downturn.

The market was in a downtrend till mid-December, but the stock indices ended the year around 20 per cent higher over the previous year. This was no mean achievement, given the storm that roiled Asia during the second half of the year.

---

I continued to meet up with Lucky over drinks, and in one of those sessions unwittingly mentioned my deal with Mouse to him. Lucky proposed that the three of us should meet, and against my better judgement, I agreed.

Mouse was reluctant to meet Lucky, but I managed to persuade him. The three of us met for dinner at the Jewel of India in Worli the following week. As the dinner progressed, I began to regret having arranged the meeting.

I could see that Lucky was subtly trying to flatter Mouse and tempt him with visions of big money. More worryingly for me, after a couple of pegs, Mouse was no longer his reserved self and seemed eager to impress Lucky. I tried signalling to him to quiet down, but Mouse was on his own trip, becoming more effusive by the minute. I was annoyed and let it show.

After the dinner, Lucky offered to drop Mouse home. I thought Mouse would decline the offer out of civility since Lucky would have to go out of his way to drop him. To my irritation, Mouse agreed.

The next day, I called up Mouse at his residence and apologized for being a bit brusque with him the previous evening. Mouse said he did not feel offended and was in fact worried if he had blurted out something unwittingly. For the next couple of weeks, I was regularly in touch with Mouse, and he passed on the information I sought from him.

He then suddenly stopped taking my calls. This went on for a few days. I suspected that he had switched his loyalty to Lucky. Finally, when I managed to get him on the phone that weekend, I gave vent to my anger and accused him of deceit.

Mouse heard me out patiently and then said: 'Fair enough, Lala, but you have been exploiting me all this while by giving me a pittance for such valuable information. I am now getting ten times what you pay me every month. I can help you out once in a while for old times' sake, but don't expect me to be at your beck and call.'

I was furious. 'So you have sold yourself out to Lucky,' I railed.

'You can think what you like,' he replied calmly.

'I am going to write a letter to your seniors and inform them about your side business,' I said.

'Do so by all means. But that would mean implicating yourself as well. Even if that does not happen, you may still end up making some powerful enemies,' he said, and hung up.

I had played my final card, and lost. I had no doubt that Mouse was now taking orders from Lucky. I was mad at being cheated out of a source of precious information. That evening I dialled Lucky and gave him a piece of my mind.

'B★$#c@%d, M@#%★$d, you call me a friend, talk about trust, and is this how you honour friendship? By stabbing me in the back?' I yelled at him.

'Calm down now, Lala, what's the matter?' he asked.

That made me angrier, and I abused him some more. He still kept his cool.

He then rang me a couple of days later. I ignored him.

Lucky persisted. Finally, I answered his call.

'B$#@c★★d,' I said by way of greeting, '. . . isn't it enough that you cheated me once? Or is there something more you want to rob me of?' I had got over my rage, but was not going to forgive him so quickly.

'Your anger is perfectly justified. Abuse me some more if it helps you get over it. But after that let's talk like grown-ups,' Lucky said.

The following evening I drove down to Lucky's place at Khar. He greeted me warmly, and then asked with mock fear: 'I hope you don't have a gun or knife on you.'

'That would be being kind to you. I was thinking of something more painful,' I replied.

He told me that he had arranged a meeting for me with his influential mentor that evening. Before heading for the meeting, Lucky apologized for what he had done.

'Look Lala, don't take this personally. I can assure you one thing – your loss will be more than made up,' he said.

'Let's see,' I said, somewhat sceptically.

We met up with Lucky's godfather at his office on Hill Road in Bandra. He appeared to be in his mid-forties, a tall man who bore a passing resemblance to the yesteryear Bollywood star Navin Nischal. He had that same tranquil and dreamy look about him. His hair was dyed black, and he wore it slightly long. He was good-looking though his once sharp features were slowly running to fat, and I suspected it had to do with a fondness for booze. I mentally nicknamed him Monk.

'My pleasure to have you here, Lala,' he said, with a warm smile and a firm handshake. 'I have heard of you from some good people, and had been wanting to meet you for a while now. Better late than never.'

Monk spoke fluent English, and certainly did not sound like a seasoned stockbroker. An investment banker, perhaps.

Having introduced us, Lucky left, saying he had some other work to attend to. I knew this was pre-planned.

Monk and I discussed the markets. He wanted to know my view. I said I was bearish for the moment.

'So is everybody on the street,' Monk said. 'I think we may have hit the bottom for the time being. Still, Asia will take a while to settle. I don't see a bull market any time soon.'

Monk's interests went beyond markets. He followed politics closely, collected antique stuff and called himself a 'serious amateur' photographer. I discovered he was a good listener too, though I was not sure if he was genuinely interested in what I had to say or if it was just a pretence. 'How did you then end up in this field, doing what you are doing?' I wanted to ask him, but checked myself.

I don't know why, but I instinctively took a liking to him. Lucky was right. The man was too polished to be a stockbroker, let alone an operator involved in dodgy deals. I had heard GB mention him a few times, but he never aroused enough curiosity in me to find out more about him. From the little I knew about him, his speciality was mid-caps.

It was late in the evening. Monk asked if he should call for some food. We finally settled for *bhel* from the vendor on the street below.

'Good stuff, you won't regret it,' Monk said.

He was right, except that it was a bit too spicy and made my eyes water.

Over *bhel* and masala tea, Monk came to the point.

'I understand you are pretty upset with Lucky, and I won't blame you for that. Not Lucky's fault, as you would have realized by now. I put him up to it. But that's the way this market works. If I hadn't poached your man, somebody else would have, sooner than later. Admit it, Lala, you were paying him a pittance for the kind of information he was giving you. But I am impressed by your resourcefulness in developing a contact like that,' Monk said.

Munching on *bhel*, he went on: 'What has happened has happened. But I would like to have you for a friend, Lala. Of course, it is up to you, whether you feel the same way. And I want to make good your loss. So I have a proposal for you.' He paused.

I nodded.

'Have you ever thought of having a broking card of your own, Lala?' Monk asked.

'To be honest, the thought has crossed my mind a few times. But I wonder if it is worth sinking in Rs 1 crore. Besides, there are other expenses too. You need an office, and then there is the cost of maintaining the office. Besides, I am doing well for myself without all those headaches. In short, I am happy in my present situation,' I said.

'Undoubtedly. But don't you want to grow in this profession and swim with the big fish in the deep seas?' Monk asked.

'Perhaps, but that also calls for a sizeable investment, which I am not so confident about making at this point,' I said. But I had a vague idea of what was coming.

'Fortune favours the brave. Next year could be tough, but I see the opportunity for big money over the next two to three years. What if I were to fund half the cost of the BSE card and arrange for office space for a reasonable rent?' Monk asked.

'Sounds interesting, but I am not comfortable taking such a big favour,' I said.

'Fair enough. Treat my contribution as a soft loan. Repay me whenever you can . . . in one year, three years, five years . . . Is that good enough?' he asked.

'And what do I have to do in return?' I asked.

Monk leaned back and smiled.

'You are quick . . . and blunt as well. Exactly what I had heard. Yes, in return you can do a few trades for me occasionally. Brokerage and margin money won't be a problem. But don't expect to survive purely on the business I give you,' Monk said.

Monk's proposition was tempting. But I wondered how GB would take it if I told him I was planning to start out on my own.

As though reading my thoughts, Monk asked me: 'Are you thinking what Govind will have to say?'

'Well . . . hmm . . . yes.'

'Don't trouble yourself over it. Govind will be happy for you. You have been with him for a while now, right? He gave you a break and you have vindicated his faith in you. What more can he ask for? And you can't be indebted to him forever. It is time to move on, Lala. Think over it,' Monk said.

'Do you know him well?' I asked Monk.

'Not personally, but I know people who know him well enough,' Monk replied, throwing me a knowing smile. I had no doubt that the Monk too did business for the big boys of the market.

I did not have to deliberate much on Monk's proposal. Two days later I called him to say I would take up his offer.

'Happy to be doing business with you soon, Lala. Just one thing. At any point, if you decide to quit the business, I should have the right of first refusal to the card,' he said. I thought that was perfectly reasonable.

The same day, I told GB about my decision. I was certain he would have got to know about it even before I told him.

He feigned surprise. 'Oh! That's good news indeed. I never realized you had made so much money to be starting your own broking business,' he said.

'Do you have to really do this, Govindbhai?' I asked.

'Do what, Lala?' GB asked.

'Pretending to know nothing when I think you pretty much know everything,' I said.

GB laughed.

'You have become smart to the ways of this market, I must say. But one has to put on a façade at times. And here's my advice to you, Lala, now that you are moving into a different league. Often, things are obvious enough for all to see, but, depending on the circumstance, it is not a bad thing to pretend otherwise,' he said. 'It's a small industry still, we will keep seeing each other, Lala. Be in touch and don't forget old friends."'

# 16

# Swimming in the Deep Sea

In the last week of December 1997, I moved into a rented space in Nariman Bhavan building at Nariman Point. The landlord was known to Monk, and the rent was quite modest for the first six months. In fact, it seemed too good to be true. There was a rider, though. After six months, I would have to pay the regular market rent.

Ideally, I would have preferred an office in the vicinity of Dalal Street so that I could hang around with friends after market hours. But Monk had suggested this place and I did not want to exploit his kindness. I hired a peon to manage the office, and was all set to take the plunge.

Sometime in February 1998, Harshad Mehta sent me feelers through one of his confidants. I was told that Harshad was planning a comeback and had zeroed in on BPL, Videocon and Sterlite as the vehicles for his second innings. Harshad's proximity to the promoters of these companies was by then common knowledge in market circles, and I was aware that he had already begun accumulating the stocks. The proposition made to me was simple: buy shares of these three companies according to Harshad's instructions. It was a pure broking transaction, but I would get a higher commission than the market rate of 50-75 basis points. Of course, a juicy commission and an assured volume of trades were not the main reason for brokers' eagerness to transact with Harshad; they were looking forward to bigger profits from front-running his trades.

I had heard stories that Harshad would sometimes delay payment to his brokers, both for margin payment to the stock exchanges and for the shares he would take delivery of. Surely, Harshad knew his brokers were making easy money off him. Delaying payments was one way of making his brokers earn their keep. Often, he would offer shares instead of cash as collateral towards margin payment. Instead of paying Rs 100 as margin money to the broker (which the broker had to deposit with the stock exchange), Harshad would give the broker shares worth Rs 100. If a broker should demur, he would talk tough or turn on his charm, depending on the person he was dealing with.

When the offer was made to me I was tempted to take it up. And, while I had not been in touch with Harshad for a long time, our relations were still cordial. Still, I was a bit miffed at his reaching out to me through his confidant instead of picking up the phone and talking to me directly. I gave the offer some thought and finally decided to turn it down. For one, I knew that the authorities would be keeping a hawk's eye on Harshad this time around and do everything in their power to ensure that he did not become the force he was in 1992. That was the last time I heard from Harshad.

The Sensex was on a tear in April, and so were shares of BPL, Videocon and Sterlite. Brokers who had signed up with Harshad were making money hand over fist, much to the envy of those who were not part of that circle. The party on Dalal Street would have continued for some more time but for the government's decision to carry out nuclear tests at Pokhran, which caught investors off guard.

Even before the government could finish savouring the public adulation for its feat, India was hit with economic sanctions. From the market's perspective, it meant two things; FII money coming into India would dry up, and our companies would find it difficult to raise capital globally.

Oddly, even as the overall market was in a downtrend, shares of BPL, Videocon and Sterlite continued to rise, thanks to relentless purchases by the Big Bull and his syndicate of brokers. Regularly, trading in the three stocks would be frozen for want of sellers. It was an open secret that Harshad was the driving force behind the spectacular surge in their prices. There was speculation that he may have once again managed to tap into the coffers of some government banks for his stock market operations. But Harshad was smart enough not to go anywhere near a bank this time. Instead, he got the promoters of the companies to bankroll his operations.

By the first week of June, share prices of BPL had nearly trebled from four months ago, and those of Sterlite and Videocon had almost doubled. In the process, Harshad was also getting to enjoy what he loved doing – squeezing the bear traders who bet against him.

Harshad avoided some of the mistakes he had made the last time, but one flaw remained – his desire to be in the limelight. Had BPL, Videocon and Sterlite shares fallen along with the rest of the market, it would have only seemed natural. But by pushing up their prices even as blue chips were not finding takers, Harshad managed to draw market attention to himself. Maybe he was trying to convince himself that he was still the Big Bull of old who could sway the market with his purchases.

The bear operators tried to bring him down by short-selling the stocks. Each time, Harshad drove up the prices and forced them to cover their positions at a loss. This went on for some time until the bears decided to back off and wait for an opportune time to hit back.

Despite the eye-popping gains in these stocks, fund managers were not willing to touch BPL, Videocon and Sterlite shares for fear of being associated with Harshad. This meant the only buyers for these stocks were Harshad and his group of brokers. So long as the prices kept rising, it was not difficult for Harshad & Co to keep carrying forward their positions to the next settlement. Still, at some point, the bulls had to pause for breath. And indeed they did, and the three stocks stopped in their tracks, staying level for about a week.

The bears now smelt blood, aware that the bulls were finding it difficult to book profits without depressing prices. In the middle of June, the three stocks started tumbling rapidly. Somebody in the syndicate had to liquidate his positions under duress, and all hell broke loose for Harshad and gang. The same stocks that had seemed to be defying the laws of stock market gravity till a couple of weeks back were now obeying another law of stock market physics – the faster the climb, the harder the fall.

Trading in the stocks was frozen on many days for want of buyers, and their free fall continued. There were many theories – ranging from the ridiculous to the plausible – as to what may have triggered their collapse. One was that

Harshad's wife too had been holding shares in them and had decided to sell some of her holdings to fund the renovation of their home. The broker selling the shares took this as a sign that the Big Bull was looking to exit the stocks, and this spread panic in the bull camp, which then started cashing out. I had heard a variation of the same theory as one of the reasons for the end of the bull market in 1992.

The other theory was that the bear cartel had managed to convince some fund managers holding shares of the three companies to sell out. These fund managers sold a sizeable chunk of the stocks during the week. Harshad kept buying the shares thinking it was short-sellers at the other end of the trade, whom he could squeeze at the end of the settlement cycle.

A third theory was that Harshad's rivals managed to smuggle out shares of BPL, Videocon and Sterlite from the BSE clearing house (demat had not picked up in a big way then) and had sold them in the market, triggering a crash in the stocks. They then bought the shares from the market at lower prices to deposit them back in the clearing house.

Years later, at our evening out, a dealer friend of mine bragged about how he was instrumental in bursting the BPL-Videocon-Sterlite bubble. One of the private firms through which Harshad was building positions in the three stocks was a client of the brokerage where my friend worked. He had a suspicion that the private firm's purchases were on behalf of Harshad. As the purchases kept getting bigger, my friend became wary, and insisted that his client deposit cash towards margin obligations instead of shares of the three companies. The firm kept buying time by offering to give more business to my friend's brokerage firm. But once the prices stagnated, my friend sensed trouble ahead and threatened to liquidate the positions unless the margin money was deposited. But the Harshad firm stopped taking his calls. Left with no option, my friend liquidated the positions in BPL. That turned out to be the beginning of Harshad's problems. When the BPL stock fell sharply, other brokers with positions in that stock too began booking profits to be on the safer side. This then set off a chain reaction, as the selling spread to Videocon and Sterlite too. At some point, Harshad's financiers must have become averse to putting up more cash, and once that happened there was no way the share prices could be supported.

Almost all the brokers who did trades for Harshad lost heavily as they were unable to sell the shares they had loaded up on, there being no buyers. They may have made good money in the first few months as the shares were rallying, but the crash put many of them out of business. BSE had to keep its systems open all night to allow insertion of trades that allowed the cash-strapped bulls to sell their positions to brokers who were in turn funded by the companies to avoid a payment default on the exchange.

As I was grappling with my trading losses because of the overall market downtrend came another bit of bad news, this time from the home front.

'Lala, I get sudden attacks of dizziness these days, and my cough too has not fully subsided even after medicines,' my father told me one morning as I was heading for work. Bauji was pushing seventy, but in very good health for somebody his age. The same evening I accompanied him to our family doctor, who recommended a CT scan and referred us to a pulmonologist.

A few days later, I was sitting across the doctor as he studied the test reports. I could sense he had some unpleasant news to give and that he was struggling to find the right words and break it to me as gently as he could.

'I am afraid I have some bad news for you, Mr Lalchand . . . Your father doesn't have much time left,' he said. 'It is cancer of the lung . . . now in its final stage.' The words hit me like a punch in the chest; I was overcome by a sudden wave of breathlessness and was too stunned to respond.

'This . . . this cannot be . . . my father is very healthy, and except for the recent cough and the occasional dizziness, he never had much to complain about,' I told the doctor when I finally gathered my wits.

'Often, the disease spreads across the body without a warning and is discovered very late. I am sorry, but there is little that can be done at this stage,' the doctor said, trying to sound as sympathetic as he could.

'How much time does he have?' I asked.

'At best, two months,' the doctor replied.

'Is there anything at all that can be done?' I asked.

'If your question is whether spending money on treatment will help, I would say that you could lessen the pain a bit, but not necessarily prolong his life,' the doctor said.

'If I can't save his life, I shall do everything within my power to ensure that he suffers as little as possible in his final days,' I said.

'But let me warn you that the treatment will be expensive, and will not make much difference to the final outcome,' the doctor said.

He told me that the drugs and chemotherapy could set me back by nearly Rs 10 lakh. I had reached a stage where

Rs 10 lakh was affordable, but the incident also showed up to me the limitations of money. Yet I was thankful to God for helping me get to a position that allowed me to make things easier for my father in his final days.

The difficult part now was to get my father to agree to chemotherapy. I had told him he was absolutely fine. Naturally, he would ask why he had to undergo treatment if there was nothing wrong with him. Bina and I finally managed to convince him that he had to take the medicines and undergo treatment as there was an infection in his lung and it could be cured faster this way. We never mentioned the word chemotherapy to him.

I booked him into one of the opulent, sea-facing rooms in Breach Candy, and requested the doctors that on no account should he get to know of his ailment. His condition had suddenly taken a turn for the worse and we had to wheel him into his room. I had this sinking feeling that he may not return home.

Surprisingly, he responded well to the first round of treatment, and was able to walk out of the hospital. We did not tell Ma about his condition, and I did not want to tell my brother and sister either. None of them would have been able to handle the news, and my father would have learnt from their faces that he was not going to recover.

I was under tremendous strain those two months. Not only did I have to accompany my father for his treatment, I was also worried that he may get to know about his illness. I knew that at the chemo sessions he would be getting to meet other cancer patients.

One day as we were having dinner, my father suddenly said: 'Cancer is such a dreadful disease.'

I almost choked on my food.

Warily, I asked him: 'Why do you say that?'

'You know, Lala, there were nine of us at the hospital today waiting for treatment. Seven in the group were suffering from cancer. I and another man from Malad were the only ones who did not have cancer. That is when I realized I should not complain to God about anything,' he said. There was little solace in the realization that I was not the only one who was lying to a dying parent.

The market continued to drift lower but I was too distracted to be able to focus my energies on trading. Sensing that my lack of concentration was leading to errors on my part, I kept my positions to the minimum. It was nearly two months since Bauji's treatment had begun, and he was making good progress. In fact, he had become healthier, despite the doctor's verdict that there was no possibility of a complete recovery, I was hoping against hope that he would pull through.

We had another scare, though. Father had to get an X-ray done every time before his chemotherapy. One of the assistants at the lab happened to be the son of Bauji's friend. He asked my father why he was getting X-rays done regularly. My father said he was undergoing treatment for a lung infection. The friend's son's intention may have been good, but he ended up causing me a lot of anxiety that day.

'You do not take regular X-rays for treating a lung infection, maybe your doctor is making a fool of you,' he said, and referred my father to a lung specialist. Thankfully, the lung specialist was available for consultation only in the evenings. After the X-ray was done, my father called me to say he would be consulting the lung specialist recommended by his friend's son. I lost my temper and scolded him for listening to people who had no knowledge about these things.

'There is no need to see any other doctor, just get back home,' I told him. He agreed, but my trader's instinct told me I had ended up making him suspicious.

I immediately called Bina and asked her to have a word with him. Sure enough, he had made up his mind to see that doctor. Bina told him it was a good idea, and managed to get the doctor's contact details out of him. Somehow, I managed to get a call through to the doctor before he could see my father.

'Doctor, I know this may be against your ethics, but my father Mr – is coming to see you for a second opinion. He is suffering from cancer and does not have much time left. I have so far managed to conceal the fact from him. But if you were to diagnose him correctly today, he will lose his willpower to battle the disease. My humble request is that you do not tell him his true condition at any cost,' I told him.

God bless the doctor, he agreed to play along.

That evening my father was even more cheerful at the dinner table.

'I am sorry, Lala, but I did go to the doctor after all, just for my peace of mind,' he said.

'That's okay. What did the doctor have to say?' I asked him in an innocent tone.

'Well, he said it was a minor problem, and prescribed me a cough syrup. I picked it up on the way,' he told me.

Bina and I were relieved, but the stress of those few hours was unimaginable. I was glad I had not taken up any big positions earlier in the day.

The downtrend in the market continued, and the reasons were both internal and external. The currency crisis in Southeast Asia the previous year had crippled the economies of the Asian tigers like South Korea, Indonesia and Thailand, which had been growing at a scorching pace until then. Japan continued to be in recession, and because of the problems in Asia, Russia was hit hard by a slump in demand for its two key exports, crude oil and non-ferrous metals. In mid-August, another global crisis erupted as Russia devalued the rouble, defaulted on domestic payments and suspended interest payment on foreign loans. This further alarmed global money managers, who were still dealing with the aftershocks of the previous year's Asian currency crisis.

A further strain on liquidity was the crisis at Long Term Capital Management (LTCM), one of the largest US hedge funds. LTCM suffered a colossal loss on its bets in Russia and had to be bailed out with a $3.5 billion package put together by the US Federal Reserve and a consortium of top US financial institutions.

The Indian economy was on the mend after a steep decline in GDP growth the previous year, but inflation was a headache for much of the year, peaking at 8.8 per cent in September. At one point, onion prices climbed to Rs 60 a kg and tomato prices to Rs 40 a kg, which would be the equivalent of at least Rs 240 and Rs 160, respectively, at today's prices adjusted for inflation. Of course, the problem of inflation was not chronic back then, as it is now.

It was a bleak Diwali on Dalal Street that year as the index struggled to stay above 3,000. Among the worst hit blue chips was Tata Motors (TELCO), which saw its losses mount because of the sluggish economy. From a high of Rs

354 at the start of the calendar year, the stock crashed to Rs 98 by Diwali. Some brokers declared they would buy it only when the price touched Rs 50, a level they were confident they would see by end-December. These were the same brokers who, when the stock was at Rs 150, said they would buy it only when the price fell to Rs 100. They never got another chance. By new year's eve, the stock was quoting at Rs 170.

In November, the Companies Act was amended to include clauses for buyback of shares by companies, and SEBI notified the guidelines. The market had been eagerly looking forward to it, in the hope that it would be a big sentiment booster. When the rules were finally announced after a wait of more than eighteen months since P. Chidambaram first mentioned it, the market reacted with indifference. Given the overall downturn, it was unlikely that companies would be in any rush to buy back their shares.

Amid the general gloom in the market that year, one man's stars were rapidly on the rise. Thirty-seven-year-old Ketan Parekh, who hailed from a family of traditional stockbrokers, was an operator of repute, but yet to be counted among the A-listers of Dalal Street. He was quite active on CSE too, where the ITC stock was seen to be his favourite quarry. The previous year, his rivals had spread rumours of his alleged suicide on a Friday – the last day of settlement on BSE – to create panic among his associates so they would sell off their positions in ITC. The rumours seemed plausible, as Ketan was said to be facing difficulties in meeting his payment obligations to the stock exchange. By the time the Ketan camp managed to kill the rumours, the damage was done. It was not a crippling setback, but Ketan had to take a knock on his profits in that settlement cycle.

In May 1998, Ketan bought ACC shares in a big way. The bet backfired badly as FIIs turned bearish in general, following the Pokhran blasts. Instead of selling out his positions in ACC, Ketan bought more of the stock, convinced that his purchases could change sentiment for it. It was a terrible gamble. FIIs sold ACC shares, and Ketan eventually had to sell his position at a loss.

The ACC debacle was a talking point in the market, and most market participants, including I, thought Ketan would be out of action for a while. But what he lost in ACC was more than made up for by the killing he had made in shares of Chennai-based Pentafour Software.

## 17

# A New Bull Market with a New Big Bull

Indian IT companies were getting popular with investors, but it would be some more months before the mania of the scale seen in the US was replicated here. Shares of leading Indian IT companies like Infosys, Satyam and Wipro had a decent run in anticipation of bumper earnings for at least the next couple of years.

At the heart of this unexpected bonanza for the industry was the Y2K bug. To save on memory space, the internal clocks of computers provided dates with six digits – two for the day, two for the month, and two for the year. As there were no digits provided for a millennium change, it was feared that on 1 January 2000 computer systems across the world would automatically reset, unable to figure the '00' at the end of the date line. Fixing the problem called for massive numbers of software code writers to screen millions of lines of computer code and correct the fault.

All of a sudden the spotlight was on India. We were the only country that could provide the volume of manpower required for the job at a fraction of what it would cost in the developed world. Another unexpected stroke of fortune for India was the spurt in undersea fibre-optic cable lines between India and the US. Using fibre-optic cable-connected workstations, software engineers in Hyderabad could fix the codes of computer systems of companies in the US to make them Y2K-ready. This marked the beginning of the great outsourcing wave that would continue for many years to come.

Amid all this hand-wringing over the approaching Y2K doom, the great dotcom boom in the US was gaining strength with each passing day. 'Internet' had become the buzzword from the mid-1990s onwards, spurred by a belief that the advent of the web marked a new dawn in human civilization and would radically change life on earth, the way the invention of the wheel did. Given the investor frenzy for anything remotely connected with the Internet, many dotcom start-ups in the US managed to raise capital at outrageous valuations, despite their flaky business models that held little promise of generating meaningful profits in the foreseeable future.

None of the major Indian IT companies were dotcom players, but looked far more solid because of their pipeline of Y2K-related orders. Shares of Infosys, Wipro and Satyam, the top three listed IT services firms, were already in demand with institutional investors. The interest was spilling over to some of the second-rung companies in the sector now.

Ketan's choice of Pentafour Software to ride the IT wave was intriguing. The company, which would later be renamed

Pentamedia Graphics, was struggling financially; there was talk about it having defaulted on its fixed deposits. The poor market perception about the Pentafour management did not help either. Let alone fund managers, even self-respecting traders chose to keep away from the stock. But all that was before Ketan took an interest in the stock.

To me, Ketan's pick made sense. As the company was in trouble, the stock was available cheap; I could see that would put Ketan in a position to dictate terms to the management. Pentafour wanted to project itself as an attractive buy to institutional investors. Market perception about its management could not be changed overnight, but a jump in its stock price would certainly get fund managers interested. And, as a surge in price alone would not help, trading volumes had to be good enough for fund houses to be able to buy and sell the shares with ease.

In early 1998, the stock was quoting at around Rs 150, its daily volumes on BSE at barely 5,000. Ketan first drove up the price, which in turn attracted traders to the stock. By the end of May, Pentafour shares had soared to Rs 1,000, and daily volumes had ballooned to between 7 lakh and 10 lakh shares on BSE, and to nearly twice those volumes on NSE. Pentafour was among the top five most actively traded stocks on both exchanges. Such was the interest in the stock that it soon came to be regarded as the barometer of sentiment for technology shares in general.

Very soon, the company began making the right kind of noises in the press about its operations, such as partnerships with big companies and orders from customers. Now fund managers were interested too. Getting fund houses to buy his holdings through negotiated deals ensured that Ketan got a better price than he would have from selling his shares in the market. Dumping the shares in the market would wreck the price and even draw the regulators' attention, besides causing losses. But palming them off to fund houses would ensure that future losses, if any, would be borne by the unitholders of those funds.

The Pentafour formula would be repeated with the stocks of Zee, Global Telesystems, HFCL, DSQ Software, Aftek Infosys, Ranbaxy, and Software Solutions Integrated, to name a few that Ketan manipulated, over the next couple of years. There were plenty of smaller companies, mostly in the media space, in which Ketan played the same game.

Ketan would ask for a slice of the promoters' shares at a steep discount to the market price. He and his associates would then boost volumes in the stock by trading the shares among themselves. Being a qualified chartered accountant, Ketan could understand balance sheets and earnings models very well. Yet, barring a few, his choice of stocks showed he was not really bothered about the fundamentals of the company.

His skill lay in figuring out which 'story' could be marketed as a 'multi-bagger' in the making. A stock that could double in price was touted as a two-bagger, one which would treble a three-bagger, and so on. His Pentafour Software story projected the company as a provider of high-end animation software to Hollywood studios, and not as a plain vanilla outsourcing outfit.

Having identified the story, Ketan's next step was to analyse the floating stock in the market so that he could control the stock price. Floating stock refers to the shares held by persons other than the promoters of the company. Analysis of the floating stock involved trying to figure out which big investors in the stock were likely to sell their holdings, and when. Ketan also had to identify fund managers who could be induced to time their sales so that they favoured his trading positions. On the other side, there had to be fund managers who could be persuaded to buy stocks off him. Ketan would also have to figure out how much stock the promoters held through their *benami* entities. This was critical, because promoters would often try to double-cross operators by selling their shares through their *benami* accounts while the operators were trying to push up the stock price by buying.

Some promoters paid cash to Ketan to inflate their stock price (some like Zee would later claim that the funds they gave him were for buying other companies' shares), while some allotted shares of their companies to Ketan and his associates way below the market price. Later, the Joint Parliamentary Committee probing the stock market scam of 2001 would name Adani, HFCL, DSQ Software, Cadila Healthcare, Essel, Kopran and Nirma among the companies that provided funds to Ketan.

Stocks that took Ketan's fancy soared to unbelievable levels, making him the new Pied Piper of Dalal Street. On tip-offs, traders blindly lapped up the stocks he was supposedly buying, whether it was true or not, fuelling their rise. If Harshad Mehta was the face of the 1991 bull market, Ketan Parekh was the undisputed poster boy of the bull run that began in January 1999 and lasted about eighteen months.

But to say that Ketan alone was responsible for the spectacular rise in every stock that he had spotted first would be to overrate his trading prowess. There were limits to how much even the most skilled of operators could influence fund managers and stock prices once trading volumes crossed a certain threshold. In the face of frenzied retail action or herd behaviour among fund managers, operators are quite ineffective.

Some of the stocks Ketan identified as potential multi-baggers subsequently fetched a huge following among institutional investors, more as a result of the worldwide craze for technology stocks rather than for the business models of the companies. Like Harshad before him, Ketan was not the one who created the wave; he merely rode it skilfully.

Harshad and Ketan were studies in contrast, though it was widely believed that Ketan was being mentored by the erstwhile Big Bull. By a strange twist of fate, Ketan's rise to fame coincided with the declining fortunes of Harshad, whose comeback attempt through BPL, Videocon and Sterlite flopped miserably.

Harshad was brash and flamboyant, and loved to be in the headlines. Ketan managed to keep a low profile for a long time, only too aware of the perils of being in the spotlight. But as the size of his positions kept growing, it became harder for him to stay in the shadows. If Harshad was outspoken and flashy, Ketan was soft-spoken and reclusive. One of Harshad's major weaknesses, according to those who knew him well, was his inability to sell a stock in good time. He was good at driving up prices to bizarre heights, but his judgement seemed to desert him when it came to encashing them for profits.

'For some reason, selling is anathema to him,' I have heard many a close associate of Harshad say.

Ketan had no such qualms. If the trend was bearish, he would not hesitate to sell a stock short. But there was one thing Ketan had in common with Harshad: he too could lose all sense of proportion. As the bull market progressed, Ketan would become increasingly reckless, and eventually pay for his hubris.

Helping Ketan's cause was the changed outlook towards stock valuation that rejected conventional parameters. Globally, stock markets were split down the middle. On one side were the new-economy stocks, comprising companies from the technology, media and telecom (TMT), or the information technology, communication and entertainment (ICE) space. On the other side were the old-economy stocks, also known as the brick-and-mortar companies, comprising the rest of the sectors.

The traditional yardstick of price-to-earnings (PE) multiple for valuing a stock was now considered irrelevant as far as new-economy stocks were concerned. For one, most IT companies were flush with Y2K-related orders from the West, and were logging strong growth quarter after quarter. It was felt that these growth rates could be indefinitely sustained. Another rosy view of the knowledge economy held that unlike their brick-and-mortar counterparts, which had to invest in plant and machinery to increase output, technology firms could easily scale up their operations by simply adding more people. The truth was, nobody knew how to value these companies because there was no precedent.

By the time the curtain fell on 1998, shares of most of the IT companies had risen three-to-five-fold during the year. Because of my misgivings about the sector, I had missed an opportunity to make some good money. I occasionally punted in a few IT stocks, but lacked the confidence to take big positions because of their steep price rise. I decided to become a convert and embrace the technology faith, but I did not have the conviction necessary for it. I conferred with GB and Monk on the matter.

Both were not very sure themselves about how long the party in technology stocks would last. But, as usual, GB had his own interesting take on the trend.

'If you ask around, you will find more believers than disbelievers in the technology story. Experience tells me that it is a good sign to have some disbelievers. So long as people are sceptical, the rally can continue. It is only when everybody tells you to buy a particular stock or a sector that you should have second thoughts about it,' he said.

Monk had a similar view, though he expressed it differently.

'It is futile to fight a trend, and the trend right now is in favour of technology stocks. As to whether these stocks are worth these prices, only history will tell,' he said. During the course of the year, I realized that Monk was quite close to Ketan. I made this inference from the stocks Monk was buying through me.

I need not have worried about being late to the new-economy party. Despite the fairly steep appreciation in stock prices, the action was just starting actually. In March 1999, Infosys raised around $70 million from investors in the US, becoming the first Indian company to be listed on Nasdaq. In October that year, Satyam Computer Services' subsidiary Sify raised $74 million, listing on the New York Stock Exchange (NYSE). Wipro would join the league six months later. Indian IT companies had finally arrived on the global scene.

The unprecedented boom in technology shares over the next eighteen months would swell my net worth beyond my wildest imagination. Young traders like me had gained the most – though I must admit I was a sceptic who later converted – as we were not weighed down by baggage from the past. But our seniors were, and when share prices of software companies surged, veteran brokers predicted that the IT boom was no different from other stock market fads of the past and would end up giving grief to those cheering the sector.

Their scepticism was understandable, considering IT stocks were quoting at PE multiples far in excess of what blue chips like Reliance, ACC, Tata Steel and SBI had seen even at their peak. The veterans refused to acknowledge the new-economy companies to which the conventional approach to stock investing did not apply. In the stock market, too much experience can sometimes be a drawback rather than a virtue.

I remember one senior broker telling me: 'Lala, what is this sudden excitement over the computer? After all, it is only a modified version of the typewriter, right? When the typewriter was invented, people had predicted it would change the world. Has it? No. And the same will be true of the computer too.'

The broker was partly right in that barely a handful of the 'world beaters-in-the-making' survived the bust that followed, and many investors lost more than they had made during the bull run. And no, the technology boom did not revolutionize life on earth immediately as expected, though it did lay the foundation for the huge changes in the coming years. The dizzying rise in IT and other new-economy shares would defy logic for about two years. But during that period, there was easy money to be made; it was a period when you were better off not understanding balance sheets, and profit and loss statements. Traders who kept short-selling IT shares, convinced that the fantastic valuations were unsustainable, were nearly driven to ruin. Those who just bought blindly without trying to figure out the reasons for their rise gained the most.

The bull run hardly presented an uninterrupted, smooth ride to riches; two speedbreakers during the year nearly halted it. But to everybody's surprise, the market managed to take both events in its stride.

Year 1999 had started off well for the bulls. Inflation was slowly going down, and with it, interest rates too. The government appeared to have regained its footing as the infighting within the top leadership subsided. Technology shares were the flavour of the season, and investors slowly began making a beeline for even the lesser known and sometimes downright dubious companies in the sector. Even news of an old-economy company launching its website was sufficient to get investors excited. Some companies renamed themselves, adding fancy prefixes like 'technologies' and other IT terms to attract investors. Of course, most of these companies had nothing to do with technology.

There was this story about a Calcutta-based software firm that suddenly became a big hit with retail investors. Only later did the buyers realize that Soft Wear was a hosiery firm and not a software firm.

Sentiment for IT shares was further fired when the Budget offered a tax break to companies making their computer systems Y2K-compliant. It proposed that all expenditure incurred by companies on Y2K-compliance should be allowed as revenue expenditure in the coming financial year. This meant companies could deduct these expenses from their tax liabilities. On the whole, it was a good Budget from the market's viewpoint, and the bulls showed their approval by lifting the Sensex around 600 points (18 per cent) over the next couple of weeks.

But clouds of political uncertainty started gathering when the AIADMK withdrew support to the government in the second week of April. The big guns of the market were confident that the BJP would be able to prove its majority in Parliament the following week by making new allies. What followed was an anticlimax. In the narrowest ever loss in a no-confidence motion, the NDA government was defeated by one vote. The Sensex crashed 7 per cent on the news, and many traders suffered huge losses as a result of their overconfidence in the prospects of the NDA. I lost a good chunk of my trading profits, but fared better than many of my peers.

'Never take huge bets on political events,' Monk had told me a few days ago. 'Markets may be irrational, but are far more predictable than politicians.'

The BJP would have won the trust vote but for the Bahujan Samaj Party and National Conference member Saifuddin Soz switching loyalties at the last moment. Surprisingly, the collapse of the government and the prospect of a third general election in four years did not dampen the bullish mood. This, even as tension was building up on the Kashmir border after Pakistani infiltrators seized India's forward posts in Kargil and refused to back off. A war looked imminent after Indian armed forces mobilized troops in large numbers to reclaim its positions. India began air attacks in the last week of May, and it would be two months before the last of the infiltrators were driven out.

Logically, a combination of war and political instability should have sent investors fleeing for cover. In fact, the mood in the market was downcast during the first few days of the war at the prospect of a long-drawn conflict. But the market shrugged off these concerns quickly, and by the time India formally declared victory in the last week of July, the Sensex had rallied nearly 30 per cent.

Technology stocks were on fire. Making money had never been so easy.

'To make money in this market, all you have to do is show up for work and buy a technology stock at random,' Monk told me one day, when I visisted his office for some work. 'But this also means that the bull market could be nearing its end,' he added.

The eye-popping rise in technology stocks – upstarts as well as leaders – had attracted ordinary investors in hordes. Like the professionals, the greenhorns too had it easy, making money by trading stocks. This encouraged them to take even bigger bets without much thought as to the consequences. This was a worrying sign for the seasoned players because traditionally, bull markets have peaked whenever retail investors have stampeded their way through the bourses.

A stock can be traded only if there is both a buyer and a seller for it. If there are no sellers, buyers will not be able to buy. Trading in scores of stocks would be regularly frozen for want of sellers. Prices would leap 8, 10 or 16 per cent, depending on the intra-day limit set by the stock exchanges for the stocks.

As the ICE stocks chased each other to new highs, the pedigreed old-economy names floundered in the absence of investor interest. The list of ignored stocks included

Reliance Industries, Tata Steel, TELCO, ACC, Grasim, SBI, ITC, Hindustan Lever and Bajaj Auto – once the most sought-after stocks on the bourses and indicators of market sentiment. These companies were spoken of disparagingly by fund managers and brokers, many of them now convinced that these firms had outlived their utility and would be driven out of business before long.

As for the much-acclaimed new-economy stocks, the majority of them were quoting at unrealistic prices that had long lost all connect with the stock fundamentals. I have never believed in the concept of a fair price for a stock. Price is something that investors are willing to pay at any particular point in time. Almost 99 per cent of the time, stocks are quoted below or above their true worth. My theory is that there is a price at which you can hope to make a decent return, and that price need not be a fair one. But right now, it was the 'greater fool' game in full swing. People bought stocks at ridiculous prices, confident that somebody else would buy them at even more preposterous prices.

Value investors like Radhakishan Damani, Rakesh Jhunjhunwala and many old-timers considered technology stocks overvalued, and short-sold them. But the stocks rallied even more, forcing them to square up their positions at a loss. The bears would wait for a while, and again short-sell at a higher price, hoping to recoup their losses. The effect would be the same; they were simply making more losses as the stocks continued to climb. It was an open secret that many stocks owed their lofty valuations to promoters funding brokers and operators to rig their price. Bears had reason to believe that they would eventually triumph. After all, the market could not ignore fundamentals forever, they argued.

In the past, many promoters had tried to inflate their stock prices. More often than not, these attempts had culminated in a wrecked stock price and regulatory action. In 1992, the bears had made a killing when the securities scam finally surfaced, when only a couple of days before it seemed certain that many of them would be driven to bankruptcy. In 1998, the bears had again dealt Big Bull Harshad a crushing defeat in the BPL, Sterlite and Videocon stocks.

They thought the same approach would work with technology stocks too. There was nothing wrong in the basic principle of going after overvalued stocks. Except that this time the frenzy was too widespread for any chance of success for the bears.

One evening, I happened to be in Rakesh Jhunjhunwala's office along with a few of his associates. He was not in the best of moods as most of his bearish calls on technology stocks had gone wrong. The topic of discussion was, naturally, the tech boom.

'I tell you, this tech boom simply cannot sustain,' Rakesh said, looking at the prices on the screen. 'As share prices start climbing, IT companies will issue stock to raise money. The more their floating stock, the slower prices will rise. That is because there will more people selling every time the price rises. IT shares have been rallying so far partly because of a self-fulfilling prophecy. People buy, share prices rise, and more people buy, thinking the price will climb further. But once share prices stall, people will stop buying. Then the vicious cycle will begin. People will start selling, prices will fall, and there will be more selling. The stocks will then simply collapse as everybody rushes for the exit door together,' he said.

'This logic is indisputable, Rakesh. The stock prices will collapse at some point. But the question is, when?' asked KD, one of his close friends. That was true. Nobody could predict how long the stock prices would climb before running out of steam. Few could have said that to Rakesh's face and got away with it. I was half expecting Rakesh to get into an argument with KD to prove his point. But Rakesh said nothing. KD was among the few whose views he respected.

Promoters dabbling in their stocks was nothing new. Usually they were discreet about it. This time around, stock-rigging by operators with help from promoters seemed to have become institutionalized. Promoters appeared unfazed by market talk linking them to operators.

There were some other unhealthy developments too. I learnt from my friends that quite a few politicians were becoming active in the market, picking up stakes in shady companies through 'fronts'. Earlier, politicians were content with a fixed pay-off from promoters in return for policy favours. But having realized that there was more money to be made as 'equity partners', many of them had decided to tweak their 'business models'.

Forever in search of the best performing markets, FIIs had stepped up their investments in Indian equities in 1999. Many of them chose to route money through investment companies registered in Mauritius. The Double Taxation Avoidance Agreement (DTAA) India had signed with the island nation in the early 1980s allowed for Mauritius-based entities to pay capital gains tax at Mauritius rates and not India rates. As Mauritius did not tax capital gains, the FIIs did not have to pay any taxes on their capital gains in Indian stocks.

Given that the rules allowed for it, there was nothing wrong in what they were doing. But the overwhelming majority of the so-called investment companies claiming to be based in Mauritius were nothing more than 'post box' companies. They merely had a postal address. Their funny business did not end there. For a juicy fee, many FIIs were willing to open what was called a 'sub-account' for Indian promoters and market operators.

On paper, a sub-account was meant to be a scheme managed by the FII for foreign individuals or foreign corporations wanting to invest in India. Sub-accounts could not invest directly in India; they had to do so through an FII registered with SEBI. There were also entities called overseas corporate bodies (OCBs), which were overseas corporations, partnership firms or trusts with non-resident Indian ownership of at least 60 per cent.

At that time, disclosure requirements for sub-accounts and OCBs were pretty lax. As a result the identity of their actual owners was a mystery. In most cases, the owners were the promoters and operators controlling these vehicles, directing the FII on what to buy and sell. But the market had no idea about this. Routing purchases through sub-accounts and OCBs had an added advantage; it would improve sentiment for the stock because of the illusion that an FII was buying the stock.

Quite a few companies indulged in what was known as 'round-tripping'. This effectively consisted of promoters stealing money from their companies by fudging the account books and transferring the money overseas, either through *hawala* or through a seemingly legal but shady transaction. At times, money earned through dubious export/import transactions was directly credited in a foreign account. The promoter then gave this money to a friendly FII that usually managed a cluster of funds investing in various markets across the world.

The FII would use one of the many sub-accounts managed by it to route the promoter's money back into India. On paper, it would be the FII investing in particular stocks, but behind the scenes stood the promoter deciding which stocks the FII would invest his money in. News of an FII buying a stock would improve the perception of that stock in the market. But usually, when the FIIs bought shares of a particular company, the sellers were entities controlled by the promoters. I have mentioned earlier that many promoters held shares in *benami* accounts, which ordinary investors were ignorant about.

Another way to bring the promoters' illegal funds back to India was through a private placement of shares by their companies. This allowed the company to offer shares to investors of its choice. One of the investors 'buying' the shares in this private placement would be the FII with whom the promoter had parked his money.

There were times when the scorching rise in share prices made many of us nervous. We would book profits, only to see share prices climb again. It did not require great intelligence to know that this kind of mad rise in stock prices could not go on indefinitely. But I was reminded of Warren Buffet's oft-quoted saying: 'Markets can remain irrational for longer than you can stay solvent.' The bears were realizing this the costly way.

October brought cheer to the market as the BJP-led NDA coalition returned to power with an improved tally of seats.

The Sensex touched the psychological mark of 5,000 for the first time ever on 8 October, and the BSE governing board and other senior brokers celebrated it by floating balloons printed with the number 5,000 from the terrace of the BSE building. The picture appeared in a couple of financial dailies the following day, and some cynical brokers said this was a sure sign of the market having peaked. But this bull market was not going to end so easily.

The price appreciation that year alone in many stocks, particularly those in which Ketan had an interest, was simply unbelievable. Pentafour, which was quoting at Rs 700 at the start of 1999, jumped to Rs 3,000 by the end of the year. The stock had risen nearly four-fold the previous year too. Zee shares climbed from around Rs 640 to nearly Rs 11,000, even after a near seven-fold rise the previous year. Somebody who had invested Rs 10,000 in Zee shares at the beginning of 1998 was now sitting on Rs 11 lakh! Global Telesystems shares rallied from Rs 74 to Rs 1,000 in a year, Himachal Futuristic Communications Limited (HFCL) from Rs 37 to Rs 700, Aftek Infosys from Rs 45 to over Rs 2,100, Ranbaxy from Rs 270 to nearly Rs 1,000 and Software Solutions from Rs 600 to Rs 2,200.

'Radhakishan or Rakesh will never be able to take the prices of their favoured stocks to the dizzying levels that a Harshad or Ketan are capable of,' GB remarked one evening, when we were discussing the trading styles of the top players.

'Unlike Harshad and Ketan, RKD and Rakesh are not reckless. They know when to exit a stock as well as they know when to get into one. Also, Rakesh and RKD believe in the intrinsic worth of a stock and are convinced that no stock can sustain an artificial price beyond a point. That is not the case with Harshad and Ketan, who think that no price is too high for a stock, whatever its fundamentals,' GB said.

But the meteoric rise in their share prices was not the only crazy feature of the new-economy companies. Barely a month after its NYSE listing, Satyam Computer's subsidiary Sify paid an astounding $28 million (Rs 122 crore at that time) for a 24.5 per cent stake in Indiaworld Communications. Promoted by IIT graduate Rajesh Jain, Indiaworld owned thirteen websites, including khel.com, bawarchi.com, khoj.com and samachar.com. The deal included purchase of the remaining 75.5 per cent stake in Indiaworld for $75 million (Rs 325.4 crore), with Sify paying $12 million (Rs 51.3 crore) for the option of buying that stake.

All this for a company with a turnover of Rs 1.3 crore and a net profit of Rs 25 lakh. The media and the market cheered the deal, but in private many suspected that the deal was just a front for siphoning out money from Sify. It was pointless to voice such doubts publicly. Loss-making Internet companies in the US were quoting at even more outrageous valuations, and there was nothing wrong in a profit-making company being bought for Rs 500 crore, argued many analysts.

Financially, 1999 was the best year of my career. But on the personal front, I had to endure a huge loss. Bauji's condition started worsening around September. Finally the end drew near, and the tests showed that now there was no delaying the Grim Reaper who had been repulsed for the last twelve months.

I asked the doctor if Bauji's last days would be painful.

'Yes, they will be. The growth has completely taken over his lungs. He will cough his way to death, spitting blood,' he said.

When I heard the doctor's verdict, I cursed myself. It would have been better if I had let Bauji die when he had just two weeks to live. I had spent money on prolonging his life, only to see him die a painful death. I really wished the growth in his brain had continued at its normal pace and granted him a painless exit. As I was lost in my thoughts that evening in office, Bina called, saying Bauji was acting strangely. He was not recognizing people and was indifferent to everybody around. The next day, I took him to the doctor for a check-up. The doctor said the growth in his brain had resumed, and that it was now a matter of days. Two days later, Bauji lapsed into a coma from which he never recovered.

## 18

# Rumblings of Another Crash

Even Ketan's closest associates found it hard to keep track of his trading calls. He would be bullish on his favourite stocks but frequently book profits when prices rose, only to buy them back when prices fell. Every such profitable trade meant his average cost of acquisition would reduce further.

'Most of his so-called investment bets are downright dubious, but when it comes to trading skills, he does not have an equal,' GB had once remarked.

Such was the speed with which he got in and out of positions that it left the market guessing. Also, Ketan traded through a vast network of brokers to confuse anyone trying to piggyback his bets. He could be buying through a group of Mumbai brokers and simultaneously selling an even bigger quantity through Calcutta brokers. Sometimes it was the other way round, his buy orders exceeding his sell orders.

By itself, there was nothing surprising in this tactic, since operators sometimes had to create a trend contrary to the position they wanted to take. If they wanted to accumulate a big lot, they would first try to depress the price to be able to buy cheap. The trick was to push the price below a key level and panic day traders and retail investors into selling out. If the operators wanted to offload a big position, they would try to boost the price and generate demand by buying a small quantity. This time, the price had to be pushed above a key level to tempt retail investors and day traders into buying.

At times, the brokers with whom Ketan placed orders would try to profit from front-running his orders. A few would get away, but Ketan got to know about most of them and punished them severely. He came across as soft-spoken and down-to-earth, but could be pretty ruthless with people who tried to double-cross him.

Monk told me of an episode when Ketan learnt that one of his brokers was cheating on him. That broker's rival squealed on him to Ketan, who checked out the information to find, after a couple of deals with the suspect broker, that it was true. Two days later, Ketan gave him an order to buy a stock that had been rising the last few days. The broker bought a good-sized chunk for himself before executing the order. Minutes after he had placed the order, Ketan offloaded a big lot of that stock through his other associates. The broker suffered a huge loss and rushed to Ketan's office pleading for help. A few other brokers too were chastened in a similar fashion. But despite Ketan's efforts to keep his brokers under his thumb, there was always somebody or the other who would try to front-run him. There was no way he could control every single one of them.

---

Not long ago a recluse who took pains to stay away from the spotlight, Ketan slowly began shedding his reserve. He now seemed to delight in flaunting his success and connections, and could be regularly seen socializing with Bollywood moguls and stars. Great was the surprise when Ketan threw a grand New Year party at a beachside resort in Mandwa, a short boat ride from the Gateway of India, to welcome the new millennium. The guest list included rising IT czars, Bollywood celebrities, senior corporate treasury officials, fund managers and Ketan's associates in the industry. For an industry that thrived on secrecy and discretion, Ketan's brazen show of power upset many of the old-timers.

'The guy is drawing the attention of the government and tax department on us; there will be trouble before long,' one of GB's friends said.

'Not to mention the underworld,' remarked another, '*Saala, khud toh doobegaa hi, saath mein hum sab ko bhi duba dega* (he will sink, and drag us down as well).'

And if you are wondering whether I was invited, all I can say is I was yet to show up on Ketan's radar. He would have known of me through Monk but did not think me important enough to meet with yet. That hurt my pride not a little, I must say.

These hiccups apart, it was an exceptionally lucrative year for me. It was the same for most of the others in the market, except for the minority that kept short-selling technology shares to prove a point. The Sensex rose around 40 per cent during the year, even though most of the revered old-economy stocks struggled through the year. Two things worked against these stocks. One, their earnings growth was nowhere as high as that of their ICE counterparts. Two, many investors sold their blue chip holdings to buy more of the new-age stocks, convinced that market leadership had permanently changed.

Intoxicated by the fantastic run in stocks, most players expected the coming year to be even better. The logic was that FIIs would allocate more money to India since it was among the best-performing markets globally.

The new millennium dawned without any disaster arising from the Y2K bug in computer systems, as was widely feared. One would have expected the bulls to be a bit cautious after the 40 per cent rise in the Sensex the previous year. If anything, it only emboldened them to the point of recklessness.

The index rose 375 points (7.5 per cent) in the very first trading session of the year. I was told that operators were buying stocks, confident that they would be able to shortly offload them to FIIs. GB's friend was not mistaken about Ketan's actions attracting the attention of the tax department. In the second week of January, income tax officials surveyed Ketan's offices and found evidence of undisclosed income. Some of Ketan's favourite stocks weakened briefly, as did the Sensex, but the rebound was quick.

No adjective can sufficiently describe the bull market that raged from January to the second week of March that year. Even the word 'madness' cannot fully describe what we witnessed in those two and a half months. It was as though everybody in the market had taken leave of their senses all at once. I will let the stock prices speak for themselves. Infosys soared from Rs 14,500 to Rs 28,000, Satyam from Rs 2,200 to Rs 7,200, Wipro from Rs 2,600 to Rs 9,800, Global Telesystems from Rs 960 to Rs 3,550, Himachal Futuristics from Rs 677 to Rs 2,550, and DSQ Software from Rs 950 to Rs 2,700 (I am providing rough figures). Compared with these stocks, Zee was a modest performer, rising less than 50 per cent, to Rs 1,600 from Rs 1,100. But it must be remembered that Zee was now a paid-up share of Re 1, which meant it was worth Rs 16,000 for shareholders who had bought the paid-up stock of Rs 10.

By now, the mania for ICE stocks in India was mirroring that on Nasdaq. The phenomenal rise in share prices made a mockery of the price targets that analysts would assign for these stocks. Twelve-month price targets would be achieved in two months, leaving analysts scratching their heads over how to justify the new prices. And, despite many stocks rising tenfold or even more in less than two years, most stockbroking firms were reluctant to rate them as 'sells', even though they were quoting at bizarre PE multiples. Of course, there were the odd 'sell' ratings, but minuscule compared with the 'buy' reports that broking firms were enthusiastically bandying around. Analysts then started justifying the high valuations on the basis of something called the price earnings growth (PEG) ratio, which is not as commonly used as the PE ratio. All it did was to help the valuations look slightly saner. I remember GB once remarking that when stocks became overvalued and people tried to justify it rather than admit they were expensive, it was time to book profits.

Broking firms could not afford to antagonize the companies from whom they stood to earn fees for helping raise capital or acquire other companies. And the brokers' institutional clients too wanted to buy the high-flying stocks so that their fund performance did not lag behind that of their competitors. Few brokers or fund managers had the conviction to stand apart from the crowd for fear of appearing ridiculously contrarian.

Another danger was building on account of the laxity on the part of brokers in collecting margin money from their retail clients. With prices rising almost by the day, the clients' outstanding positions would always show a credit. Many investors used this credit to buy more shares, prodded on by their brokers eager for more brokerage. The day of reckoning did not seem too far away now.

On 11 February, the Sensex topped 6,000 for the first time ever, but closed below that psychological level. That was a Friday, and we celebrated the landmark over drinks at the Harbour Bar in Taj Mahal Palace overlooking the Gateway of India. There were about a dozen of us. After the third or fourth peg, everybody present agreed that the market was absurdly overvalued and that it was time to sell out.

After we broke up, GB and I had a short stroll by the seaside. There was a slight nip in the air, even as winter was in retreat.

'You know, Lala, every time people attend a funeral, they become philosophical and return home promising to become better human beings the following day onwards. But after a good night's sleep they are back to being their usual selves,' GB said. 'I am sure the same goes for all those who tonight vowed to reduce their positions after a few pegs. If anything, they will buy more as prices rise.'

The following Monday, the Sensex hit a new peak of 6,150 intra-day, but again closed below 6000. By now the bulls were delirious with excitement and buying stocks at whim, confident that the index would hit 7,000 by the end of the month. I was surprised to see some of the most level-headed fund managers I knew behaving like momentum traders, chasing stocks on their way up.

One particular fund manager at a domestic fund house who, until a couple of months ago swore by Warren Buffet's principles of value investing, suddenly turned hyper-bullish on new-economy stocks. At a press conference announcing a new fund, a journalist asked him what value he saw in Zee at around Rs 14,000 (unadjusted for stock split) a share.

'People who go by the absolute price of a stock and say that Zee is expensive do not understand the business of the company,' the fund manager replied. He was lucky that nobody in the audience asked him to elaborate further.

A week later, the Sensex topped 6,000 a third time, but again failed to close above that mark. Some technical analysts saw this as a sign that the market was on the verge of peaking out, if it hadn't already. But nobody took much notice of the slackness in the Sensex. After all, technology stocks were reaching highs by the day. So long as there was money to be made, what difference did it make where the Sensex was?

The Union Budget further fired up market sentiment. It raised the FII ceiling in listed Indian companies to 40 per cent from the earlier 30. Only a month ago, Indian companies had been allowed to raise funds through issue of American depository receipts (ADRs) and global depository receipts (GDRs) without prior government approval. ADRs and GDRs were the equivalent of shares, except that they were offered to investors in overseas markets. ADRs are listed on a US stock exchange (either Nasdaq or NYSE), and GDRs on the Luxembourg Stock Exchange.

The government also allowed Indian companies to use up to 50 per cent of their ADR and GDR proceeds to acquire companies in overseas markets. In the coming months, a few companies would raise money through GDRs, and the promoters would siphon off the funds by acquiring dubious companies abroad. The modus operandi consisted of the Indian company buying a foreign firm with whose owner the Indian promoters already had an understanding. The Indian promoter would pay a certain amount for the acquisition, more than half of which would be returned by the foreign owner later.

---

I am embarrassed to tell you what my paper wealth had grown to by the last week of February that year. All I will say is that it was substantial enough for me to have lost count of it.

'Lala, has it occurred that you must have made more money than Shah Rukh Khan over the last one year?' Monk remarked the day after the Budget, when a group of us had gathered at a restaurant. I mentally calculated my net worth, and was flattered to realize that Monk was right after all.

'I never thought of it that way, but I guess it must be true,' I said, both delighted and embarrassed at the same time.

'Of course it is true, Lala. Tell me something, why are you still working after having made so much money?' Monk asked with a grin.

'For the same reason that you come to work every day despite having made more money than perhaps Shah Rukh Khan and Aamir Khan put together,' I said.

My repartee drew laughter from everybody at the table. I thought I saw a flash of anger briefly flicker in Monk's eyes before he joined the others in the laughter.

I knew I had overstepped my boundaries with Monk and had to make amends quickly. Monk could discuss my net worth in public, but I was not to take the same liberty with him.

'. . . for the same reason Ketan Parekh comes to work every day or, for that matter, even Warren Buffet, to make more money,' I continued.

Monk smiled. Sipping his drink, he said, 'What I like about Lala as a trader is that he is good at sensing market trends and will quickly get out of a loss-making trade.'

Nobody at the table caught what Monk was getting at, but I did.

---

Three days before the great US stock market crash of 1929, the economist Irving Fisher famously said, 'Stock prices have reached what looks like a permanently high plateau.'

A similar delusion seemed to have gripped most of the market experts in India, given the stupendous rise in technology share prices. Some veterans feared the worst, given the way prices were rocketing. For some time now they had been saying a crash was imminent. But after repeatedly being proved wrong they kept their wisdom to themselves, not wanting to appear ridiculously old-fashioned. Also, it made bad business sense; clients did not like brokers preaching caution when stock prices were shooting through the roof every day.

The normally adventurous Prakash was among the handful who managed to retain a good chunk of his profits.

He reduced his trading positions to near-zero by mid-February, and decided to go on a vacation.

'Honestly, Lala, I don't think we will see a run like this again in our lifetime,' he told me when I drove him and his wife to the airport. 'In fact, I have half a mind to quit this profession altogether. Even when this party ends, we will keep hoping to double or treble our money every two months.'

---

The party on Nasdaq ended abruptly on 14 March with a 4 per cent drop, sending the index tumbling to 4,707. And suddenly, investors in technology shares around the world were racing to exit the stocks, as if everybody had simultaneously realized at that magic moment that the business models of most of the technology companies were unsustainable. Overnight, these stocks – ardently pursued by fund managers and individuals until so very recently – became pariahs.

The scene was no different on Dalal Street. The panic selling over the next one month halved the prices of the technology darlings. Many investors saw their paper wealth diminish considerably, or even vanish. When the slide began, many traders and investors held on to their positions, thinking it was another of those bull market corrections that would reverse quickly. By the time they realized the gravity of the situation, trading volumes had dried up. In many stocks, trading was frozen because there were only sellers.

Like most of the others in the market, I too saw my paper wealth diminish. But there was plenty still left.

## 19

# From Bad to Worse

It was a bleak Diwali on Dalal Street, with the Sensex having fallen to around 3,700 from its peak of 6,000-plus Even the most diehard of bears would not have expected the fall to be this steep though they had anticipated a downswing.

The aura of invincibility around Ketan had faded now, though he still called the shots in a few of his favourite stocks. He still had access to funding from friendly promoters, could tap into the coffers of Global Trust Bank and Madhavpura Mercantile Co-operative Bank (MMCB), and had fund managers whom he could count on to buy or sell shares on his instructions. He had also the support of the Indian brokerage arms of global investment banks like Credit Suisse First Boston and Dresdner Klienwort Benson, which entered into synchronized buy and sell trades with him. This arrangement helped create the impression of huge trading interest in a stock to attract other market players. Ketan would later tell the Joint Parliamentary Committee probing the 2001 stock market scam that these arrangements were not aimed at creating artificial volumes, but were pure financing deals where the brokerages were loaning him money at a price.

A typical arrangement would consist of Ketan directly transferring shares held by him into the brokerage's account and receiving cash for them upfront. This facility was known as delivery-versus-payment (DVP), and the transaction was not routed through the stock exchanges' clearing house. The clearing house route – the normal procedure – would have meant another ten days before Ketan could receive funds for the shares.

Having bought the shares from Ketan, the brokerages would immediately put through a sell order for the same block at a slightly higher price, the buyers being Ketan and his associates! This time the deal would be routed through the clearing house, giving Ketan about ten days' time to settle the trade as the payments had to be made only in the week following the weekly settlement cycle. Whatever Ketan's claim to the JPC about this web of dealings, the public thought of these large trades as a sign of FII interest in a stock.

With the market showing no signs of revival, Ketan's troubles were now mounting by the day. When the market had been on the rise, some politicians and their affiliates had given sizeable sums to Ketan to work his magic and multiply their money. As was to be expected, Ketan invested most of it in the stocks he operated. With the prices headed south, he was now in no position to return the principal, let alone get returns on them. The powerful people who had given him money had not the faintest clue about how the stock market worked, and did not care to know either. All they were bothered about was their money.

The bears were now striking at will, aware that Ketan would not be able to support prices with the same ease he did during the bull market. Also, Ketan had unwittingly antagonized politically powerful people. His proximity to Amar Singh worried some of the big guns in the BJP. The Samajwadi Party and the BJP were fierce rivals, particularly in Uttar Pradesh, and there was a growing feeling that Ketan had become an important source of funds for the SP.

Then there were the old-economy industrialists who had to endure the double agony of investors ignoring their stocks and upstart technology companies growing in market capitalization by the day. Thanks to Ketan pumping up their stock prices, many technology companies were now in a position to raise huge sums from the market with minimum equity dilution. This allowed them to expand operations at a much faster pace. The new entrants were not a direct threat to the established brick-and-mortar companies, but the latter found it hard to digest the fact that companies with barely any physical assets were commanding exorbitant valuations. In short, Ketan was seen as arming the challengers and threatening to upend the established order.

The Union Budget in February 2001 brought brief cheer to the market. However, unlike the previous couple of Budgets, this one had little for the information technology sector. In fact, there was some bad news. Export-oriented units and units located in export processing zones, free trade zones and software technology parks had been granted a tax exemption on 25 per cent of their sales in the domestic market until then. This was removed in the Budget. The ceiling on FII investment in a company was now raised to

49 per cent. But this did not really matter at a time when FIIs were fleeing India.

The bears intensified their assault soon after the Budget, sensing that the overall sentiment had taken a turn for the worse.

'Ketan is foolishly trying to support the prices of his favourites in the face of relentless selling; the bears will make a meal of him this time,' Monk told me over the phone after he had placed an order through me.

I had observed that Monk had been a heavy seller in the Ketan favourites like Global Telesystems, Himachal Futuristics, Zee and DSQ over the past few weeks. Initially, I thought he was unwinding the long positions Ketan had built in these stocks through him. But his remark about Ketan made me think otherwise.

Had he switched over to Ketan's rivals and was now executing trades on their behalf, I wondered. Or was he short-selling the shares in his personal capacity, on the hunch that Ketan's game was up?

'But Ketan is known for his ability to make a comeback when least expected,' I said, trying to confirm my suspicion.

'Not this time. He has been done in by overconfidence. He has taken on unmanageable positions, believing he can get prices to obey him irrespective of the market trend. That would have been possible around a year ago. From what I hear, he is now struggling to pay margin money to his brokers,' Monk said.

Things were rapidly going downhill for Ketan. In a desperate attempt to prop up the prices, he asked his key brokers in Calcutta to buy on his behalf. Share prices, however, continued to melt away. The authorities saw the market fall as the work of a bear cartel that was unfairly trying to beat down prices for their personal gains. No doubt, heavy short-selling was putting pressure on prices; but when the bulls were ramping up prices a year ago and the bears were losing money, the authorities had seen nothing wrong with that.

By now, bad news was pouring in from every corner. Just two days after the Budget, BSE president Anand Rathi called up the surveillance department of the exchange and asked for confidential information on broker positions in certain stocks. Rathi would later claim that he had sought the information to see if the crash in the Sensex that day was caused by institutional investor selling or speculative selling, and direct risk management measures accordingly. Whatever his justification, this was in violation of the code of conduct for BSE governing board members. The taped conversation between Rathi and the surveillance official was leaked to the press by a BSE official, and Rathi was accused of seeking the information for his personal gains and of passing it on to the bear cartel. Subsequent probes could not prove the charge against Rathi that he personally gained from the information. But the damage was already done. Less than a week after the revelation, SEBI dismissed the entire board of directors of BSE.

The already beaten-down technology shares were hit by another thunderbolt when NIIT Technologies – among the darlings of the market – announced a profit warning. That soured the mood for a host of second-line IT services stocks such as VisualSoft, Polaris and KPIT Infosystems.

Amid a growing perception that bears were to blame for the chaos in the market, SEBI tried to arrest the slide by banning naked short sales. This ban meant a trader could only sell shares that he owned. He could not short-sell and then square up his position by buying an equivalent quantity of that stock later. On paper, this measure was expected to boost stock prices as rattled bears rushed to cover up their positions by buying the quantity of shares they had sold. Instead, the ban had the opposite effect, and the Sensex shed another 500-odd points over the next three sessions following the ban.

'The bears may have stopped short-selling, but those with delivery are still selling. To support the market you need buying, which is simply not there,' GB told me when I asked him for his view.

There was more bad news for the country coming. Only a couple of days after the BSE board was fired, a sting operation by the investigative website Tehelka.com showed senior defence officials and politicians from the ruling NDA coalition taking bribes in return for favouring a fictitious arms company. This was a big blow to the credibility of the government, which had always claimed it would not tolerate corruption. The government alleged that the exposé was deliberately timed to further dampen stock market sentiment. That was because Shankar Sharma of First Global Stockbroking was a key shareholder in Buffalo Networks, the holding company that owned Tehelka.com.

Shankar Sharma, Radhakishan Damani, and Nirmal Bang were accused of acting in concert to hammer prices, and were the target of raids by the Income Tax Department and Enforcement Directorate. There were others who were raided too, but they were not so high profile. A SEBI probe found that entities related to Nirmal Bang and First Global had entered into synchronized trades to give an impression of heavy selling to beat down share prices. On appeal, Bang and Damani were able to prove that their trades were not large enough to depress prices and that they had not violated any rules. Sharma's ordeal continued for much longer.

All through March, Ketan's situation was getting worse by the day. The raids by investigating agencies and the consequent freezing of his bank accounts cut off his access to funds. Ketan asked brokers in Mumbai and Kolkata to buy stocks on his behalf and promised to pay them interest for holding the shares on his behalf. He also placed some of his stocks as collateral with these brokers for margin obligations.

Many in the market now felt he had become emotionally attached to the stocks whose prices he was going all out to support. Some claimed the promoters of the companies had beseeched Ketan to save their stocks, and he had agreed to oblige them, overestimating his own ability. The truth was simpler. Ketan tried to support the prices in an attempt to save himself. It was a desperate gamble, but he had little choice. When prices move up or down sharply, they tend to create self-reinforcing loops. Ketan was hoping that if he managed to stabilize the prices through small purchases, the selling pressure would ease and the prices would rebound, giving him some breathing space. The alternative was to dump his existing positions, but that would have caused prices to fall even more steeply, and he would still not be able to exit his positions fully. Sitting still and waiting for the selling fury to abate would not have helped either. With prices in a free fall, he would have to pay marked-to-market margins to the stock exchanges, which called for funds. In the marked-to-market margin system, an increase in the value of your outstanding positions gets you a credit in your account, while a decrease in the same requires you to deposit the difference as margin to the stock exchange.

In a final throw of the dice, Ketan chose to support the prices of his chosen stocks, hoping to arrest their slide at least temporarily. On CSE, his associates were loading up on DSQ, Himachal Futuristics and other such junk stocks, and then attempting to carry forward the positions. But their prices continued to flag.

Sensing trouble, many of Ketan's brokers started offloading his positions. Others dumped the stocks he had placed with them as collateral. These actions set off a vicious cycle, the falling prices triggering off selling, every wave of selling leading to a further fall in prices, and so on. Trading in many stocks was frozen for lack of buyers, and brokers, unable to unwind their positions fully, defaulted on payments to the exchanges.

Ketan's situation was made worse by many badla financiers deciding to withdraw funds from the market at the same time that he was badly strapped for cash (too much of a coincidence, I thought). Badla rates shot through the roof as the handful of remaining financiers then asked for a steep premium. Undoubtedly, those Ketan had caused heartburn to on his way up the ladder of fortune were now tightening the screws on him.

On CSE, there was a major payment crisis as Ketan's associates who bought on his behalf were unable to make their payments to the exchange. There was a cumulative shortfall of Rs 106 crore across three settlement cycles, even as the exchange somehow tried to complete the settlement by invoking bank guarantees and appropriating the margin money of the defaulting brokers. In addition, the exchange dipped into its trade guarantee fund to bridge the shortfall. But all these measures were still not good enough to tide over the defaults.

With all exit routes closed, Ketan decided to go for broke. He got MMCB to issue him a pay order for Rs 137 crore and pledged his shares, by now worthless, as collateral. This was not the first time that the bank's chairman Ramesh Parikh had accommodated Ketan. In fact, the bank had been facing liquidity problems since early March when it became common knowledge that Ketan had a free run of the bank. Parikh was loaning funds to Ketan far in excess of the limits set by RBI, and that too without collecting adequate collateral. Unnerved by rumours that the bank had given a hefty bank guarantee to the latest Big Bull on Dalal Street, wary depositors started taking their money out of the bank, effectively sealing its fate.

Ketan was a major reason for the bank to go under, but he was not the only reason. Ramesh Parikh's son Vinit Parikh was an active player in the stock market through his firm Madhur Capital, and was said to be dipping liberally into the bank's coffers to repay his trading losses. At the time of issue of the pay order to Ketan, MMCB had already been hollowed out. Ketan presented the pay order to Bank of India, which released the money to him. When Bank of India presented the pay order to MMCB for the money, the pay order, naturally, bounced.

Only too aware of the fate that befell the officials at SBI who allowed Harshad more time to settle his accounts, Bank of India chairman V. Krishnamurthy showed no such leniency to Ketan. He promptly called in the CBI, and on 30 March, a Friday, Ketan was arrested after market hours.

Interestingly, the market shrugged off the development. The Sensex fell barely 40 points on Monday.

'Looks like people don't have anything left to sell,' Prakash remarked, when we discussed the market that evening.

A major casualty of the stock market crash was UTI's flagship mutual fund scheme US-64. Just before it went under in July 2001, the scheme had 1.9 crore unitholding accounts – 99 per cent of them belonging to retail investors – and around Rs 16,500 crore of funds under management. A flawed pricing mechanism meant that the price at which investors purchased US-64 units, as well as the price at which they sold the units back to UTI, had no relation to the NAV – or the true value – of the scheme. UTI would increase the sale and repurchase of US-64 by 20 paise every month. To a large extent, these fresh inflows helped pay the unit holders who wanted to exit. Such a pricing mechanism gave certain returns to existing and exiting investors, but also created the perception among investors that US-64 was an 'assured returns' scheme without any risk. Till the early 1990s, equity investments accounted for 20 per cent of the US-64 portfolio, and debt instruments for the rest. By June 2001, as the bull run was in its death throes, equities accounted for 75 per cent of US-64's portfolio, and included a good many dubious stocks purchased for nefarious reasons.

Despite its deteriorating asset quality, the scheme had managed to stay afloat for longer than most people thought it would. As with Ponzi schemes, the steady inflow of fresh money from new investors helped pay off the exiting investors in US-64. But once inflows dried up, around March 2001, it became an uphill task for US-64 to meet redemption requests. Rumours of a crisis at UTI started doing the rounds, leading to more redemption requests from unitholders. Corporations and institutional investors started pulling out in droves from May onwards, sensing their investments were in danger. The losers were individual investors who had no inkling of the true health of US-64 and stayed invested.

It was obvious that the unusually heavy redemption pressure in May and June had to do with inside information that UTI would announce a halt in repurchase of US-64 units at its 2 July board meeting. In what was a clear breach of confidentiality, SBI, which had a nominee on the board of trustees of UTI, redeemed Rs 355 crore in May. UTI had borrowed heavily from many banks in June to meet redemption requests. Each of these banks was an investor in US-64, and, knowing the scheme's perilous financial health now, joined the queue for redemption.

At its board meeting on 2 July, UTI announced that it was freezing redemptions in US-64, stunning the market and shattering the faith of millions of individual investors. The scheme was restructured, and a repayment schedule was worked out, but almost every US-64 investor had to take a knock on his original investment. Worst of all, the crash also claimed a few lives. There were newspaper reports of at least half a dozen investors committing suicide after incurring massive losses in speculative trades. Some of them owed huge sums to brokers and financiers, and feared a far worse fate if they failed to pay up.

The quarterly earnings season brought more bad news for the IT services sector. Satyam's numbers were good, but the management said it was 'cautiously optimistic' about the year ahead. Anybody reading between the lines could make out that the booster growth rates seen till a quarter ago were unlikely to be repeated for a while. The slowdown in the US following the Nasdaq crash was now beginning to pinch Indian software firms.

The following day, Infosys too made a similar statement; its revenue guidance for the year provided for a growth of 30 per cent, which, given the company's track record, was a modest target. Some of the second-line IT companies like Mastek announced very sorry earnings figures. And, quite suddenly, the market appeared to have got over its obsession for technology stocks.

Looking back, I wish I had been a bit more cautious in investing my profits from the dotcom craze or bubble, whichever way you look at it. I survived the meltdown in ICE stocks, which is not to say that I did not make any losses. The market snatched away roughly 40 per cent of my peak paper wealth, but I still had a substantial amount left. I invested in a dozen-odd start-up firms that seemed to show a lot of promise. Or maybe I should say the entrepreneurs did a good job of convincing me to invest. There were all kinds of ideas on which the start-ups were founded, many of which were actually quite absurd. Some of them were ahead of their time and, launched a few years later, would perhaps have done much better.

Of course, I was not alone. To use a pun, I was in good company. I was hoping that even if two of them did well, I would still be able to at least double my overall investment. Over the next years, the majority of them turned out to be duds. I managed to exit a couple of them at a modest profit. But on the whole my start-up portfolio was a disaster.

Nevertheless, it was a good experience in terms of understanding some of the business models and the aspiring businessmen.

# 20

# Penny Wise, Pound Foolish

Prakash may have retained his trading profits, but most of the gains in his long-term portfolio slipped through his grasp as he could not bring himself to sell in time. There were some others who suffered sizeable losses despite having cashed a good chunk of their paper profits in time. Bina's distant cousin Pankaj belonged in this unlucky category. He managed his family business of trading in grains and oilseeds. He had grown the business with his hard work and acumen, and now made a net profit of around Rs 50 lakh annually. About a year ago, he developed an interest in stocks. As a professional trader, Pankaj felt he could replicate his success in grain trading with stocks too.

He began cautiously, and thanks to the bull market, made good money with his initial bets. From modest positions of a couple of hundred shares, he increased the size of his trades to a couple of thousand shares, that too in high-priced technology stocks. His wife and parents were worried, but Pankaj was certain he had mastered the game.

To my irritation, he offered me a few tips on trading when I ran into him at a relative's wedding around Diwali.

'The man will be in trouble before long, and I am willing to write it on stamp paper,' I told Bina that evening.

When stock prices leapt to unimaginable highs in February and March, Pankaj's paper profits on his outstanding positions amounted to Rs 50 lakh. When he boasted about it to his parents at the dinner table, they told him to cash the profit. They did not understand stocks, but were wise enough to know that the paper wealth represented one year's income. Pankaj refused to listen to them. His wife then rang Bina and asked me to speak to him. I knew it was easier to convince a professional stock trader than an amateur who mistook luck for skill. Still, I managed to convince him to book profits. But instead of taking the money out right away, Pankaj let it lie with the broker. When the stocks went into a tailspin, Pankaj thought there was quick money to be made by buying them at lower levels and selling them at the first opportunity. A series of mistimed trades later, Pankaj not only lost every rupee of his profits, but had to pay his broker an additional Rs 15 lakh. His father paid up the money, and that was the last time Pankaj ever mentioned stocks at home.

Another relative of mine lost a fortune, simply because he wanted to save on capital gains tax by holding on to the shares for three months.

---

On Nasdaq, investors were punishing new-economy shares with a vengeance. The selling frenzy reached a crescendo on 14 April when the Composite Index was hammered 10 per cent in a single trading session. It was now down around 35 per cent from its peak barely a month ago.

On Dalal Street, many of the late entrants among retail investors had been wiped out by the fall. But those who had got in early still had some cushion left and chose to play on.

By the first week of April the Sensex had fallen to around 4,700. But within the next week, it rallied to over 5,500, convincing many that the bull market had resumed and that India would be able to stand apart from other global markets. Also, many of the high-flying stocks appeared cheap against their earlier peak values, something new entrants found tempting, as they felt a steep fall presented a good opportunity to buy stocks and make the kind of profits their friends, colleagues or relatives claimed they had.

For instance, Infosys was going for around Rs 15,000, against its high of roughly Rs 28,000; Wipro was available for under Rs 5,000, attractive considering its peak of Rs 10,000 in late February; Global Tele could be bought for around Rs 1,700, against its high of Rs 3,500. The list was pretty long.

Of course, the buyers failed to notice that the stocks were not exactly cheap, but only seemed so when compared with their peak prices. Retail investors also have this misconception that once a stock touches a new high, it will definitely cross that price in the foreseeable future because there are smart people who bought the stock at its peak.

The rebound in the Sensex to 5,500 turned out to be short-lived. By the end of April, it again sank to 4,500, and by the last week of May, slumped below 4,000.

Many retail clients defaulted, causing losses to the brokers who had to honour the trades with the stock exchange, whether or not their clients paid. Brokers had only themselves to blame for not collecting adequate margins and for allowing clients to take up positions without bothering to check if they could pay up when the chips were down. Any investor you spoke to in those days would invariably say these words, 'If only I had . . . ' at some point during the conversation.

'Indiscipline has cost even the best of traders a lot of money,' GB told me when I visited his office one evening. 'And I can say that because I handle their trades. But to be fair, nobody has seen a rally like this before. They became too comfortable as prices kept rising. Any professional trader will have a price target at which he must take his profit and another target at which he must cut his loss. In the past, these operators would stick to their targets on the upside and downside, no matter what.'

But this time, they felt it would not hurt if prices fell some more because their average cost of purchase was quite low. Once overconfidence creeps in, it creates room for indiscipline, and bigger errors of judgement follow. Because of the large positions they carry, they have to time their exit well. Theoretically, it may have looked safe to hold on to their positions and even buy some more when prices began to weaken. But their experience should have told them that if prices fell further, there would be many weak sellers at lower levels, all looking to exit at the same time. That would make it difficult to unload large positions without breaking the price.'

The Sensex showed some signs of stabilizing in June, when it ranged between 4,300 and 4,800. In the first week of July, it again topped 5,000, raising hopes that the bull market was still alive. But that turned out to be a false dawn. ICE stocks continued to melt as fund managers and retail investors tried to salvage whatever they could of their paper wealth. By now, most of them had reconciled to the bitter truth that the technology party was well and truly over. In February, you were seeing prices that nobody could have ever imagined, and just a few months later, you were again seeing prices few would have thought possible even in their worst nightmares.

Like most of the players in the market, I too had lost money. But thankfully, it was only a loss on profits. You may find this a bit hard to believe, but I was relieved that my profits had shrunk to more realistic levels. Had I cashed every rupee of profits when my portfolio was at its peak, I would not have known what to do with the money. Many get a kick out of being known as a 'Rs xxx crore net worth fellow'. Not I. This is partly due to fear of attracting the attention of the tax department and the underworld, and partly due to the fear that too much money may blunt my trading skills. I own a portfolio of shares, but have absolutely no delusions about being a value investor and no aspiration to be counted among the investment gurus.

I bought the shares on the recommendations of the people whose wisdom and judgement I trusted. Over the years, my faith in their investment calls would pay off handsomely. Still, trading was what I enjoyed most, and I wanted to be in the game for at least a decade more.

When I told GB all this, he did not take me too seriously.

'Lala, you will be here for a long time, don't worry,' he said in his usual dismissive style.

'Why do you think so?' I asked.

'First, you have managed to stay in business for ten years. That says something about your trading skills. Had you not been a competent trader, the market would have forced you out by now. Second, this profession leaves you unfit for any other trade, because nowhere else can you make or lose lakhs in a day. Perhaps it is not just the money but the excitement, which you cannot find in any other job,' GB said.

The man made sense.

Despite the market crash, it had been a good year for me. I invested in land outside Mumbai, acquired a bigger flat in Ghatkopar and bought myself a red Opel Astra.

# 21

# Back on the Slow Track

Just when it seemed the market had stabilized, the 9/11 attacks on the twin towers of the US World Trade Center plunged markets worldwide into another spell of gloom.

Over a period of less than two weeks of the attacks, the Sensex slid 15 per cent to slump to an eight-year low of 2,600. More foreign brokerages closed shop, and so did scores of small brokers. In less than twenty months, the mood in the market had swung from euphoria to one of utter despair. Many of us traders, including I, wondered how long we would be able to survive if the situation continued. In the previous bear market, people had been talking about companies closing down. Now some were talking about stock exchanges shutting down. The 9/11 attacks deepened the recession in the US, and the ripple effect was felt in economies across the world.

---

In January 2002, Bharti Tele-ventures announced its IPO, the first 100 per cent book-built issue in the history of the

Indian capital market. In a book-built issue, the price is discovered by gauging investor demand for the shares. This was different from a fixed-price IPO, where the company offers shares to the public at a price decided by it. Mobile phones had gained in popularity by then, but most people thought it would be a privilege of the well-off for some time to come. Consequently, the ambitious projections by the company in the run-up to the IPO were mostly ignored by prospective investors. The dotcom debacle was still fresh in everybody's minds, and people were sceptical of IPOs in general.

The company announced a floor price of Rs 45, which eventually became its issue price too because of the lukewarm response from investors. At Rs 834 crore, the issue was fairly big for a market still trying to find its feet after the previous year's crash. The overall bearish mood was mainly to blame, and the raw deal that minority shareholders in Bharti Telecom got when that company was delisted in 1999, made some prospective investors wary.

As for me, I had no such qualms. IPOs never excited me, except for the grey market in them. What put me off about IPOs in general was having to buy shares at what the promoter decided was the right price for him. I bought Bharti shares after they listed and kept adding to my positions over the months. Bharti's IPOs were subscribed to around 2.5 times – no mean feat considering the depressed market environment. The decision paid off handsomely a few years later as the mobile phone went on to become an amenity rather than a luxury.

'Many companies will be out of business soon,' I remarked to GB one day as we were discussing the precipitous erosion in stock prices. 'Ah, don't worry about that,' GB said. 'The stock prices may have been hammered, but that does not mean the companies' customers will stop giving them business. The market may think of many of these promoters as shady and most of them actually are. But their products and services are trusted by clients. And that trust is what it takes to stay in business, not a high stock price.'

The market remained lacklustre through 2002 and all the way till May the following year. I was now truly on my own, having split with Monk. He was probed by SEBI because of his dealings with Ketan, and would later be penalized. Since he had routed quite a few of those deals through me, I had SEBI officials landing up at my doorstep too. They could not prove any wrongdoing on my part, but there was still a cost in terms of the time and energy I spent responding to their queries and making repeated trips to their office.

My parting with Monk was amicable, and I returned the money he had loaned me for the BSE membership card. Not long ago, the money would have been loose change for Monk. But the market crash had set him back by a good few crores, and every rupee now mattered.

'It is a small world after all, Lala, but let's be in touch,' Monk told me as I shook hands with him after handing him the cheque.

Corporate earnings kept sliding, and the intermittent rallies usually ended in grief for the bulls. The market was not ready to turn around yet. Caught on the wrong side many times myself, I reduced my trading positions considerably, not wanting to burn more capital.

And then the market changed course, without any indication. It would be a few months before players acknowledged that a bull market was under way again. The denial was only to be expected. After starting the year at around 3,400, the Sensex had sunk to 2,900 by mid-May. It then climbed to 3,500 by end-June. However, corporate earnings were still sluggish, and many, including me, were certain the rally would not endure. But the market got an unexpected sentiment booster in Maruti Udyog's IPO. Despite the uncertain market conditions, the government decided to push ahead with the public issue. To everybody's surprise, the IPO got an enthusiastic response from all classes of investors, including retail. The floor price was set at Rs 115, and based on the demand, the final price was set at Rs 125. This was the first time that a book-built issue had been priced above the floor price. The issue fetched the government Rs 993 crore.

For a market thought to be starved of liquidity and lacking buyers, the response to the IPO came as a pleasant surprise. More importantly, it drove home the message that there will always be takers for quality offerings if the price was fair. Many players were worried that the market would take a while to digest the Maruti IPO, as it had sucked out nearly Rs 1,000 crore at one go. But the shares did well on listing, and investors who made money in the issue started looking for other attractively valued stocks to put money in.

That's the beauty of public issues – they come across as liquidity guzzlers. But if the shares do well on listing, the IPO itself then becomes a source of liquidity.

By mid-October the index was closing in on 5,000, and even the most diehard of bears now had to grudgingly admit that a bull market was truly under way. Companies were eager to raise money and merchant bankers were working overtime advising them on how to go about it.

Every bull run needs a poster boy or Big Bull to look up to; that is something typical of the Indian stock market. This time the market found its hero in Rakesh Jhunjhunwala. A skilled trader, but an even better value investor, Jhunjhunwala suffered sizeable losses during the technology rally of 2000. He invested heavily in the shares of public sector firms and other old-economy companies. Simultaneously, he short-sold most of the junk technology stocks being rigged by Ketan.

The stocks Rakesh bought fell, despite the companies being fundamentally sound and even paying good dividends in many cases. And the price of the junk shares that he short-sold kept rising in value, forcing him to buy back those shares at a loss. In short, both his investing and trading calls were going wrong.

When the tech bubble finally burst, he recouped some of the trading losses by again shorting the same set of market-fancied stocks that had caused him grief in the past. But the bear market that followed shrank the value of his long-term portfolio considerably. More trouble followed, as his trades were also probed by the regulator for alleged bear hammering, post the Budget in February 2001.

But Rakesh's patience and his penchant for quality stocks began yielding fruit as the market recovered. Value investing was back in fashion, and Rakesh was the embodiment of it. His stakes in companies like Titan Industries, CRISIL, Matrix Laboratories, Geometric Software and Hawkins Cookers had appreciated significantly since the time he had started buying them. A feature on him in the October edition of *Outlook* magazine pegged the value of his 1 per cent-plus stakes in twenty-one companies at Rs 114 crore.

Of course, the market had grown too big over the last few years for any one individual to dictate the trend. When Ketan's stars were rising, the market was still shallow in terms of trading volumes and quality of stocks. FII activity was mostly concentrated in the top 20-25 stocks. Thanks to dematerialization of shares, the tech boom and the US listing of some Indian companies, more foreign investors were eager to invest in India where there was now a wider range of superior companies to choose from. Rakesh would go on to have a huge following in the market over the next few years. And while he would never evoke the mass frenzy for a stock that a Harshad or Ketan could at their prime, his investment style endured, despite a fair share of bad bets.

Soon he began to be referred to as 'India's Warren Buffet' by the media, a comparison he always resented. Rakesh credited Buffet with having far more wealth and wisdom than him, and in the same breath also maintained that he (Rakesh) was not anybody's clone.

Hounded by regulators, his mentor and close friend Radhakishan Damani took a break from the stock market to set up a supermarket chain under the brand name of D-Mart.

Year 2004 began on a cheery note for the bulls, with the Sensex closing above 6,000 for the first time ever. The success of the Maruti issue encouraged the government to arrange more stake sales through initial and follow-on public offerings. The largest of them was ONGC's follow-on offering in March, which fetched the government around Rs 10,500 crore.

A clerical error at the share registrar's end resulted in

HNIs being allotted more shares than they were entitled to. The investors were surprised to see the extra shares when they checked their demat accounts, and many of them immediately sold off their entire lot, hoping to profit from the error.

But pocketing the money was not as easy as they thought it would be. SEBI and the finance ministry swung into action and forced them to return the shares. Being regular traders and well versed with the allotment process, the HNIs could not pretend ignorance.

---

As the market continued to climb, retail investors slowly began to test the waters, and brokerages cautiously began adding staff. But the market had one big shock coming in May, which led many to think that the boom was as good as over.

The BJP-led NDA coalition decided to call for elections in April, a good six months ahead of schedule, convinced that the public mood was in its favour. But the move backfired, with the Congress and its allies winning more seats than the NDA coalition. The results came as a dampener for the market, which was rooting for a BJP win as the party was perceived to be pro-business and pro-market. Still, the bulls took it in their stride. But their resilience would be severely tested over the next couple of days.

To block the BJP from forming the government, the Left parties offered to back the Congress-led UPA, but without being part of its government. A day after it promised support, leaders of the Left parties began demanding that the government scrap the divestment policy initiated by the NDA government. That made the market nervous, and it showed its displeasure with a 330-point drop in the Sensex on Friday, the day after the election results were announced.

Matters did not end there, and worse was to follow on Monday. CPI leader A. B. Bardhan tactlessly remarked, 'Bhaad mein jaaye Sensex,' in response to a television reporter's query on the Left parties' stand on divestment. That comment sent the Sensex and Nifty crashing 10 per cent, to the lower end of the intra-day circuit filter. Under the rules, trading was frozen for fifteen minutes. But when trading resumed, there was no let-up in selling. Both the indices fell 5 per cent more and the market had to be closed again. The Sensex was now down 840 points over its previous close and the Nifty down around 290 points.

The last I had seen such a ferocious selling spree was when the Harshad Mehta securities scam had been exposed in 1992. But this was the first time that trading had to be suspended midway through a session because of such a rapid decline in share prices. Angry brokers and investors spilled on to the street facing the stock exchange building and shouted slogans denouncing the Congress, SEBI and Sonia Gandhi. Their rage was only natural, as the steep fall had almost entirely snatched away nearly all their profits painstakingly earned in the last few months.

Trading resumed again for the day a couple of hours later. Congress leaders tried to pacify the rattled market participants by promising to stay on the path of reforms. Simultaneously, LIC and other government-backed institutions stepped in to steady the market with their purchases. The nosedive had triggered margin calls at many broking firms, and most clients were not in a position to arrange additional funds at short notice.

The build-up to disaster had begun the previous week, when the Sensex and Nifty fell around 10 per cent each over the week. In particular, Friday's 330-point fall in the Sensex had many bulls on the ropes. The stock exchanges imposed ad hoc margins on some large brokers with significant positions in shares that were most vulnerable to a further fall. Trading terminals of many brokers who had been unable to meet margin obligations on Friday had been disabled.

Their finances already wearing thin, many traders had little option but to liquidate their long positions to meet the demand for additional margins. The exchanges would later deny that they had imposed ad hoc margins, but I knew of brokers who had got faxed instructions to collect higher margins from clients in certain stocks.

As soon the market opened on Monday, a deluge of sell orders hit the trading screens as many traders liquidated their long positions, unable to pay the additional margins. A SEBI probe would reveal exactly a year later that the maximum damage was caused by sell orders from UBS Securities Asia.

The Swiss broking firm dumped shares worth Rs 188 crore within minutes of the market-opening. SEBI found that the broking firm had short positions of a cumulative Rs 726 crore in Nifty index futures and some stock futures. When share prices fell sharply, the index and stock futures too moved lower in tandem. The investigation showed that UBS made a loss of around Rs 17 crore on its cash market sales, but gained around Rs 59 crore on its futures positions.

On the face of it, UBS stood to gain if prices fell sharply.

UBS initially told SEBI that it had sold the shares in its proprietary account. Later, it changed its version, saying it had sold the shares and futures on behalf of clients who had exposure to India via participatory notes.

Participatory notes – P-notes or PNs – were derivative instruments issued by SEBI-registered FIIs. The buyers of these instruments were overseas investors who were either ineligible or chose not to register with SEBI. Often, the supposed buyer of the P-note was merely a front for another investor, and that investor too was often a front for still somebody else. And the chain was so long the ultimate beneficiary was well shielded from the regulator's gaze. The Joint Parliamentary Committee probing the 2001 securities scam had found plenty of instances of wide misuse of PNs during the technology boom of 1999-2000.

Promoters found PNs a convenient tool to launder black money and to prop up their share prices. The peculiar structure of PNs made it difficult for SEBI to trace the true owner; more so if he/they/it happened to be domiciled in a tax haven where banks could refuse to disclose the identity of their customers, citing confidentiality laws.

SEBI asked UBS to disclose the identities of the beneficiaries of the PN accounts. UBS stonewalled SEBI, saying its clients were refusing to cooperate. Under the rules, FIIs were required to be aware of the identity of their PN clients and provide their details to the regulator when asked for them. UBS's inability or reluctance to disclose the names only strengthened the suspicion many had about PNs – that they were mostly a conduit for round-tripping and money laundering.

The SEBI order indicting UBS highlighted the misuse

of PNs but could not prove that UBS had deliberately sold shares in the cash market to profit from its derivatives trades. And the punishment for UBS? A one-year ban on issuing PNs for a year. UBS promptly appealed against the order to the Securities Appellate Tribunal, and in less than two months, won the appeal.

SEBI moved the Supreme Court, but in January 2009 the matter was settled through a consent order. UBS paid a penalty of Rs 50 lakh to SEBI without admitting or denying the charges against it.

---

The UPA government's maiden Budget had a pleasant surprise for stock market investors. The 10 per cent long-term capital gains tax was abolished and the tax on short-term capital gains was reduced to 10 per cent from the income tax rate applicable earlier. For those in the 33 per cent income tax bracket, the short-term capital gains tax had more than halved. And investors did not have to pay tax on any shares held for more than a year.

'All in the name of encouraging retail investors,' GB smirked, when he heard the announcement. 'Actually it is the promoters who will benefit the most since they are the ones who trade more often.'

To make up for the revenues lost by way of the new capital gains tax rates, Chidambaram introduced a 0.15 per cent Securities Transaction Tax (STT) on all stock market trades. A key reason for its imposition was the notoriety of stock market players for evading capital gains tax by showing fictitious losses. Also, since this tax was to be collected by the stock exchanges at the time of the trade, players would not be able to escape it. For the government, STT was both an efficient as well as low-cost source of tax.

But the STT sparked a furore among day traders who played for spreads as low as 5 to 10 paise. Unlike capital gains tax, STT had to be paid whether or not the trader made profits from his trades. Capital market players, with support from the stock exchanges, made presentations to the finance ministry, arguing that trading volumes would dry up if day traders stayed away because of STT. Day traders – also known as jobbers or arbitrageurs – were an important source of stock market liquidity. An absence of speculators would make stock prices volatile and hurt even genuine investors, they argued.

The government refused to repeal the tax, but agreed to modify the STT rate. For delivery-based transactions – buy and sell – the rate was reduced to 0.075 per cent. For non-delivery-based transactions, the rate was reduced to 0.015 per cent, and for derivatives transactions, the new rate was 0.01 per cent. Traders and investors could also claim a rebate on their tax liability to the extent of STT paid.

The government had to take a huge hit on its tax estimates for that year because of this revision in STT rates. But an illiquid stock market could have cost the government even more.

It was one of those rare occasions when the powers in Delhi had to soften their stance in the face of sustained protests from the broking community.

Before long, the ingenious brokers would exploit a loophole in the STT and help clients lower their tax liability for a cut of the savings they made. The government hit back by scrapping the rebate after a few years.

After a long gap, 2004 turned out to be a busy year for merchant bankers, with 26 companies raising around Rs 12,400 crore through IPs. They included the Rs 5,420 crore IPO of India's number one software services exporter, Tata Consultancy Services (TCS). The issue drew an enthusiastic response from investors, even as the overall market was recovering from the post-election drubbing in May. The retail portion of the issue was subscribed three times, and the issue fetched 12.5 lakh applications. Overall, the issue was subscribed 7.7 times.

Again, concerns that the TCS IPO would cause a liquidity squeeze in the secondary market turned out to be unfounded. Another Rs 23,000 crore was raised by companies through the year by way of FPOs, preferential issues and rights issues. Despite the massive capital mop-up, the Sensex made a new high by December.

I decided to upgrade my Opel Astra to a Mahindra Scorpio.

# 22

# In the Name of Wealth Creation

It is a standard practice for most promoters to siphon money out of their companies. Their business would be flourishing, but very little of the money would show up in the company's books. Only a certain portion would be booked in the company's accounts, while the rest would be diverted to the promoter's personal accounts.

But, as the bull market began to gather steam, promoters realized that there was more money to be made by showing the full revenues in the company's books, and maybe even showing more revenues than there actually were. The higher the earnings and earnings growth potential, the more value the market was willing to assign to a stock.

And so began the great game of 'market capitalization' and 'wealth creation', as many promoters went in for an image makeover, helped by market operators, analysts, fund managers and last, but not least, a friendly media.

Market capitalization is the share price multiplied by the outstanding number of shares (equity base) of a company. A huge equity base does not necessarily lead to a large market capitalization, as a large number of shares floating around would make it hard for the stock price to move up. So the key to higher market capitalization is a fat stock price. The higher their market capitalization (or valuation of the company), the easier it became for companies to raise more funds by selling the least number of shares.

By now I had become very friendly with an analyst I had nicknamed Sherlock because he was forever suspicious of promoters and the numbers companies put out. We regularly met over drinks. During our discussions, he would tell me a thing or two about his profession, and in turn I would tell him a few things about trading.

One evening we had a very long chat, during which he told me about the ways in which promoters manipulated the earnings of their firms. According to him, manipulation was more rampant in mid-cap firms, though large-cap firms too were not always above board.

'It is like this – all milk is adulterated, only the proportion of water varies,' Sherlock explained to me.

One way to manipulate numbers was to recognize revenues in the books of accounts ahead of time when there was no certainty that the company would receive the payment. A property developer's luxury residential project may be fully booked on the very first day of launch, but there could be cancellations or defaults later on. A products firm could reduce its inventory by getting dealers to overstock by offering them favourable credit terms. Companies also booked fictitious sales or showed income from non-core operations (for example, income from investments in shares, bonds, mutual funds) as sales. There were companies that dabbled in their own shares and showed the profits in their earnings. Some companies would not make adequate provisions for doubtful receivables, tax disputes and other liabilities. In the banking industry, 'evergreening' of loans is a standard procedure to lower provisions for bad loans. The banks issue a fresh loan to the troubled borrower so that he is able to repay his earlier loan with it, thereby technically avoiding a default.

In a rising market, promoters were keen to show off a fat bottom line, real or fake, as it helped them raise equity capital at fancy valuations. But in a bear market, promoters would usually revert to their old trick of siphoning off money from the company's books. They know that showing good earnings is of little help when the market is down because prospective investors are finicky about the price they are willing to pay.

The most common strategy to pilfer cash from the company's books was to suppress receipts and inflate expenses. These could relate to a wide range of items, from sales and promotional events, to capital expenditure programmes.

Merely studying the profit and loss statements of companies would tell investors little about the funds that were leaking out. Only those working in the company or in the same industry would know the true picture. In some sectors like liquor, a good deal of sales were done in cash, outside the company's books, because of the steep difference in sales tax rates across states. Many companies would under-report production to evade central excise duty, sales tax and income tax. Firms also diverted a part of their sales to associate firms in locations where tax rates were lower. Sometimes companies sold a chunk of their goods to dummy entities below their fair price. The dummy entities then sold those products at market price, ensuring the profits from the sale never reached the company's shareholders. If the company catered to export markets, promoters could take the money out of the country through this route. The company would sell its products to a promoter-controlled entity in Dubai or Singapore at a discounted rate. That entity would then sell the product in the international markets at its true price, and the difference would flow into the bank accounts of the promoters in Switzerland or the Cayman Islands.

Companies would enter into arrangements with their vendors for fake bills to show higher expenses. The excess money would later be paid back to the promoter in cash. If the vendor was an international entity, the promoter could take the money out of the company's books and divert it to his accounts in tax havens.

There were hawala operators who controlled the dummy entities, be they proprietorship firms, partnership firms, companies or trusts, in India or overseas. Promoters looking to suck out cash from their companies would make cheque payments to the hawala operator for phony expenses, and get the cash back, minus a commission, for the arrangement.

Inflating costs of plant and machinery also helped divert company money to the promoter's coffers. The inflated payment would be made by the company and the promoter would later collect the money in cash from the supplier. The higher the cost of the machinery, the higher would be the depreciation, and the lower the profits. Depreciation money was set aside for replacing the equipment when their useful life was over. The promoter would then find some way or the other to take this money out.

The 'other expenses' head – under which several miscellaneous operating expenses were aggregated in the profit and loss statement – made for a rich conduit for leakage. A sharp rise in 'other expenses' in a depressed market or slowing economy could point to money being drained from the company.

There were quite a few instances of acquisition of foreign companies that were nothing but contrivances by promoters to take money out of the company. In some instances, the promoters had raised capital specifically for overseas acquisitions and then bought out little-known companies at exaggerated valuations. These 'arrangements' ensured a chunk of the payment would find its way back to the promoter.

---

One of the unintended consequences of dematerialization was the encouragement of speculative tendencies in promoters. In the days of physical shares, promoters would learn the identity of the buyer or seller only when the shares came to them for transfer. But with dematerialization, they could know within a couple of days which fund manager was buying or selling their stock. The promoters would then use this information to take up positions using shares in their *benami* accounts. Or, they would approach fixers who would negotiate a deal with the fund managers. If a fund manager was buying a big chunk of the company's shares, the promoter would offer him shares from the *benami* account at a slight discount to the market price. Or, if the fund manager was selling, he would offer to buy the entire block of shares so that the price did not weaken.

In 2005, SEBI had tried to make large deals more transparent by naming the buyers and sellers. For all trades in a stock where the total quantity of shares bought or sold was more than 0.5 per cent of the equity base of the company, brokers had to disclose to the stock exchanges the name of the client and the traded price. But operators and promoters managed to find a way around this too.

If a promoter or market operator was transacting a deal of this size, the trade would be routed through a clutch of privately owned finance companies in such a way that no one entity violated the 0.5 per cent threshold. The information on the stock exchange website would only show the name of the fund house and not the details of the counterparty.

---

With the market once again in the grip of a bull run, Ketan Parekh was back in action. Since he had been banned by SEBI till 2017, he had to operate through fronts. Interestingly, he still had friends among fund managers, and his services were sought by promoters of many mid-cap companies, eager for lofty valuations for their shares.

But there remained the problem of finding brokers to trade through. Following the stock market crash in 2001, brokers who had dealt for Ketan had suffered huge losses. And since his bank accounts were frozen and investigative agencies were closely watching his every move, Ketan could not repay them legally, even if he wanted to.

So he made them a proposal. He would trade through them using fronts. If he profited on the trade, a chunk of that money would go towards repaying his debt. The only way his erstwhile brokers could hope to recoup the money Ketan owed them was to execute his trades. If he lost money on the trade, the broker got nothing, and what was more, he could not complain to the regulator either. After all, Ketan should not have been allowed to trade in the first place.

Still, many brokers took up the offer.

To my surprise, Monk refused to do business with Ketan until his previous dues were cleared.

I asked Monk why.

'Ketan had planned his game very well,' Monk told me. 'Having been in the business of trading for so long, he knew that no trader, however skilled or lucky, could escape the law of averages. In his case, he knew that the losses would be huge enough to wipe out his net worth, given the outsized bets he was taking. While agreeing to manipulate the stocks of a few promoters, he prevailed on them to allot him a good chunk of shares from their *benami* accounts at throwaway prices. Of those, he transferred a sizeable portion to his accounts abroad masquerading as OCBs.

'He used the rest of the shares to generate artificial volumes in the stock through circular trading. Finally, when the technology bubble burst globally, Ketan knew he would no longer be able to support the inflated prices of his favourite stocks. He then played his final card. He placed orders with his brokers, including me, to buy shares of the companies he had been manipulating. We bought the shares, unaware that the sellers of those shares were overseas entities controlled by Ketan.' I could sense the bitterness in Monk's tone.

He did not have to complete the story for me; I could see how the story would have played out. On the day of settlement, the money was debited from the brokers' accounts by the stock exchange towards the payment for the shares. Unknown to the brokers, the money flowed into the 'foreign investors' accounts and out of the country. When the brokers approached Ketan for payment for the buy orders he had placed with them, he must have bluntly told them that he did not have the money to honour their commitments. There was nothing they could do.

# 23

# A Booming Primary Market

The IPO boom continued in 2005 too. While more companies were listed than a year ago (fifty-five versus twenty-six in 2004), the amount raised was lower by around 20 per cent (Rs 9,918 crore against Rs 12,402 crore).

If TCS was the blockbuster IPO of 2004, then Jet Airways and Suzlon Energy were the most sought-after offerings of 2005. Investor enthusiasm was natural, considering both Jet Airways and Suzlon were the market leaders in their respective sectors – aviation and wind turbines. Jet raised close to Rs 1,900 crore and Suzlon around Rs 1,350 crore.

Long-term investors in both stocks would lose heavily in the coming years, as the companies' financial performance kept worsening steadily.

To be fair to Suzlon, the stock delivered handsome returns through the bull market. Offered at Rs 510 to the public, the stock peaked at Rs 2,300 in the second week of January 2008 before its downhill journey. But investors who had bought the stock during the IPO still had a chance to make some profits, as it was only towards the end of October that the share price fell below the issue price. But Jet Airways turned out to be a disappointment for IPO investors in less than a year after its listing. In fact, many investors started to regret their decision within a month's time of their purchase. It must have caused all the more heartburn considering Jet was tipped to be a sure winner because of its dominant market share.

There was some heartburn in store for merchant bankers too.

Till August 2005, merchant bankers to a public issue could decide which institutional investors to allot shares to, and how much, whenever the issue was oversubscribed. This arrangement helped the merchant bankers favour their important clients by allotting them a higher number of shares than they did to the smaller institutional players. Domestic mutual funds, in particular, got a raw deal as merchant bankers gave priority to FIIs. Peeved at this discrimination, many of the marginalized institutional players complained to SEBI.

The regulator scrapped the discretionary powers and ruled that all institutional investors should be allotted shares proportionately if the issue was oversubscribed. Merchant bankers protested, saying the power to decide allotments helped weed out the short-term players among institutional investors looking to make a fast buck on listing. Encouraging short-term players would increase fluctuations in the stock price and scare away retail investors, they argued.

I found the argument hollow. The main reason for their opposing the removal of discretionary powers was the fear that it would diminish their importance among institutional clients. Also, there was no way to prove that the so-called 'long-term investors' actually stayed invested for the long term. I have seen plenty of flippers (investors who buy shares in IPOs to sell them on listing day) among long-term investors too.

Try as hard as they would, their arguments did not wash with SEBI.

Another good thing the regulator did was to ask institutional players to deposit 10 per cent of the value of the shares at the time they applied for them. Until then only retail investors had to pay up for shares – that too, the entire amount – at the time of application. This inequity allowed institutional players to bid for any number of shares since their money was not getting locked in.

Often, merchant bankers and even promoters would ask some of the reputed institutional investors to bid for a large number of shares in their issue. This would help create the impression that the issue was in demand with fund managers. Since merchant bankers had discretionary powers of allotment, the fund managers would not have to buy all the shares they had bid for either. In effect, these investors were lending their names to ensure the success of the issue.

In book-built issues, the friendly fund managers would bid for a large quantity of shares at the upper end of the price band. The other investors too were now persuaded to bid high or risk not being allotted shares if the final price was at the top end of the band. Having to put 10 per cent of the money on the table at the time of application did help curb some of the exaggerated bids by institutional investors.

The IPO boom nearly got derailed by a SEBI probe, which revealed that shares reserved for retail investors in the Yes Bank and IDFC IPOs were cornered by a group of racketeers who opened fictitious demat accounts. The matter first came to light sometime in July when, during an income tax raid on businessman Purshottam Budhwani, it was found that he controlled 6,000-odd demat accounts. The Income Tax department then tipped off SEBI, which began its probe by examining the allotments in the IDFC and Yes Bank IPOs.

The findings enraged retail investors who were either not allotted shares or got fewer shares than they might have because of the scam. Yes Bank shares had risen more than 50 per cent in less than three months since their listing in October. Shares of IDFC had more than doubled since their listing in August.

SEBI widened the probe to IPOs dating back to June 2003. It brought out a detailed report in April 2006. The investigators found that in 21 IPOs, shares meant for retail investors had been cornered by a group of 85 financiers working through 24 players fronting for them. Based on the listing-day gains, SEBI concluded that the financiers and their fronts had together made a profit of Rs 72 crore through this theft of shares.

In all, around 59,000 *benami* demat accounts were opened, and applications for shares in IPOs were made by these fictitious entities. Nearly 84 per cent of the accounts were opened by the depository participant (DP) Karvy. A DP is an agent of a depository, an intermediary between the depository and the investor. A large number of such *benami* accounts were opened at other DPs too, the notable ones being HDFC Bank, Centurion Bank of Punjab (which was later acquired by HDFC Bank) and ILFS.

In every case, the DP had not diligently checked for proof of identity and proof of address of the entities opening demat accounts. They were required to do so under the Know Your

Customer (KYC) norms. Strangely, none of the DPs found anything suspicious about accounts with common postal addresses being opened in bulk on the same day. No red flag was raised either when the IPO shares allotted to the *benami* accounts were consolidated in a select few demat accounts to which they were transferred just before listing day.

At many DPs, hundreds of demat account holders had identical postal addresses. It was common for many retail investors to have multiple demat accounts. This was a throwback to the days when retail investors would make multiple applications in a public issue to increase their chances of share allotment. Since there was nothing such as a Permanent Account Number (PAN) at the time, these investors got away. A household of four – the husband, wife and two children – could apply under at least half a dozen combinations of names.

When dematerialization was introduced, investors who jointly held shares in various combinations had to open as many demat accounts under those exact combinations to get their shares dematerialized. As a result, many households had multiple demat accounts. So multiple demat accounts with identical postal addresses were not uncommon. But when hundreds of accounts had the same address, it should have set the alarm bells ringing.

The SEBI probe found that the depositories imposed fairly steep penalties – up to Rs 3 lakh in some cases – if employees at the DPs did not have NSE's Certification in Financial Markets (NCFM). And in bizarre disproportion, the penalty for violation of account opening rules was between Rs 500 and Rs 1,000. Despite DPs repeatedly violating account opening rules, the depositories did not take any action beyond imposing paltry monetary fines. This showed the casualness with which the depositories inspected the DPs.

Market players thought the SEBI report would dampen retail investor interest in public issues. But the IPO juggernaut continued to roll on, with 75 companies raising Rs 24,779 crore in 2006 – more than twice the sum raised in 2005.

# 24

# No Stopping the Bulls

The Sensex hit the historic 10,000-mark in February 2006. By now, a sense of euphoria was again suffusing the market. Emerging markets were the flavour of the season across the globe, and India was no exception to the trend. FIIs were buying everything in sight, and the retail money flow into mutual funds too was steadily on the rise. By the last week of April, the Sensex had rocketed to 12,000, and was not showing any signs of fatigue.

Reliance Petroleum was the blockbuster IPO of the year, with the company raising Rs 2,700 crore. The 45 crore share issue, priced at Rs 60 apiece, was subscribed a whopping 51 times, reflecting the frenzied mood in the primary as well as the secondary markets.

As stock market history shows, steep climbs are often followed by equally steep declines. A combination of rising commodity prices, firming up of interest rates globally, and concerns about expensive valuations of emerging market stocks triggered a worldwide fall in equity markets.

The Sensex fell below 9,000 by June, its 30 per cent fall the steepest since the bull market had started in May 2003. Many felt the bull market was as good as over.

GB was among those who had a contrarian view of the situation, thanks to his proximity to top market operators.

'The economy still appears to be in good health. Companies are still in expansion mode, earnings are growing and jobs are being created. I would not be too worried,' he told me. I knew he was echoing the views of either Radhakishan Damani or Rakesh. Damani had still not returned to the market, so in all likelihood it would have to be Rakesh's views.

—

The crash affected investor appetite for the IPOs that hit the market between June and August. GMR Infrastructure's issue had to be priced at the lower end of the bidding band of Rs 210-250. The issue was subscribed close to seven times. The institutional portion was subscribed eleven times, but retail investor response was poor. The shares got a lukewarm response on listing day, and could barely manage a 2 per cent premium before ending the day at the issue price of Rs 210.

I wondered where all the institutional investors who had enthusiastically bid for the issue had vanished. If the institutional portion was subscribed eleven times, it meant those who applied had got only one share for every eleven they had bid for. When the share was available close to its issue price on listing, these investors could have bought the remaining shares they had wanted. That there was hardly any demand on listing day suggested that some strings had been pulled to ensure that the issue got a decent response. Still, investors who subscribed to the issue and held on for a year had no cause for regret, as the stock appreciated nearly fivefold over the next eighteen months.

---

By the end of August that year the global markets had settled down, and in the following month had resumed their climb. The Sensex was crossing 1,000-point milestones at the strike rate of Sanath Jayasuriya in top form. In October, it reclaimed the 12,000 mark, on the first day of November, hit 13,000 and in the first week of December, it topped 14,000.

The mania in the secondary market notwithstanding, one of the high-profile public issues of the year turned out to be an anticlimax for the company as well as its merchant bankers.

Cairn India, the Indian arm of UK-based Cairn Plc, was looking to raise over Rs 6,000 crore through an IPO. Until then, only ONGC had raised a bigger amount – Rs 10,500 crore – through a public issue. But everything seemed to go wrong for the IPO, right from the moment the issue opened for subscription in December.

The issue, with its price fixed at Rs 160-190, was fully subscribed on the first day of bidding itself. But many institutional investors reduced the size of their bids and revised downward their bid price, with quite a few withdrawing their bids altogether. This had a cascading effect, as many retail investors too chose to withdraw their bids sensing institutional investor apathy. By the last day, it appeared that the issue may not be fully subscribed.

The pedigreed merchant bankers to the issue then had to fill the shortfall by paying from their pockets. Had the issue not attracted enough bids in the first place, the merchant bankers would only have had their reputation to worry about and not their pockets. But with investors withdrawing their bids, the merchant bankers were obliged under their agreement with the company to bridge the shortfall.

The issue was just about subscribed on the last day at the lower end of the price band. In private, the merchant bankers would say that a powerful rival of the company had prevailed on many of the institutional investors to withdraw their bids.

Cairn Plc may have got the satisfaction of raising Rs 5,788 crore through the issue, but more embarrassment lay ahead. The issue had a floppy debut on the bourses in the second week of January, closing at a 14 per cent discount to the offer price of Rs 160.

---

The year 2007 would turn out to be the high noon of the IPO boom, as 100 companies together raised close to Rs 34,000 crore. With property prices shooting through the roof across the country, realty stocks were a big draw with investors. Little wonder, then, that nearly 43 per cent of all the money raised through IPOs that year was by realty companies.

The chartbuster public issue of the year was the K. P. Singh-promoted DLFs, which raised around Rs 9,200 crore. The company's road to stock market listing was a long and bumpy one. Some of the potholes are said to have had been created by Singh's rivals who did not want him to become too powerful.

Realty stocks were soaring to new highs, and 'land banks' was the buzzword as real estate firms touted the value of the land owned by them to pump up their valuations. In many cases, the land parcels they claimed to own did not have clear title deeds. Also, investors paid little attention to the execution capabilities of the company, its profit margins, the regulatory hurdles and other challenges in developing the land. An even bigger problem was the lack of transparency in the financial statements of the property firms, given that a lot of their dealings were in cash.

But how did all that matter as long as land prices and stock prices were rising by the day? When the bubble burst the following year, real estate stocks would bear the brunt of the selling fury. But that was still a few months away.

In March, SEBI issued a directive that real estate companies could get land banks valued only if a clear title deed existed. And while the rule was directed at real estate firms in general, DLF's valuation did take a bit of a knock as its merchant bankers had been pitching the issue on the strength of the company's land bank.

When DLF's plans to go public started doing the rounds in 2006, talk was that the listing would make K. P. Singh the richest person in the country and pitch DLF among the top three companies in terms of market capitalization. When the issue finally got all the required clearances, the number of shares on offer as well as the issue price were less than what had been talked about in merchant banking circles.

The year 2007 was also the high-water mark for the Indian broking industry. In May, the Nirmal Jain-promoted India Infoline poached four senior executives from the French broking firm CLSA. The quartet of Bharat Parajia,

H. Nemkumar, Anirudh Dange and Vasudev Jagannath were paid a sign-on bonus of Rs 11 crore each. Parajia and another CLSA colleague Abhijit Raha had become legends in the broking industry by propelling CLSA to the top of the broking league tables. CLSA managed to retain the top slot for a good many years, despite bigger and more established global investment banks snapping at its heels. This was a record sum in the broking industry, where sign-on bonuses had rarely topped Rs 1 crore earlier.

Not just the broking industry, but outsized pay packages appeared to be the flavour of the season across the corporate world, as companies were making massive profits. Just two days before India Infoline had disclosed the details of the compensation package for its new executive hires to the exchanges, Prime Minister Manmohan Singh had corporate India in a tizzy when, at a public function, he urged restraint on 'excessive remuneration to promoters and senior executives'. India Inc countered Singh's remarks, saying it was easy to target top corporate executives because their source of income was public knowledge. On the other hand, most politicians who were known to have huge sums of unaccounted money could safely conceal those from the public.

In the last four months of 2007, as the market continued its climb, three well-known brokerages – Motilal Oswal Securities, Religare Enterprises and Edelweiss Capital – issued IPOs. All the issues fetched overwhelming response, and the stocks got off to a flying start on listing. Shares of Motilal Oswal and Religare Enterprises more than doubled in under two months. Shares of Edelweiss Capital surged 83 per cent on listing day itself.

Lucky were the investors who cashed out soon, because after the market crash of January 2008, shares of broking firms would be available for a fraction of their dizzying highs and stay depressed for a long time. And for many years ahead, the main source of income for these firms would be their lending business and not stockbroking.

# 25

# Margin of Error

With the unprecedented bull run, some dubious dealings too gained currency. Thanks to the fantastic run-up in share prices, there were now plenty of mini-operators with a net worth of between Rs 50 crore and Rs 100 crore. These 'jockeys', as they were known in market parlance, were in demand among small- and mid-cap company promoters looking to boost the valuations of their shares.

In addition, there were operators who could even double up as investment bankers for small companies wanting to go public. These operators would have shell accounts abroad masquerading as FIIs, which would subscribe to small-sized IPOs. These operators also provided dummy HNIs to subscribe to the non-institutional portion of the book. In the first week of the stock's listing, volumes and prices would be driven up through circular trading and the shares then dumped on unsuspecting investors.

Many brokerages also allowed their clients to take up excessive leveraged positions through the NBFC margin-financing route. In a margin financed trade, an investor would put up part of the money required to buy a stock, while the lender would put up the rest. SEBI rules permitted brokers to finance clients only up to 50 per cent of the transaction value, and only in stipulated stocks, with the position to be disclosed on the websites of stock exchanges.

At the same time, there were no clear guidelines on margin financing by NBFCs, which would at times lend up to 70 per cent of the transaction value. There were also no restrictions on the stocks that could be funded in this way, and the positions did not have to be disclosed on the stock exchange websites, since NBFCs were regulated by RBI and not SEBI. Ingenious brokers who figured this out provided margin funding to their clients through their NBFC arms.

The regulators finally woke up to the havoc this practice caused, but years later. In August 2014, the RBI would bar NBFCs from lending more than 50 per cent of the value of shares pledged to them, and restrict such lending to shares that fulfilled certain liquidity criteria.

# 26

# An Assured-Return IPO?

Even as the bull market was gaining in strength with each passing day, it was hard to ignore the signs of trouble surfacing in the global markets intermittently. But the tide of liquidity washing up the shores of the Indian market was so strong that it had managed to temporarily suspend the law of gravity in share prices. Analysts were devising newer ways to justify the bizarre share valuations, which were now factoring earnings three to four years ahead. The engines of the economy were running at full power; tax collections were at a record high; and the profit and loss statements of companies were not in good health.

Going short turned out to be suicidal for the handful of traders who were convinced that fundamentals did not justify the high valuations and that stock prices had to correct. They were right in their assessment of valuations, but lost money trying to stand up to a crowd that was willing to pump in funds without any thought to fundamentals. Also, promoters of most of the mid-cap companies were dabbling in their own stocks, using money borrowed by pledging their own shares.

Over the years, I had developed my own set of indicators to warn me of impending danger in the market. One such indicator was the ease of making money. The easier it becomes to make money off shares, the closer you are to the day of reckoning. By now the point had come when all you had to do to make money was to show up in front of a trading terminal. Pick any stock at random and you would still be able to sell it 10 per cent higher the following day. To me, this was a sure sign that the bubble could burst any time.

But getting the timing right is the most difficult feat for any trader, no matter how experienced he is. Traders who tried to call the top in realty and infrastructure firms in recent months had taken a nasty licking. Many of them had even become converts, turning buyers in those very stocks they had shorted, in the hope of recouping their losses. This was similar to the trend seen in technology stocks during the dotcom boom of 2000.

I was reminded of a stock market adage: a bull market does not start till the last bull has given up hope and a bear market does not start till the last bear has given up hope. One could already see many bears throwing in the towel after repeated failures in their attempts to profit through short sales. In fact, bears never stood a chance in the face of the tidal wave of FII money. By mid-October, FIIs had ploughed in a record $18 billion into Indian equities for the year so far, lifting the Sensex above 20,000. The Fed's decision to cut benchmark rates in the US by 100 basis points in two tranches from mid-August was one of the key factors fuelling money flows into emerging markets, including India.

In two months, the Sensex had risen 5,000 points, setting off alarm bells in the government and the regulatory bodies. Strong capital flows was a good thing, but excess of it spelt trouble as it would make the rupee too strong, and by extension, Indian exports uncompetitive. The torrent of dollars had already lifted the rupee to a record high of 39 to the greenback. This apart, the dollar deluge made the Indian market vulnerable to a sudden withdrawal of 'hot money', if FII outlook on the country changed for some reason.

Hedge funds had become hyperactive, and a big chunk of their money was coming through the participatory notes route. It worried the government and regulators that there was no saying who the actual investors behind the P-notes were. They could be politicians, Indian promoters, the underworld or even terrorists! The fact of the matter was that a good chunk of the P-notes were just a sophisticated form of *benami* investment.

To rein in the marauding FIIs, SEBI signalled its intent to clamp down on P-notes. In a discussion paper released on the evening of 16 October, the regulator proposed an immediate ban on fresh issue of P-notes that had derivatives as underlying assets. It also proposed that renewal of outstanding P-notes be disallowed, and the positions be unwound over the next eighteen months.

The proposals rattled foreign investors, mostly the variety that wanted to play the Indian market by remaining anonymous. And the market had, by now, become addicted to hot money. Even though the P-note restrictions had been aimed at moderating capital flows into the country, a short-term collapse in stock prices looked imminent as P-note holders went about liquidating their positions. This would undoubtedly have had a domino effect as players tried to offset losses in one set of stocks by selling others in which they were still sitting on paper profits.

Traders who were heavily long on the market got behind their desks the following morning expecting the worst. And their fears were proved right. Frontline indices crashed 10 per cent – the Sensex tanking 1,745 points – within minutes of the market opening, triggering a one-hour shutdown.

SEBI and the finance ministry immediately swung into damage control mode, trying to pacify jittery foreign investors. Finance Minister P. Chidambaram said the idea was not to ban P-notes but only to restrict the flow of money through this route. SEBI chief M. Damodaran said the regulator would try to simplify the process of registration for FIIs so that more of them could directly invest in India instead of in a roundabout manner. That assuaged investors briefly, but the selling spree resumed the following day. In three trading sessions since the discussion paper on P-notes was floated, the Sensex had plunged nearly 1,500 points.

However, things turned around quicker than expected, as many FIIs that invest with a longer time horizon saw the correction as a good opportunity to buy into India. Typically, FII activity tends to taper off in December as most money managers head out on vacation. But this year, FIIs resumed their purchases with a vengeance in December, pumping in around a billion dollars, bringing their cumulative net purchases for the year to $17 billion – the highest ever in a single calendar year. The party in the stock market was on in full swing, even though there were telling signals that investors were beginning to lose their sense of proportion, and many companies their sense of propriety.

In addition to this FII interest, there was also the upcoming IPO of Reliance Power, the largest ever IPO in the history of the Indian stock market. The issue size was around Rs 11,500 crore, but looking at the demand in the grey market, the subscription would be many times that. Assuming the issue got subscribed ten times, over Rs 1 lakh crore would be sucked out from the market temporarily. The grey market for shares of Reliance Power was sizzling, and they were quoting at a premium of Rs 35 in November even before the price band for the issue was announced.

Lastly, there was the gigantic build-up of leveraged positions in the futures and options market. Worryingly, too many retail investors had got into a game meant for deep-pocketed players. To maximize commissions, brokers were encouraging their retail clients to recklessly build positions without any thought to the consequences if prices were to move sharply against them.

GB pointed out one more warning sign to me.

'One sure sign of trouble is when businessmen and traders outside the stock market start heading here, convinced this is the place to make good money. In the right proportion, their investments are welcome, and even good for the market from a liquidity perspective. But the problem arises when they start ignoring their main business and start chasing easy money,' he said.

Wherever I looked, the signs of a foolhardy euphoria were unmistakable. And yet, I was not sure if it was the right time to start going short on the market. The market kept climbing all through December, and both my trading positions and portfolio were turning in handsome returns.

Yet, I was beginning to get uneasy. After topping 20,000 in late October, the Sensex was now moving in a narrow range, but many small- and mid-cap shares continued to make new highs every other day.

Even though I was wary of going short on the market, I began reducing my trading positions mid-December onwards. I then evaluated my portfolio, and decided to encash the stocks that had doubled over the last one year. These stocks were unlikely to rise at such a scorching pace in the near future. I had to curb my temptation to reinvest the profits; not an easy thing when you are surrounded by noise that the Sensex is going to touch 25,000 before the middle of next year. But I reminded myself that I was not getting any younger. A misstep at this stage of my career could set me back by a few years. I was no longer worried about going bankrupt, but recouping big losses would not be as easy as it was, say, five years ago. As I kept winding down my positions, I became more relaxed. Bina was happy too as I got home much earlier than before, and was able to spend time with her and the kids.

It had been yet another fantastic year for the market, the fifth in a row since the bull run began in 2003. True, there had been at least one sharp correction during the course of each of these years. There were phases when traders like me lost a packet, but the market had been kind enough to give us enough opportunities to get back into the game.

There was a New Year party planned at an influential market operator's weekend home in Alibaug. I was not very keen on going, but GB insisted that I go with him.

'Don't be a sissy, Lala. Come, let's have a good time. More importantly, listen to what some of the best people in the trade have to say about the market,' he said.

'If you say so, Govindbhai,' I said. GB was one person I always found hard to turn down.

As I was driving down to Alibaug, a friend called to say that RBI had issued a circular permitting FIIs to short-sell equities. Short-selling by FIIs was nothing new. Even if the rules had forbidden it until now, many hedge funds were known to have been borrowing shares held by foreign brokerage houses in P-note accounts, and selling them in the hope of buying them cheaper later on to return to the lender. The RBI circular would legitimize such short sales, going forward.

Also, there was a perfectly justifiable reason for RBI to allow FIIs to make short sales, as I saw it. The market was beginning to overheat because of the heavy purchases from both institutional and retail investors. Traders who had so far tried to short the market had been routed. The result was an absence of effective counterbalances in the market, should sentiment change for the worse. Perhaps by allowing FIIs to short-sell, RBI was trying to rectify the imbalance in the system. But whichever way I looked at it, the signs looked ominous.

I immediately called GB to inform him about the development.

'Yes, I heard about it too . . . hard to say what impact it could have in the short term,' GB said. 'None, so far as I can see, as long as the overall trend remains bullish. But the day the trend reverses, rest assured that there will be slaughter. The bears are now armed; only, they will have to wait for a suitable opportunity to deploy the weapon for maximum impact.'

At the party, everybody was upbeat about the coming year. The seasoned hands knew a correction was in the offing. They had seen too many bull markets to believe that this party could go on indefinitely, even if they consoled themselves saying every bull market was different from the previous one. And the immortal line – 'it's different this time' – seemed to ring true. The last time anybody present at the party had seen a bull run of such ferocity was during the peak of Harshad Mehta's powers in 1992, when ACC had touched a dizzying Rs 10,000 per share, throwing every conventional method of valuation out of the window.

Deep in their hearts, many knew the current round of madness was likely to end in grief for a lot of investors, as had every other bull market in the past. There was nothing like an orderly unwinding of a bull market, much as traders and investors would have loved it.

After everybody had downed a few pegs, our host cracked some witty but risqué remarks for which he was known.

One broker said he was waiting for a particular stock to make a double bottom on the price chart before he bought it. Double bottom is when a stock price falls very low, rises briefly, again falls to that earlier low, and again rises. This is an indication that the stock is unlikely to slip below that low price in the future.

'Double bottom?,' the operator asked the broker: 'My suggestion to you is that you install mirrors in front of and behind your commode. Whenever you sit there you can see as many bottoms as you want.' He had all of us in splits.

He then tried to take the discussion to an intellectual level. He launched into a monologue on sub-prime loans and the trouble brewing in the banking sphere of the developed world. He was well read (too well read for a market operator, I sometimes thought) and clued into the trends in global markets, but he was not on firm ground when it came to the complexities of sub-prime mortgages and its derivative products. Of course, barring the analysts who created those funny products, nobody had a clue as to what exactly they were about, or what risks they posed to financial markets. Like most of us present, he too knew what the basic problem was – too many people in the US having borrowed money beyond their means to buy homes. The banks that had recklessly lent to them had repackaged these loans as derivatives and sold them off to investors chasing higher returns. If house prices fell more steadily than anticipated, there would be widespread defaults on the loans, which would affect the entire chain.

'Something is not right about this sub-prime . . . you see, there could be trouble . . . in fact, this could be the trigger for a big market correction,' he kept repeating, trying to sound as convincing as he could, yet unable to articulate his thoughts well. Most of the party was a bit too high by then to be paying enough attention to his words.

Not I, though. I had taken just a few sips of my first drink of the evening. I wanted to keep my wits about me to hear what some of the best in the industry had to say about the market.

'I believe Japanese investors are waiting on the sidelines armed with a few billion dollars, looking for a suitable opportunity to invest,' somebody said.

'I heard that some of them have already started deploying the money,' another said.

'Ah, one should be careful then, I guess. Next to retail investors, the entry of Japanese investors is the surest sign of a market top,' somebody else said, prompting laughter from the crowd.

The conversation then veered to how India was the best bet among emerging markets, and how India's GDP growth would surpass China's before long.

'People say India is expensive. Still, foreigners will have no choice but to buy at these prices or even higher. After all, how many countries other than China can boast of a GDP growth like ours?' one gentleman said.

Somebody mentioned the Reliance Power IPO and the risk of a liquidity squeeze in the short term. This concern was immediately brushed aside.

'*Arre baba*, you have no clue about the money waiting on the sidelines. Even if two issues like Reliance Power were to be launched simultaneously, they would be absorbed without much trouble,' one mid-level market operator remarked.

The others nodded in agreement and raised another toast to the market.

It seemed to me that nobody wanted to talk about the possibility of a correction or a fall for fear of being laughed at. I saw this as another sign of irrational exuberance, strengthening my theory that a steep fall would not be long in coming.

The market began 2008 on a sedate note, with the Sensex climbing just 15 points. By the tenth of the month, the Sensex had made a fresh record high of 21,206, but ended the day nearly 300 points below the previous close. The index was struggling to close above 21,000 despite having topped that mark during three consecutive sessions. A few days before this, Reliance Power had announced a price band of Rs 405-450 for its 26 crore-share issue, which would be open for subscription from 15 to 18 January. For all the talk of ample liquidity in the system, an issue of this size was indeed bound to soak up a sizeable chunk of the money sloshing around.

Within hours of the announcement of the price band, the premium for Reliance Power shares in the grey market shot up to over Rs 200. The rule of thumb when it comes to grey market prices is that the premium is reflective of the minimum gains an investor in an IPO can expect on listing day.

I was amazed at the frenzy over Reliance Power shares. Premiums in the grey market climbed to Rs 450 a share over the next couple of days, baffling even the most diehard of bulls. If the grey market premium was a true indicator, then an investor who got shares in the IPO would almost double his money on listing day.

The company had no earnings worth talking about, and yet people were willing to buy its shares at absurd prices. The IPO was not being seen as an equity investment any longer; rather, people appeared to think of it as some kind of scheme where you were assured of doubling your money in less than a month. This drew even more people to the IPO, feeding the mania further. Wherever you went, the conversation would soon steer to Reliance Power. You could not miss it in even on autorickshaw and taxi rides, as the drivers had learnt from their friends that the IPO was a sure-fire way to double their money. I doubt that another IPO such as this one will be seen, one that will generate the kind of mass hysteria that the Reliance Power issue was creating. Friends and relatives whom I had lost touch with suddenly began calling me, asking if they should be investing in the IPO.

Depository participants (DPs) had a windfall, as first-time investors rushed to open demat accounts so that they could buy the shares. I heard stories about *kirana* store owners hawking IPO forms and even offering to help their customers open demat accounts.

Bina was taking driving lessons at the time. One evening there was an unexpected visitor as we were sitting down to dinner. It was Bina's driving instructor; he had come with Rs 25,000 in cash, wrapped in a polythene bag.

'Sir, *hum ko Reliance Power ka shares khareedna hai; madam keh rahi thi ki aap* stock market *mein hain, aap meri madad karenge please*,' he said, in all earnestness. He wanted to know where I could get him the form to apply for the shares and what documents would be required to be shown.

The man was in his early thirties, and had never invested in the stock market before. I was a bit annoyed with him, but soon more amused than annoyed. The people who had sought my advice on the IPO had some basic knowledge about shares and the stock market, and were occasional investors in the market, getting lucky once in a while. But here was a person who had not the foggiest idea about the stock market, eager to invest a decent chunk of his savings in what appeared to be a risky bet.

'But why do you want to invest in Reliance Power?' I asked him.

'Because my friends tell me that I will be able to double my money in less than a month,' he replied.

I was tempted to tell him to get lost and instead try the racecourse, the matka bazaar, or, for that matter, any of the Ponzi deposit schemes, which promised fantastic returns in a short time. Bina could almost read my thoughts, and looked at me pleadingly not to be rude to the man. I relented. After all, he was her teacher, even if only till the end of the driving course next month.

I saw little point in talking this man out of his dream. There was a possibility that he would make decent returns on listing day, but I thought it highly unlikely that his investment would double. I promised to put him in touch with a sub-broker friend of mine who would guide him through the process. That was enough to make him happy.

Until that point, I had been thinking of putting some money in the IPO myself. But looking at the madness around me, I wondered if it would be a good idea. I had little doubt that the issue would be priced at the upper end (Rs 450) because of the phenomenal demand for the shares from all classes of investors. I decided to invest in the IPO, but not with borrowed funds, as that would raise my break even point so high that the probability of losses would be greater.

The IPO signs were ominous. A day before the issue opened for subscription, the Sensex tumbled 100 points. The Nifty, however, inched up 6 points, masking the nervousness in the market. Some pressure was expected, given the sheer size of the issue. Many investors would be liquidating positions in other stocks and using that money to apply for Reliance Power shares.

The issue was sold out within the first minute of its opening on 15 January, a record for an offering of that size. By the end of the day, the issue was subscribed nearly ten times. Even as money was pouring into it, the main market took a beating, with the Sensex plunging 477 points and the Nifty, 124 points.

Mid-cap stocks suffered even more, especially the stocks in which there was a huge build-up of futures and options positions. Too many weak players had taken up positions in the derivatives segment, lured by easy returns when stock prices were rising almost every other day. Unlike in the cash market, traders betting on futures and options had to pay just 25–30 per cent of the total value of their positions. When the market was racing north, the returns on investment in F&O were much higher compared with those in the cash market.

But when prices fell sharply, these players had to square off their positions in a hurry. They could pay additional margins and hold on to their positions, but few traders had the resources to cough up margin money during a crisis. Brokers started liquidating positions of clients who were unable to deposit additional margins. This added to the pressure on stock prices and set off a vicious cycle wherein falling prices forced many more weaker players to sell out their positions.

I had by now got out of nearly 90 per cent of my long positions, even taking losses on some of them towards the end. Somewhat cautiously, I had begun short-selling Nifty futures. Still, I was not confident enough to go short on the market in a big way.

That evening (the first day of the Reliance Power IPO) as I was chatting up one of my friends at a prominent retail broking house, he said something that made me prick u my ears.

'The craze for R-Power is unbelievable; most of my clients have withdrawn every rupee in their trading account to subscribe to the issue,' he said.

Clients usually keep some extra funds with their brokers. This could be a safeguard against sudden margin calls, if they were regular traders, or it could help them buy a stock at short notice if it was available for a bargain.

The market was beginning to overheat, and a correction looked imminent. Prices of many stocks had more than doubled or, in some cases, even trebled in less than six months. My gut feeling was that the market had changed course. But I needed more indications to confirm this. I called a few more of my contacts at other retail broking houses to check if their clients too were acting the same way. Sure enough, they too had the same story to tell. Retail and HNIs were pulling out the spare money in their trading accounts to invest in the Reliance Power IPO.

This would turn out to be the clinching factor that would ravage the market in less than two weeks, when the market suddenly reversed course. I thought over this piece of information hard. Were the market to fall sharply for some reason, most retail investors and HNIs would not have money to meet their margin requirements, leave alone take advantage of the correction by buying at lower levels.

I decided to take a very bold gamble: I would short Nifty futures as heavily as I could first thing the following morning. Like a giant vacuum cleaner, the R-Power issue was sucking out more liquidity from the system than was good for the market. I did not have to count on a major trend reversal to be able to make a killing by going short. A precipitous fall over a few sessions would be good enough, and right now the market did look vulnerable to a bruising fall.

The following morning I started hammering away at Nifty futures as soon as the market opened for trading. I knew that at least two other respected names in the market had taken a similar view and were short on the market. One of them was a value investor who also had sizeable trading positions; the other was a trader who managed the proprietary book of a top US investment bank.

The sense of uneasiness among brokers and investors was now giving way to panic. In three trading sessions, the Sensex had fallen nearly 1,000 points and the Nifty around 260 points. There was mayhem in the futures of many mid-cap stocks as brokers squared off client positions when margin calls could not be met. Amid the carnage, the Reliance Power issue got subscribed over 65 times, making history in terms of bids received. The institutional portion of the book (50 per cent) was subscribed 82 times, the non-institutional portion 160 times and the retail portion around 10 times. In all, the company received over 50 lakh bids collectively worth Rs 7.5 lakh crore. To put this figure in perspective, it was equivalent to the Plan and Non-Plan expenditure estimated by the government in that year's Budget. Given such strong demand, the issue price was fixed at the top end of the price band, at Rs 450 a share. Retail investors would be allotted the shares at Rs 420 apiece, 5 per cent lower than the issue price for institutional investors, HNIs and corporations.

Two weeks later, the company would say that around 4.5 lakh retail applicants who had applied for less than 225 shares had not been allotted any shares. The massive subscription in the non-institutional portion spelt bad news for HNIs who had applied for the shares using borrowed funds. They would be getting only one share for every 160 they had applied for, while the interest they paid on borrowed money would be applicable for 160 shares.

Big traders and operators were not too bothered about the Reliance IPO as they were staring at a far worse problem. The stunning fall in share prices during the week had caused heavy losses on their positions in multiple stocks, and the situation would get worse if they were unable to deposit additional margin money with their brokers.

Most of the market players I knew spent their weekend scrambling around for cash. With the mood turning on its head, the proverbial tide of liquidity that had lifted every boat suddenly seemed to have drained away.

I did not get too many calls for help, because most of my fellow traders assumed that I too had suffered heavy losses and was scouting around for cash. Unknown to my friends, I was sitting on a handsome pile of profit.

From what I could see around, the bloodbath was expected to become even more gory on Monday. There was just not enough money in the system for investors to be able to take advantage of the steep fall in prices. I foresaw more margin calls being triggered on Monday, setting off another round of panic selling. But I now had to think about winding down my short positions. Not even the most experienced trader can rightly call a market top or bottom. Of course, once in a blue moon, your trade might be the last one just before the market reverses course either way. But that trade would be merely of academic significance. The Nifty had closed at 5,705 on Friday. My instinct and my reading of the trading screen over the last week told me that the index could break below 5,000 at least once even if it did not stay there for long. As was expected, the turmoil on Monday was by far the worst in the market since it had started falling a week ago. Stocks went into a free fall from the moment trading began. Players unable to put up additional margins were selling out at whatever price they could, sending prices hurtling into a death spiral. Adding to the downward pressure was massive short-selling by hedge funds, which were adept at exaggerating market trends, whether up or down, through their heavy purchases or short sales. Also, these funds could now legitimately borrow shares from whomever was willing to lend to them, and dump those shares in the market.

As the carnage was playing out, the stock exchanges added fat to the fire by hiking margins on various stocks and then insisting on brokers paying up the margins ahead of the usually permitted time. Brokerages did not have a choice; if they did not fork out the margin money, their trading terminals would be shut down. Brokers were now caught between the devil and the deep sea. Trading terminals being shut down in a falling market amplified the risk for the broker if he had long positions and prices were continuing to slide. Brokers responded by liquidating their clients' positions. In some cases, clients promptly wrote out cheques towards margin payment. The RTGS facility for speedy transfer of funds had still not caught on in a big way, and their cheques would take at least two days to clear. Two days was a long time in a panic-stricken market such as this one. Besides, there was no saying if the clients actually had sufficient balances in their accounts, given that many of them had suffered heavy losses. A climate of fear and mistrust had settled in the market.

On their part, the exchanges were right in demanding additional margins to ensure there were no defaults by brokers. But the situation would not have come to such a pass had they been gradually increasing margins instead of hiking them at one go when things began to go out of control. Keeping margins unchanged in a rising market encourages players to build up positions recklessly. As long as prices were rising, the credit in the trading accounts was good enough to take care of the margins. It did not occur to anybody that the margins would be woefully inadequate if the prices fell sharper than they had in the past.

After the 208-point fall of the Sensex on Friday, most players did not expect an even sharper decline in the next trading session. Many felt the market would rebound, even if briefly, considering it had been falling consecutively for the last five sessions. But the market was not through with its brutal punishment of the bulls.

The Nifty fell to a low of 4,977 on Monday before trimming some of its losses to close at 5,208. It had fallen around 500 points for the day and the Sensex by 979 points. I had squared off nearly 60 per cent of my positions by the end of the day after realizing a profit that would have caused heartburn to anybody who got to hear of it.

My big worry was that the government may direct the LIC and maybe even some of the state-owned banks to support the market by making purchases. Something like that would help stabilize the market and prompt bears like me to start covering my positions. By now, many players were short on the market, and if all of them rushed to cover at the same time, the market might just take off.

There was no public statement by the finance minister or any other senior ministry official. But if the market fell any further, there would surely be some soothing words from the government to assuage the rattled investors. Or maybe SEBI would declare a ban on further short sales just before the market opened, setting off a stampede among bears to cover up their positions. Still, my trader's instinct told me there was one more round of sell-off coming, as many brokers and traders were still struggling to pony up cash to pay margins on their outstanding positions.

I slept fitfully that night. Despite all the money that was waiting to pour into my bank account, I still had this niggling worry that the market could once again change course abruptly and dent my profits. After all, I still had outstanding positions. Perhaps my sleeplessness reflected my guilt complex, as I had been making money while many of my friends were in dire straits.

I had strange dreams that night. In one of them, I was arguing with my friends who had accused me of being selfish and not helping them out even though I had the resources to. In another, a cop turned up at my doorstep with an arrest warrant, saying SEBI had identified a set of people who were spreading terror in the market through short-selling. Ignoring my pleas, he walked me through the streets with handcuffs on, much to the delight of the onlookers who were clapping in glee.

When I protested, the cop told me he had orders to make an example out of me so that people would stop short-selling. Perhaps this particular segment of my dream had to do with an inflated sense of self-worth that I was behind the market crash.

As I headed to work next day, the nightmare of my arrest and parade through the streets was playing on my mind. But my run of luck continued that morning, with the indices crashing 10 per cent within minutes of the start of trading, leading to market-wide circuit filters being triggered. Trading was suspended for an hour, according to rule.

Sure enough, the finance ministry swung into action to calm the agitated market players who did not know what had hit them. Banks were asked to extend additional credit lines to brokers, and finance ministry officials assured the market of enough liquidity in the system. State-owned banks were told not to offload shares that had been deposited as collateral with them in a hurry, as this would further aggravate the downtrend in share prices. Some of the bank chiefs remarked on the strong fundamentals of the economy, some others promised full support to brokers through additional credit, and a few even spoke about increasing their capital market exposure as they felt valuations were attractive. Later, many brokers would complain that banks were offering them additional short-term credit, but at interest rates as high as 24 per cent.

The finance minister himself stepped in to say that all was well with the country.

The market opened for trading an hour later, and there was some semblance of sanity. Still, every rise was met with heavy selling, and the Nifty finally ended the day at 4,900, and the Sensex at 16,729. With a near 25 per cent dive from its peak over just seven sessions, the bull market appeared to be over.

Many small-timers and part-timers in the market had been wiped out for good. It would be years before they fully got over their trauma, and could even bring themselves to think about the stock market. Some of the larger firms and players too had just about managed to avert serious setbacks. For many, that dream house, dream car, or the month-long sightseeing tour of Europe would not be possible for some years to come.

As for me, I was a rich man. I had made the boldest bet of my career so far, and it had paid off handsomely. But it was not entirely about the money. My satisfaction lay in my decision to stand up against the market right in the midst of a raging bull run and coming out on top.

I thought of celebrating my triumph in style by taking Bina and the kids out for dinner at a five-star hotel that night, and gifting them a grand vacation in April to any location of their choice. For some reason, I decided against it. Maybe it had to do with a subconscious feeling of guilt, or not wanting to tempt fate. Instead, I chose to unwind at home over music and a long chat with Bina.

I was gripped by conflicting emotions. On the one hand, I wanted the world to know of my success, and yet, I was not comfortable at the thought of the envy it would evoke at a time such as this. I would also be drawing attention to myself, something I had always avoided. It would not be long before the size of my pay-out became the talking point in the industry. That was something I could not avoid, no matter how hard I tried.

## 27

# The Denouement

The troubles that had seized the market were not fully over yet.

The final act of the dark tragedy was pending – R-Power's debut on the bourses two to three weeks away.

The first indications that the stock's listing could be an anticlimax of sorts came from the grey market, of course. The premium, which had climbed to as high as Rs 450 at one point – suggesting that Reliance Power shares would list at a 100 per cent premium to the issue price irrespective of the wider market mood – was now down to Rs 200 after the indices had shed 25 per cent in a week's time.

Even though their expectations had toned down considerably, investors in the issue still believed they could make a decent return. The massive demand for the IPO was the foundation on which this hope rested. If investors had got only a fraction of the quantity they had applied for, it stood to reason that they would be eager to buy the remaining quantity from the open market when the shares listed.

11 February was fixed as listing day for R-Power shares. The market appeared to be stabilizing in the run-up to the listing, and many players felt the worst was over. A good showing by Reliance Power could even get the market climbing again, they felt. The premium in the grey market, however, kept dipping, with not many deals taking place.

Outside of the grey market, everybody was looking forward to what was likely to go down as a historic moment in the annals of the Indian stock market.

There could not have been a bigger anticlimax.

At 9.55 a.m., R-ADAG group chairman Anil Ambani sounded the gong on the floor of BSE to signal the listing of the shares. He might as well have rung a dinner bell signalling to a sloth of starving bears to dig their claws deep into his stock.

The shares briefly topped Rs 500, but not many trades happened at those prices. On BSE, the highest price for the day was Rs 599 and on NSE Rs 530. But this was just a flash in the pan. Within minutes the share price sank, hitting a low of Rs 355 before ending the day at Rs 372, 17 per cent below the issue price. The average price during the session was Rs 416.

It was possible that the overall downtrend in the market aggravated the slide in Reliance Power shares. Later, Anil Ambani would accuse corporate rivals of having orchestrated the debacle by hammering the prices to force existing investors to sell out and scare off potential buyers. Those who had bid with such enthusiasm for Reliance Power shares during the subscription period did not turn up to buy more shares even though they would have got them much cheaper.

Only a handful of investors managed to exit their positions at a decent profit. And even those who got a good price may not have been able to offload as much of their stock as they would have liked to, as the stock price fell so fast.

The tremors of the disastrous listing were felt in the grey market too, where many players reneged on their commitments after suffering heavy losses. The grey market is illegal and functions purely on trust; there is no way you can drag somebody to court for going back on his word. Still, this market had stood the test of time, which is proof that players rarely wriggled out of their commitments. But this incident shook the faith of players in the grey market. It would be a very long time before their confidence in it returned.

Stung by bad press in the wake of the debacle, Reliance Power, on 24 February – a Sunday – announced a bonus share issue solely for its non-promoter shareholders. Investors were to get three bonus shares for every five shares they held.

What many failed to understand was that even if the bonus share issue reduced the average cost of purchase in absolute terms, the market price would automatically adjust lower, to the extent of the extra shares in circulation after the bonus. The bonus issue itself would not assure investors of good returns; there had to be a fundamental reason for the stock price to go up if investors were to make meaningful returns. Looking at the price charts and the trading screen, I was convinced that the stock price would crack sooner than later. I wasted no time in going short on the stock.

The market now appeared to be stabilizing in the 17,000-18,000 range after a series of bruising sell-offs since January. The easy pickings for bears appeared to be over for the time being. Just when they were running out of bullets came unexpected ammunition from none other than the finance minister himself. In the final Budget of the UPA's tenure, P. Chidambaram announced a Rs 60,000-crore relief package for farmers, including complete waiver of Rs 50,000 crore of farm loans to small and marginal farmers.

To the stock market, this was a clear signal that the government's main priority now was to win the Lok Sabha elections due next year. That meant more populist measures in the offing, something the market dreaded. Emboldened bears went on the offensive, knocking nearly 3,000 points off the Sensex over the next three weeks, dragging it to below the psychological 15,000 mark. Even the most diehard bull now had to admit that the near five-year bull run had finally ended.

What allowed bears to sustain their attack was the steady stream of bad news pouring in from global markets, the US and UK markets in particular. Investment banks, which were at the forefront of the sub-prime loan boom, were now haemorrhaging capital as borrowers defaulted. Faced with a severe liquidity crunch, these banks were pulling out whatever money they could from other markets they had invested in.

The dramatic change in sentiment had hurt the fund-raising plans of other companies, as fund managers appeared to have developed cold feet for IPOs. Wockhardt Hospitals was looking to raise around Rs 750 crore and Emaar MGF – a joint venture between Dubai-based Emaar Properties and India's MGF Development – hoping to collect Rs 6,400 crore through IPOs. Both public issues had to be shelved.

I decided to take a well-earned break from trading, and went on a vacation with my family to Sri Lanka. I tried not to get distracted by market news, but kept track of events that were rapidly unfolding across the globe.

I could afford to do nothing for the rest of the year but watch from the sidelines. But the thrill of trading in a market that was changing course at whim was too much to resist.

It was evident that the market trended lower every time it attempted a climb after a bout of selling. Adding to the pressure on stock prices was the short-selling by FIIs who were borrowing stocks held in P-note accounts. Unknown to investors in P-notes, the broking firms holding the shares on their behalf would loan their shares to other FII clients for short-selling. This was a lucrative business for the broking firms as they could charge a juicy fee for this 'loan'. The FIIs would first sell the borrowed shares, then buy them back at lower prices and return them to the broking firm.

Since the mood in the market was bearish, these 'borrowed' short sales, while earning handsome profits for the FIIs, further collapsed share prices. Ironically, the stocks that bore the brunt of this selling fury were among the favourites of institutional investors only a few months ago. Many panicky FIIs dumped their holdings and fled to safer havens.

Over the years, I had come to like bear markets and the art of making money through short-selling. Any novice can make money in a raging bull market but only a truly professional trader can profit from a falling market. Short-selling tests a trader's nerves in a way that going long does not.

I still remember GB's explanation as to why there were always more bulls than bears in the market and why most traders were loath to short-sell in a falling market as aggressively as they would go long in a rising market.

'Human beings are by nature optimistic, and traders are no exception to the rule, even if they are only concerned with making money in whatever way possible,' he had told me many years ago. 'It is easy for a trader to buy a stock and hope that it will go up, rather than sell a stock and then hope that it will decline. If you buy a stock for Rs 100, you know that at worst the price can go down to zero, and that the maximum you stand to lose is Rs 100. Of course, a stock price will never go down to zero. If you short-sell a stock at Rs 100, there is no limit to which the stock price can rise.

'So a trader long on the stock can sustain his hopes even if the stock price falls to Rs 90. But most traders short on a stock at Rs 100 will start squirming the moment the stock price climbs to Rs 110. To begin with, many of them are going against their natural tendency when they short-sell, and will be uneasy till they see the price slipping below the rate at which they have sold. That is why it takes a really courageous trader to go short, even if the market can give up in a week the gains that took months to build. Traders are more disciplined when it comes to short sales and, in general, end up losing less than what they would from long trades.'

The crisis in the global financial markets was growing steadily worse, reaching a flashpoint on 15 September. That was the day when Lehman Brothers filed for bankruptcy after being denied a federal bailout, and Merrill Lynch got taken over by Bank of America in a distress sale in the space of a few hours. Between them, the two storied investment banks had a history of nearly 252 years. On Wall Street, rumours were swirling thick and fast that it was a matter of time before Morgan Stanley, Citigroup and even the seemingly invincible Goldman Sachs went belly up.

In a matter of just six months, three of the Big Five US investment firms – Lehman, Merrill, Bear Sterns – had become history, and the surviving ones – Goldman Sachs and Morgan Stanley – had changed in character, altering the landscape of Wall Street forever.

It was hardly a surprise that financial sector stocks in the US were being hammered out of shape. Fearing that more banks could go under if the share prices continued to fall at this rate, the Securities and Exchange Commission (SEC) announced a temporary emergency ban on short-selling the stocks of all companies in the financial sector.

I was hoping that SEBI would not imitate SEC's strategy and impose a similar ban here. On Dalal Street, the sector that had the most to fear from the marauding bears was real estate. Stocks like DLF, Unitech, HDIL, Sobha Developers, Anant Raj, Omaxe and Orbit Corp were down 60-70 per cent from their peaks in January, and it still did not look as if the stocks had bottomed out.

The 'land bank' fad, which I have described earlier, had pushed up the prices of these stocks to dizzying highs. Investors valued these companies on the basis of the large parcels of land owned by them, though the title deeds of many of these parcels were in dispute. Also, it was a case of counting the chickens before they hatched, as it would take a while before the land was developed and buyers emerged. Real estate prices had been on a tear, as it always happens in a bull market, and everybody felt property prices would be on the upswing for many years to come, if not in perpetuity. Investors had also overlooked the poor corporate governance standards in the sector, a good chunk of whose dealings were done in cash that would never show up in the account books. Promoters of most of the realty companies were also known to play their own stock, and many had raised funds by pledging shares held in benami accounts. But now that the cycle had reversed, the same investors who had once chased prices were now exiting.

Even a ban on short sales in real estate stocks by SEBI would have provided little more than temporary respite to the sector. The market had realized how hollow these companies' valuation models were, and its disenchantment with the sector was so strong that despite the massive collapse in prices, no price for realty stocks seemed too low. Juxtaposed against the better managed and fundamentally sound companies available at good prices, the real estate stocks looked all the more ugly.

Even as bulls were licking their wounds, there followed an even more brutal sell-off in October. This one was triggered by the appreciation of the Japanese yen against the dollar, and the unwinding of what is known in market parlance as the yen 'carry-trade'. In a typical carry-trade, investors borrow in a currency with the lowest interest cost, convert it into dollars and invest the funds in assets – usually risk assets like equities, commodities, currencies or high-yield bonds – that offer a handsome return after adjusting for the currency conversion costs.

In a yen carry-trade, the money is borrowed in Japanese currency. After borrowing in yen, an FII would convert the funds into dollars and then again into the local currency of the market in which it intended to invest. On the way back it would have to convert the local currency back into dollars, and the dollars back into yen to repay the original loan.

There was a cost to each of these conversions, and the overall returns would have to be well above the conversion costs through the entire round trip. This trade works well as long as the currency (yen in this case) in which the funds are borrowed remains stable or even depreciates relative to the dollar. At the same time, the assets in which the funds are invested have to keep appreciating.

But it is bad news when the yen appreciates to the dollar, because it means the investor will need more dollars to repay the original yen loan. It is worse if, in addition to this, the assets in which the funds are invested start depreciating in value. And that is precisely what began to happen from September onwards, when prices of emerging market equities, commodities and risky bonds like mortgage securities went into a free fall, triggering margin calls. The carry-trade had begun to gradually unravel towards the end of 2007, and accelerated after the events of September 2008. As investors unwound their carry-trades and began to convert dollars into yen to repay the loans, the demand for the yen rose, strengthening the Japanese currency against the dollar. This double whammy of a rising yen and falling asset prices set off a vicious cycle, triggering more unwinding of carry-trades, the tremors of which were felt across global financial markets.

In a desperate measure to staunch the huge outflow of FII money, SEBI reversed the restrictions it had put on P-notes the previous October. But FIIs were in no mood to invest fresh money in Indian equities, and the freedom to take up positions through P-notes made no difference to their outlook.

SEBI then tried some strong-arm measures. It asked FIIs to disclose shares borrowed from P-note accounts for short-selling. This was to send a subtle signal to the FIIs that short-selling was not welcome. The smarter among the FIIs took the hint and immediately stopped short sales. Some others persisted. Within a week, SEBI had banned FIIs from short-selling using borrowed shares. But this measure too had little effect. In the net, FIIs sold over Rs 14,000 crore's worth of shares in October 2008

It turned out to be a rough month for domestic mutual funds too. Strangely, it was not the equity portion of the business that was causing them a headache, though stock prices were in a free fall. As was the case in the US, money market funds in India too witnessed massive redemptions beginning mid-September and extending all the way up to end-October 2008 In all, corporates and HNIs pulled out Rs 71,000 crore during this period.

Many investors in money market mutual funds shifted their funds to banks, which were offering much better interest rates, besides being safer. Money market funds invest in certificates of deposit of companies, in debentures and in commercial papers (unsecured short-term borrowings by companies with a high credit rating). Swamped with redemption requests from investors, money market funds tried to sell their assets. To their dismay, they found no takers for those securities. They tried borrowing from banks to pay off their unitholders, but banks were stingy in honouring their credit lines to the stricken mutual funds. For a long time now, banks had been nursing a grudge against mutual funds as their (mutual funds) debt market schemes were direct competitors to the fixed deposits they offered. And while banks may have had sound reasons for not lending too much to mutual funds in the current situation, they secretly enjoyed the spot mutual funds were finding themselves in, and were now legitimately extracting their pound of flesh.

Banks charged mutual funds anywhere between 11 per cent and 24 per cent, and there were a few cases where some fund houses were charged 39-46 per cent interest for two- or three-day loans. Banks were also refusing to accept the Certificates of Deposit (CDs) of private banks as collateral for loans. RBI had to intervene with an emergency lending window at concessional rates, and the finance ministry had to prevail on banks to lend money to mutual funds at reasonable rates and to accept CDs of private banks as collateral.

Another notable incident in October was the near run on ICICI Bank, which became the centre of nasty rumours following the demise of Lehman Brothers. The stock tanked from Rs 450 to Rs 305 in three trading sessions on market chatter that its foreign subsidiaries had suffered massive losses as a result of a sizeable exposure to securities issued by Lehman Brothers. I have little doubt that the rumour was a well-planned operation by a cartel, which hoped to profit from an ensuing crash in the stock price.

The overall environment was such that people were willing to believe the worst. And a falling stock price would definitely lend credibility to the tittle-tattle that something was wrong with the bank. As speculation about the bank's financial health spread, panicky investors lined up at ICICI Bank branches to withdraw their money. This was the second time that ICICI Bank had to face such a situation, the first time being in April 2003, when its branches in south Gujarat faced massive withdrawals.

I was tempted to join the mob in bashing the stock when I first heard the rumours, but checked myself. If I decided to go short on the stock, the size of my position would have to be big enough to give me a decent profit. Inevitably, there would be a probe later on, and all the big sellers would be investigated. I would then have to waste time explaining to investigators that there were no ulterior motives behind my trade. I decided it was not worth the headache that was likely to follow.

I had an unbelievable winning streak right from January all the way till April. My performance the following months, up to September, was average, as I lost money on some positions betting on a rebound. But then, one can never be right all the time, and I was perfectly content to yield to the law of averages without my ego getting in the way.

Most of the stocks I had shorted were purely my own calls. Then there were stocks in which I traded as part of a group – hunting for prey in packs, as I loved to call it. Our favourite targets were stocks in which promoters themselves were known to dabble heavily. The strategy was simple; together we would hammer the prices of the stock futures. As the price of the futures fell, the stock price too would move lower in tandem, in turn triggering stop loss limits and margin calls, aggravating pressure on the stock as weaker players started selling out. Stocks favoured by short-term players like hedge funds too fitted the bill. However, even as a group we were not able to influence the price of a large-cap stock beyond a point. But with a little bit of planning, we could call the shots in many of the mid-cap stocks.

Sometime in October, GB suggested that we go after this energy player, which was a darling of fund managers at the peak of the bull market. This stock too had taken a pounding in the market downtrend. But there were additional factors weighing down the stock. Some ill-conceived acquisitions and glitches in the company's products had soured sentiment for the stock, and by mid-September, its price had nearly halved from its record high. By early October, the stock price had fallen below Rs 100, which was when GB suggested the stock as a potential target for a bear raid.

I looked at its price chart and told GB that it did not look very appealing to me.

'The stock is already reduced to one-fourth of what it was at the start of the year; assuming there is still some downside left, how much lower can it go?' I asked GB.

'You forget one of the market truisms I told you long back, Lala: bull markets have no tops and bear markets have no bottoms,' he retorted.

'I haven't forgotten any of your teachings, Govindbhai. The charts are telling me that there is a desperate attempt to keep the stock price above Rs 100. And I am told the promoter is well networked with fund managers and other investors to be able to defend his stock price in a crisis situation,' I countered.

'That makes the game all the more interesting, doesn't it?' GB said.

'Maybe. But there are other, easier stocks to make money off, so why get into this one?' I said, trying to reason with him.

I was beginning to suspect that he may have a personal reason for going after this stock. 'Never let your ego affect your judgement' is one of the cardinal rules of stock trading. Some players have come to grief violating this rule, but I have also known traders who would, once in a while, indulge their egos and even get away with it.

'Trust me on this one, Lala, there is some good money to be made here,' GB persisted.

I was now beginning to feel that he may know something the rest of the market probably did not.

'I am in. So what's the inside dope, then?' I asked.

'Ah, Lala, since you are being too nosy and I trust you enough, let me tell you this: Old Fox feels the stock is ripe to be taken down,' GB said.

Old Fox was the code name for one of the most astute players on Dalal Street who had few equals when it came to both trading and investing. I trusted Old Fox's judgement, but not so much as to blindly follow him into a trade. Still, I was ready to be a part of this operation because I was curious to see how much lower this stock could be beaten down.

We kept hammering away, and the stock once again fell below Rs 100. The overall downtrend in the market helped our cause. The stock kept dropping a few percentage points every day. But to make big profits, you needed that one round of panic selling that would help you cover your positions without sending the prices shooting up.

We were waiting for that one big break, but it seemed to be taking forever, despite the weakness in both the stock and the overall market. We suspected that the promoter was doing his best to defend the stock price. The settlement of the current F&O series was barely a week away. We were wondering whether to move in for the kill and risk a loss or cover up our positions for a modest profit.

We finally got the break we were waiting for. GB got to know from a company insider that the promoter was taking a morning flight to Germany on Friday to meet some investors over the weekend in connection with the company's fund-raising plans. Old Fox proposed that on Friday morning we hammer the stock's futures with all our might.

'This could be our best shot at breaking the price; I don't think there is anybody in his absence to organize a fightback if the price falls sharply. And even if there is, I doubt that person will be as effective as Mr T (the promoter) himself,' Old Fox told GB.

As soon as the market opened on Friday, we fell on the stock futures like a pack of wild dogs. And then, we had our second stroke of luck which made me feel the gods were on our side that day. The company had been facing trouble over the quality of its products exported to international markets. Just the previous day, there had been a major problem with its products at the location of one of its US clients. This news was flashed by a foreign newswire service around noon. After that the stock price went into a free fall accompanied by heavy volumes. It finally ended the day around 40 per cent below its previous day's closing price. We covered our positions almost entirely in that fall.

'So, Lala, are you now convinced that the stock still has enough room to go down, even after having fallen 75 per cent from its peak?' Old Fox asked me the following day, when we all met for lunch at his place. I understood that GB had filled him in on my initial reluctance to participate in the operation.

'Maybe or maybe not, but I guess the bulls would have been demoralized the moment they realized that it was Old Fox that they were up against,' I replied.

Old Fox laughed. I knew he was secretly flattered.

## 28

# The Turn of the Bulls

Relentless selling by FIIs had dragged the Sensex below 9,000 and the Nifty below 3,000 by the last week of October 2008. It was the bleakest Diwali in six years. Every single support level for the indices was crumbling under the weight of panic selling, which in turn sparked off more panic selling. After the first wave of sell-off in January, it looked as if the Sensex would stabilize around 15,000 after a nearly 30 per cent drop from its peak. When that level gave way, investors thought 12,000 was the bottom. When that too was breached, they felt 10,000 was inviolable, no matter what. But the Sensex fell below 10,000 and then below 9,000 too in just two trading sessions. The Nifty dropped as low 2,252. The climate of fear made it appear that no target on the downside was unimaginable.

Stocks which had been touted as blue chips and world beaters in the making had been smashed out of shape, and their high-profile promoters had turned recluses. Last year during this time, the mood everywhere had been euphoric. And now the pendulum had swung to the other extreme –

there was intense despair all around and some were even talking about the imminent demise of equity investment. Many witty SMS's did the rounds, rubbing salt into the wounds of those who were hit so badly they could not see the humour in them.

'Now showing on Dalal Street: *Saare Zameen Par*', went one of them, taking off on the Aamir Khan hit of that year *Taare Zameen Par.*

'Full form of NIFTY: No Income For This Year', went another.

I had made my fortune going short on the market. But there are no winners really in a bear market. While most of the profit I had encashed was safe, the value of my portfolio had shrunk considerably. I had been careful, though, to stay away from the flavour-of-the-season mid-cap and small-cap shares, most of which turned out to be junk. Not that I did not invest in any second-line shares at all; but I had consciously kept them to less than 20 per cent of my portfolio. Having been around in the market for nearly three decades, I had seen plenty of upcoming blue chips vanish without a trace. The returns from the tried-and-tested frontline stocks may not be spectacular, but over a longer period of time they are both handsome as well as consistent. Trading profits are never consistent, however skilled a trader may be. And even the most disciplined of traders are known to suffer from the occasional attack of overconfidence, which can at times be fatal.

Across the globe, central banks and governments had begun taking steps to halt the rapid slide in their respective economies. 'Economic stimulus' and 'bailout package' suddenly became the buzzwords as the unravelling crisis in financial markets threatened to push the real economy off the cliff.

Back in India, many retail brokerages had started to lay off employees. The situation was to get worse in the coming months. In many cases, the brokerages themselves were to blame for the mess they had got into. In their pursuit of a higher valuation, many had embarked on a reckless expansion spree, adding branches and manpower. Private equity investors and foreign institutions, who were willing to pay exorbitant prices for a stake in broking firms not long ago, suddenly became choosy and tight-fisted. Owners of brokerages realized that they could no longer demand high valuations based merely on the number of branches they had. Brokerages knew that many of their clients had made such heavy losses that they were unlikely to return in a hurry. New clients showing up in the foreseeable future seemed altogether unlikely. The brokerages did not see the need for too many employees even at their profitable centres now.

November brought its share of misery, the developments rattling the entire nation. On the evening of 26 November, a group of armed terrorists from Pakistan entered Mumbai by sea and went on a rampage, killing 166 people, including 28 foreigners, across key locations in South Mumbai. This was the most vicious terror attack on the city since the serial blasts in March 1993 that killed 350.

Though the stock exchanges were closed for trading the following day, both the Sensex and the Nifty ended the day with modest gains when trading resumed on November 28. That the markets appeared unfazed may have been admirable, but it also revealed the merciless face of financial markets, which at the end of the day are only concerned about profits and losses that can be quantified. Calamities and deaths mean little to the markets unless it affects the economy and corporate earnings. And here lies the irony – the market moves on sentiment, and yet is unemotional. I do not really trust market reaction following a calamitous event of national or global import. My experience so far suggests that behind the market stoicism operates a desperate government, attempting to ensure that its markets send out an it's-business-as-usual signal to the world.

New Year celebrations were muted, given the losses suffered by so many. Few nursed positive hopes for the coming year. I was reminded about the conversation at the New Year party in Alibaug a year ago, where just about everybody present was emphatic that the market would continue its ascent. Where did those Japanese funds with sackfuls of cash disappear, I wondered as I replayed the discussion in my mind.

The only headline-grabbing purchase by a Japanese player during the year was Daiichi Sankyo's takeover of Ranbaxy. Daiichi bought out 34 per cent of the Ranbaxy's promoters' – the Singh brothers' – stake in the company at Rs 737 per share and made an open offer to buy 20 per cent more from minority shareholders at the same price. Daiichi eventually sold Ranbaxy to Sun Pharma in 2014 for half the price it had paid to buy it. In the interim, there were a series of regulatory raps for the company and a $500 million settlement charge for exporting adulterated drugs to the US.

I thought about the market operator who had hosted the party, and his prognosis of the coming doom because of the havoc in the sub-prime loan market. He had analysed the situation correctly, but had not acted on his own advice in time.

Not many in the market would carry pleasant memories of this year, even though they were in the thick of action while history was being made.

# 29

# Satyam's Big Lie

Year 2009 started on an upbeat note, with the Sensex surging 256 points in the first trading session. It gained another 350 points over the next three days, and everything seemed to be looking up when disaster struck again. This time, it had nothing to do with the chaos in the global financial markets.

On 7 January, before the market opened for trading, B. Ramalinga Raju, founder of Satyam Computer Services, wrote to SEBI and the stock exchanges confessing that he had been cooking the company's books for the last few years by showing non-existent revenues and bank balances. His confession was the final nail in the coffin for the company, which had been in the eye of a shareholder storm when it floated a proposal to acquire stakes in Maytas Properties and Maytas Infra the month before.

Raju's admission sent the Satyam stock crashing by 83 per cent, to Rs 30, from the previous day's closing price of Rs 179. Panicky investors dumped shares fearing that it was only a matter of time before the company would go belly up. The stock finally ended the day at Rs 40.

There was a sense of vindication among fund managers who had always steered clear of the stock and among analysts who were forever bearish on it. For a long time now, this minority group had been of the view that the Satyam story would have a bad ending. Despite being the fourth largest IT services company in India, after TCS, Infosys and Wipro, Satyam had not quite been able to convince the market about its corporate governance and accounting standards. Its PE multiple was always lower than that of its peers. In other words, even those who bought Satyam shares were reluctant to value the company as richly as they did the other three. Still, there were enough takers for the stock because the company was able to demonstrate consistent growth in earnings, quarter after quarter.

And the 'beauty' of the stock market is that even in times of utter despair, there is never a dearth of optimists, value buyers or bargain hunters – whatever you may call them. A record total of 34.67 crore shares of Satyam were traded on both exchanges that day which showed there were many investors who felt the company could still make a comeback, despite the serious mess it was in.

When I first saw the news flashed on television, I could not believe my eyes. Rarely do you have the promoter of a frontline company admitting to a fraud, that too a fraud on such a massive scale. My trader's instinct quickly took over, and I short-sold as many shares as I could. But the price had begun to sink rapidly, even before I could hit the 'enter' key on my trading terminal. The severity of the slide stunned the market, and within minutes the stock had fallen to below Rs 100. I wondered if I should be doubling my position, but decided against it. I covered my position at

Rs 90 and waited. Since there was no intra-day circuit filter on the stock, it continued its free fall, going all the way down to Rs 30 before closing at Rs 40 by the end of the day.

Satyam's troubles had started a few months earlier when the lenders with whom the promoters had pledged shares to raise money started offloading them. That Raju was pledging his shares to raise money was not common knowledge because SEBI rules did not require a company to disclose details about shares pledged by its promoters.

By the end of September 2008, promoter-holding in the company had fallen to 8.6 per cent, leaving the company vulnerable to a takeover.

Still, the stock managed to hold ground in October while the market as a whole was being battered by the yen carry-trade unwinding. But, unknown to shareholders, time was running out for Raju. There was a big hole in Satyam's books because of the fictitious cash and bank balances in it. Raju had managed to outwit the auditors so far, but at some point he would have to reconcile the books. Besides, he had to keep paying real taxes even if the revenues were fake. And, since he had pledged shares to raise money, the stock price had to be maintained, or the lenders would start dumping his shares. To maintain the stock prices, the artificial growth in revenues had to be sustained.

In a desperate measure to cover up the non-existent revenues, Raju proposed to the board that Satyam buy out the unlisted Maytas Properties (wholly owned by the Raju family) for Rs 6,240 crore, and pick up a 51 per cent stake in the listed Maytas Infra for Rs 1,440 crore.

Institutional shareholders were outraged, thinking Satyam promoters were trying to profit at the expense of minority shareholders of the company. Raju realized that antagonizing his important shareholders would draw more attention to the company's workings, and so dropped the plan.

That mollified investors somewhat. Just as Raju managed to put out one fire, another broke out a few days later. Fox News reported that the World Bank had banned Satyam from doing business with it for eight years for allegedly bribing its officials to secure orders. The company vehemently denied it, but the World Bank confirmed the development, sending the stock crashing by over 13 per cent.

Things were rapidly getting out of control for Raju. On 27 December, just two days before the scheduled board meeting to consider a share buyback proposal for the company, it was announced that the meeting was being deferred to 10 January as options other than a buyback were being considered. The company appointed DSP Merrill Lynch to advise it on 'strategic options to enhance shareholder value'.

DSP Merrill Lynch's association with Satyam dated back to 1999 when it had been lead manager to the company's ADR issue and adviser to subsidiary Satyam Infoway's acquisition of Indiaworld for a jaw-dropping Rs 499 crore. The deal, as I have mentioned earlier, had raised many an eyebrow, and there had been whispers in market and corporate circles that the promoters had actually siphoned off the cash raised in the recent ADR issue through the extravagant acquisition.

A week after its appointment as adviser to Satyam on 'strategic options', DSP Merrill issued a statement that it was terminating the assignment, saying the company was not forthcoming on some crucial disclosures.

Even though its stock had nosedived, many in the market believed the government would intervene, directly or indirectly, to salvage Satyam, given the number of jobs – roughly 53,000 – at stake, and the fact that Lok Sabha elections were barely three months away and state elections due shortly after. A section of the market hoped industry rivals would be interested in buying out Satyam at some price or other, even if the full extent of the fraud was yet to be ascertained.

Betting on this, many traders started loading up on the stock on Friday when markets resumed for trading after the holiday for Muharram on 8 January. I picked up a couple of lakh shares at around Rs 30, a couple of lakh at around Rs 25, and another couple of lakh at around Rs 20. The volume of trades was again heavy on Wednesday, but the stock price began to sink after a steady start. The latest rumour doing the rounds was that the government was unlikely to intervene and would let Satyam go under. On BSE, the stock price tumbled to Rs 11 and on NSE to Rs 7. I sold out my positions close to the lows of the day at a considerable loss. While initiating the trade, I had planned to hold on to the stock for a month or even longer, by which time there would be some clarity on whether the company would be salvaged. But the rapid descent in the stock price forced me to react as a trader would.

Most traders I knew took a hit on their long positions in Satyam, having sold out in panic. I watched the Satyam screen out of curiosity for a while, though I had sold out my position. There was heavy buying at lower levels, and I suspected that the buyers knew something that the rest of the market did not. I became more certain of this as the stock price climbed to Rs 23 by the end of that day.

I had lost Rs 90 lakh in a single trade, but took solace in the fact that there were others who had fared more miserably. When the Satyam stock had plummeted on the board's decision to buy stakes in the Maytas firms, Larsen & Toubro (L&T) had picked up a 3.95 per cent stake in the company at Rs 170 per share. At the end of the December quarter, L&T's stake in Satyam was higher than the promoter's holding, which had fallen to 3.6 per cent because of the sale of Raju and Co.'s pledged shares.

After the fraud surfaced, the L&T top boss A. M. Naik said his company would not sell or buy any more shares of Satyam. Two weeks later, the company would pick up an additional 7.6 per cent at Rs 34.52 per share, lowering the average cost of its 12 per cent stake in Satyam to Rs 82 per share. The company had little choice; it appeared almost impossible that the stock price would ever go back to Rs 170. But there was a better chance of the company being able to recoup its investment at Rs 82 a share.

Over the weekend it also became clear that the government would not abandon Satyam to its fate.

The entire incident reinforced what I had always believed: that only the promoter really knows what is going on inside a company, no matter how intensely researched a company and its stock. Satyam's low PE multiple was proof that the market did not fully trust its earnings. But analysts and fund managers could never put a finger on what exactly was wrong with the numbers.

A careful study of the cash flows, debtor outstanding, tax payments and operating margins vis-à-vis key competitors does provide an indication of the soundness of the business. But what safeguard can an investor have against a promoter who manages to forge invoices and bank statements, show fake revenues and cash balances, get them certified by a careless or complicit (as may be the case) auditor and, on top of all this, pay real tax on fictitious income? Nothing.

The Satyam episode had investors worried about more such frauds surfacing in the coming days and cast a shadow on the shares of second-line IT companies, which until then were doing fairly well in a turbulent market. If you cannot trust the numbers of a frontline company, how reliable can the numbers of smaller companies be?

The scam also punched a hole in India's claim to having the best corporate governance standards among emerging markets.

# 30

# Bulls Make a Comeback

For all his market wisdom, Old Fox had begun to overplay his hand without realizing it. In 2009, the market started climbing mid-March onwards, slowly at first, then gathering speed. The common view was that the uptrend was unlikely to sustain. Whenever there is a trend reversal either up or down, players take a while to recognize it.

When the Nifty and the Sensex had managed to top 3,000 and 10,000 respectively by the end of March, chartists and non-chartists alike were still looking for signs that the market had finally broken away from its fourteen-month-long downtrend.

Initially, I was content with small profits, unsure if an upcycle was under way. As prices rose, I would book profits, then buy again if the stock continued to show strength. All this while, Old Fox continued to short-sell with all his might, convinced that the rally 'had no legs to stand on'.

An error even the most seasoned traders are prone to is to misjudge the point at which to start cutting down positions even as you are winning. Everybody is aware of the market truism that nobody can catch tops or bottoms except liars. The experienced trader knows he will not be able to exit his entire position at the peak price or start covering his short positions at the bottom price. If the trader is not careful, he finds himself like the soldier who gives hot pursuit to an enemy and, in doing so, unwittingly enters enemy territory

Something similar happened to Old Fox this time. He kept selling even as the trend had changed from bearish to bullish, a shift that escaped his notice. A bear trader's unseen foe is the long-term investor, just as a bull operator's nemesis is the genuine seller.

As the market had kept falling over a long period of time, traders who went long in the futures market kept incurring losses. So did the short-term investors who had bought shares hoping to cash out within a month or two for a decent profit. The presence of these two categories of investors in the market had now dwindled as continuous losses drove many of them away. In their place had begun to enter investors who were willing to buy and wait it out for a year or two, or even longer. They included HNIs, promoters buying through fronts, and sometimes even the contrarians among retail investors. None of these investors buy aggressively, so it is hard to detect their presence. The market sees this trend as 'shares passing from weak hands to strong hands'. As a result of this buying, the floating stock in the market had slowly begun to decline. Most of the players who wanted to sell out had done so and the shares now rested with players who took a long-term view of their purchases. Not recognizing these subtle changes, the bears had unknowingly ventured into enemy territory through sheer overconfidence. Once prices started to climb, the rise would be sharp because of the absence of enough sellers to blunt it. And that would make it hard for the bears to cover their short positions without sending prices shooting up.

That is exactly what happened with Old Fox, who failed to realize that his opponents had changed. He was spot on when he had predicted the previous year that the market had peaked out. But he misread the signals as the market reversed trend. By mid-April, the Nifty was sniffing at 3,500 and the Sensex had topped 11,200. The bears were taken by surprise. Partly, it was their frantic short-covering of positions that added fuel to the fire and pushed up share prices.

Old Fox had to cover a part of his short positions at a loss as prices flared up. But to his credit, the Fox knew when he had been beaten and would not stick to a market view just to prove a point. He squared off his short positions and began building long positions quickly.

My winning streak that had begun in January last year, continued. I steadily increased the size of my trades and watched the profits pour in.

There was still one major hurdle for the market to cross – the Lok Sabha elections. Political analysts and psephologists continued to predict a hung parliament, and there was no strong reason to believe otherwise. Media reports showed a general disenchantment with the ruling UPA, but the Opposition appeared to be in disarray, with no strong candidate to lead the charge.

The results announced on 16 May, a Saturday, took the nation by surprise. The Congress had returned with an even stronger mandate, bagging 220-plus seats on its own. More importantly for the market, this time the Congress would not be at the mercy of the Left parties that had supported the UPA from outside for much of its previous tenure and had hobbled the government from pursuing major economic reforms.

The market move on Monday stunned everybody. Within 30 seconds of start of trading, indices leapt to the upper end of the 10 per cent intra-day circuit filter, and trading was suspended for an hour, as per SEBI rules. When trading resumed, it took only another 60 seconds before the indices surged another 5 per cent, and trading was halted for the day. The Sensex rose a whopping 2,100 points to close at 14,284, and the Nifty gained 651 points to close at 4,323.

It was the first time in the history of the Indian stock market that trading had to be halted because of indices hitting the upper end of the intra-day circuit filter. Life seemed to have come a full circle for the UPA government. Exactly five years ago, on 17 May, a tactless remark by CPI leader A. B. Bardhan soon after the UPA victory had sent the market crashing to the lower end of the circuit filter, suspending trading for the rest of the session.

Both indices cooled off over the following week, but sentiment had improved considerably by then. FIIs bought shares for Rs 20,600 crore in the net in May alone, which was seen as a vote of confidence by global investors in the India story.

The dramatic turnaround in sentiment and the recovery in share prices also caused heartburn in some quarters. On 14 May, DLF promoters sold a 9.9 per cent stake in the company to a clutch of institutional investors for Rs 3,860 crore, which worked out to Rs 232 per share. This was less than half its IPO price of Rs 525 less than two years ago.

At the peak of the bull run, the stock had touched a high of Rs 1,200. That now seemed very long ago.

The founders used the funds from the stake sale to buy out private equity firm DE Shaw's stake in group company DLF Assets Limited and also to infuse fresh funds into it. This decision would turn out to be troublesome for the promoters just two trading sessions later.

To be fair to the DLF promoters, they closed the deal ahead of the election results as there was a risk of the market mood souring in the event of a hung parliament. As share prices surged crazily in response to the unexpected UPA sweep, DLF's shares price rocketed to Rs 323 on May 18, the first trading session after the election results. By October, the stock had climbed to Rs 475.

By July, many companies decided that market conditions were ripe for another round of fund-raising through qualified institutional placements (QIPs), or sale of shares to institutional investors. For many companies there was little choice – they needed to raise money not to grow their business, but merely to stay in business. There was a floor price for this placement – the two-week average closing price of the stock – below which companies could not sell their shares. They were free to price their placements above the two-week average if they found takers for it. Many companies tried their usual tricks, like getting market operators to bump up the stock price just before bids were sought from interested buyers.

But fund managers refused to fall for the trap; they could now afford to be choosy as they were flooded with offers from companies starved for capital. The two-week average price formula meant nothing to them if they had reason to believe that the stock had been rigged or that the formula was yielding a high price only because the market as a whole had moved up and not because of the value of the stock. They drove a hard bargain, and in many cases promoters had to wait for their stock prices to cool off a bit before fund managers agreed to subscribe to their issues.

Knowing that promoters would eventually have to offer their shares at a discount to the market price, many fund managers dumped the shares they were already holding in the company, buying the same stock at a cheaper price through the QIP route. The tables had turned, and this time it was the fund managers profiting at the expense of the promoters.

# 31

# A Reality Check

But the severe bear run that had lasted fourteen months had brought about some changes that were hard to reverse. For one, even as share prices had risen sharply in the last four months, many stocks were a long way off from their giddy peaks of January 2008.

Second, the bear market had exposed the fragile business models of many companies, mostly those in the infrastructure and real estate sectors. Many of them would never regain the favour of institutional investors, even though bull operators would take a passing fancy to them once in a while.

From the perspective of the brokerage firms, the days of juicy commissions and brisk business from retail investors and HNIs had ended for the time being. Many clients had lost huge sums of money or had seen their paper profits shrink to alarmingly low levels. Many of them would not return to the market in a hurry, and some would never again have the courage to. The ones who stayed back reduced the size of their trades, biding their time till they felt safe enough to stake bigger sums.

The investors who had dabbled in stock and index futures, however, had been dealt the most devastating blow. The broking houses had led them to this. It was in the interest of the broking houses that clients traded in the more risky futures and not in the relatively safer options, the commissions on futures trades being several times higher than on options trades.

In 2007-08, as the bull market was raging, index and stock futures accounted for 87 per cent of the total turnover in the derivatives segment. The following year, the turnover in the derivatives segment declined by nearly 15 per cent, and futures turnover accounted for 64 per cent of this reduced pie. The next year it would fall to around 33 per cent. In the following years, most brokerages would earn a substantial chunk of their revenues from their NBFC (lending) business rather than from stockbroking.

The bear market of 2008 brought the high-flying promoters of many mid-cap companies down to earth, or down on their knees, as would be the more apt phrase in many cases. When the market was booming, these promoters had resorted to all kinds of tricks to ensure that their companies made it to the list of securities eligible for futures and options trading. To make the cut, the stocks had to have a minimum market capitalization, and specified minimum daily volumes for a specified period. The promoters would rope in a bull operator, and together they would ensure the stock fulfilled the criteria to make it to the F&O list. For many promoters, their stock being in the F&O list helped them manipulate prices and make a killing from time to time. These promoters used to throw grand parties on the day the inclusion of their companies in the haloed list was announced. I had myself been to at least half a dozen such parties.

Typically, the promoters, in collusion with a market operator, would corner a sizeable quantity of the company's shares, pushing up the stock price. As the stock price climbed, so would the futures price. Many traders would short-sell the futures, betting that the rise in stock price was not sustainable. But since most of the shares had already been hoarded, the stock price would stay firm, and so would the futures prices. For good effect, the operator would buy some more shares closer to the settlement day of the derivatives contracts, further driving up the futures prices. Eventually, the traders who had short-sold the futures would have to cover up their positions, and this would further drive up the futures price and further increase their losses. Some of the traders with deep pockets would carry forward their short positions to the next settlement cycle, hoping that prices would move in their favour. But so long as the promoter-operator duo controlled the floating stock, short-sellers stood little chance of winning.

In a bear market, however, the presence of these stocks on the F&O list made it easier for bears to hammer their price. The short-sellers would target companies whose promoters they knew were facing liquidity problems. The bears would then get down to short-selling the futures in a big way. Once the futures prices started to buckle under the onslaught of the relentless selling, the spot price too would move down in tandem. The difference this time was that the promoters did not have the cash to prop up the stock price. More often than not, the promoters would have raised money by pledging shares, either from the stock they officially held, or from the stock held in *benami* accounts. Once the stock price came under pressure, margin calls from the lenders would follow. If promoters were unable to deposit additional collateral, the lenders would start dumping the shares, aggravating the slide in the stock price. The bears successfully deployed this tactic in many mid-cap stocks, and in a reversal of roles, they were the ones laughing all the way to the bank while the hapless promoters licked their wounds.

Not surprisingly then, companies wrote to the stock exchanges begging that their stocks be excluded from the F&O list. Even otherwise, many companies automatically found themselves out of the list once their market capitalization and trading volumes fell below a certain threshold.

During the bull run, many promoters had tried to increase their shareholding cheaply by issuing equity warrants to themselves at a predetermined price. The promoters had only to pay 10 per cent upfront; the rest they could pay at the time of conversion of the warrants to shares eighteen months later. Since the market was in an uptrend, the promoters were confident that they would be able to convert their warrants at a discounted market price eighteen months later.

But the share prices of many of these companies fell so sharply that by the time the warrants came up for conversion, the conversion price was way above the market price. It made no sense for the promoters to convert their warrants, and they allowed them to lapse, forfeiting the 10 per cent upfront payment. A year later, SEBI would hike the upfront payment for equity warrants to 25 per cent so that promoters did not try to short-change minority shareholders.

## 32

# Making it to the Big League

Thanks to my unusually long winning streak for the last couple of years, people in corporate circles began to hear my name. By that, I mean executives on the treasury side, such as chief financial officers. I found some of the fund managers too becoming more approachable now. Thankfully, since most of my gains came from my trading bets and not investment bets (which could be easily tracked from publicly available data), I was unknown to the media. I was perfectly fine with that since I had no desire to be known beyond my professional circles. I slowly began to get invites to parties of the rich and famous, which I refused without a second thought. Promoters began to send feelers to me to help boost their share price in return for a cut. At times, there would be offers to hammer a rival company's shares. I had been approached in the past too with such requests, but the pedigree of companies that were now seeking my services was a few notches higher.

I have helped quite a few promoters to ramp up their stock prices, but as a rule I never invest in their shares. I have to trade in their stock for a certain period when I am managing its price, but my association with the stock ceases once I have fulfilled my commitment to them. It is good if promoters are mindful of their stock price; that way they may not want to do something rash that will upset the market or their key shareholders. But it is a problem if promoters are obsessed with their stock price. To me it is a clear indication that they are not focusing their time and energy on their main business. And that is a recipe for disaster. Promoters often forget that a healthy share price flows from the strength of their core business and not the other way round. A healthy stock price can at best help a promoter raise money, but he has to put the money to work and show consistent returns to the shareholders. Unless he is able to do that, his stock price will just flounder.

I got to meet some interesting market operators too. JC was the most notable of the lot, and I guess it had partly to do with his flamboyant ways. Anybody who met him once would not forget him easily. His showy ways put off many while amusing others. He had a fondness for expensive watches, and especially loved to tell people what they cost. His manner of speaking could be misinterpreted as offensive, and while that was not always intentional, he had ended up rubbing quite a few names the wrong way with his tactless remarks.

JC had been in the market since the late 1980s, but it was only in the last couple of years that he began to get noticed, for reasons right and wrong. He delighted in short-selling stocks, as though the task of chastening errant promoters had fallen to his lot. He would go long too on stocks, and had a decent-sized investment portfolio, but it was his bearish bets that got talked about and gave him the attention he relished.

He won and lost big sums, and from what I gathered, it was his stubbornness that often got him into trouble. He claimed to be a value investor and not one of those operators who colluded with promoters to rig up stock prices. That claim was only partly true because I knew that he had cut deals with some of the dubious mid-cap and small-cap companies to boost their stock prices.

He called me one day and proposed that we meet up. I agreed. He invited me to his office, which I found a bit odd. Somebody else in my position might have taken offence. But I had heard enough about JC's idiosyncrasies to take umbrage at the suggestion. His calling me over to his office was his way of subtly asserting his seniority over me in the profession and telling me 'you come and see me'.

I drove down to his office in Andheri, curious to meet the man I had heard so much about. For a man rumoured to be worth a few hundred crore rupees, he had an office that was housed in a nondescript building that was modestly furnished and had barely half a dozen employees.

His cabin was spacious, though not outsized. His arc-shaped, glass-topped table held four trader workstations. Three were placed right in front of JC, while one stood to his right. There was a packet of Davidhoff beside one of the workstations. I glanced at his watch – sure enough, it was an expensive one. A friend of mine who knew JC well had once mentioned that JC's watch cost Rs 15 lakh.

JC claimed to be more of a value investor than a trader in stocks. But most people in the market felt it was the other way round.

'I prefer companies where the managements don't try to suck up to you just because they are keen that you buy their shares,' he said, as we got chatting. 'Though not a foolproof method, I see overfriendliness as a sign that they crave a higher market value for their shares.' He said his portfolio comprised mostly blue chips and some well-managed companies that were undervalued at the moment, but held great potential.

'The blue chips are my nest egg. I never touch them. They are for the future generations. I have ensured that at least six generations of the family can get by without ever having to work. I decide on the maximum loss that I can take on my trading positions and then play within that range. I am like a kid at a video game parlour. I play for as long as the coins in my pocket last. Once the coins are over, I get off the machine.

'Till 1996, I always used to buy first and then sell. But the bear market showed me that there was good money to be made by doing exactly the opposite too. I began to short-sell at every opportunity, and though a few bets went awry, I made good money. Short-selling is not everybody's cup of tea, but I find it more challenging. Most of the time I am long on the market. For some reason, it is always my short positions that get talked about.'

'Of course they would be,' I said. 'The aggression with which you go after some of the stocks almost gives the impression that you expect the company to be out of business shortly. I have known some promoters who had trouble getting sleep at night because of your raids.'

JC grinned, and I could see that he seemed pleased with that remark.

'You exaggerate, Lala, but I try to distinguish between stocks that are overvalued because the market is convinced about their potential, and stocks that are overvalued because the promoters are supporting the stock price. The second category gets its comeuppance sooner than later. One adverse bit of news, or a sudden change in market sentiment for the worse, and these puffed-up stocks collapse like a house of cards. Of course, one has to be patient enough to wait for that break. In the interim, the promoter and operator will push up the stock and you will have to take short-term losses. I have had to suffer quite a few times, but the two or three bets that pay off more than compensated for my losses in other stocks,' JC said.

JC had warmed to me and was now freely talking about his trades.

I asked him why he had turned bullish on Aban Lloyd (a company that operates oil rigs) after having been bearish on it for a long time. I knew the reason, but I wanted to hear it from him. JC had been bearish on Aban for many months. But he lost a lot of money as the stock price kept rising even as he short-sold Aban futures. Then JC got lucky. The company's main revenue grosser, an oil rig off the Venezuelan coast, sank. The stock price halved within a week, and JC not only recouped his losses, but made a tidy profit too. Of late, the stock price was on an upswing, and had recovered significantly from the lows of the year even if it was still some way off from its recent highs.

'Having worked with some of the best market operators, I thought you would have spotted that trick, Lala,' JC said, once again smiling. 'The stock has bounced because I have covered most of my short positions,' he said, looking pleased with himself. 'Of course, the company is doing poorly. But I am unable to hammer the price down further because all the buyers have fled. I have to attract some buyers before I start hammering down the price once again. To bring them back, I have to create an illusion that the stock price is set to move up,' he said.

Earlier during the year, I had heard that JC had heavily short-sold the futures of a Mumbai-based realty company. The promoters, in collusion with a bull operator, had pushed up prices and had managed to hold them at a certain level, forcing JC to buy back the futures at nearly three times the price he had sold them for. The talk in market circles was that JC had suffered a loss of Rs 40 crore on that trade. Though it was impolite on my part, I brought the matter up.

'I heard that trade cost you a packet.'

'A little, but not as much as the market would like to believe,' JC said, looking me in the eye. But JC made no bones about the fact that he was mad as hell at the operator who helped the promoter jack up the price.

'But why make it personal?' I asked JC. 'If that operator had declined, the promoter would have enlisted somebody else for that job.'

'Maybe. But for some reason I took a dislike to that fellow after the incident. Since then I made it a point to short the stocks on which he would be long,' JC admitted.

'Now you are contradicting yourself, JC. Just a while ago you said you never allowed ego to interfere with your trading decisions. By hammering some stock just because you want to screw a rival, you risk losing money,' I pointed out.

He smiled. 'That is okay. In my position, I can afford an enemy or two. There are plenty of other stocks where you can make money.'

But JC did end up making more than just one or two enemies. According to the market grapevine, he had managed to infuriate the promoters of quite a few companies by hammering their stocks. One of them happened to be a Mumbai-based real estate company with politically well-connected promoters. The promoters first asked him to back off from their stock. JC in turn asked them to get lost. Infuriated by his gall, the promoters sent goons to his office to intimidate him. I even heard that he was roughed up so that he got the message loud and clear. To ask JC about that would be testing his patience. But I know that for some time JC was moving around with a couple of bodyguards in tow. Those who did not know the reason felt it was yet another of his antics to exaggerate his importance.

We chatted for over an hour. As I was leaving, JC came up to my car to see me off. 'You come across as an intelligent fellow to me. I think we should do business together,' he said.

I told him it was a good idea, but though we exchanged market views quite a few times after that, we never got down to doing business together.

# 33

# A Level Playing Ground

Some of the policies introduced by SEBI were now beginning to bite. In 2008, it had approved a facility called direct market access (DMA) for institutional investors. Under this system, clients could access the stock exchange's trading system through their brokers' infrastructure, but without manual intervention by the brokers. Earlier, a fund manager based out of Singapore or London wanting to trade in Indian shares would have to call the broker in India to place his order. Somebody like me who was thick with dealers at institutional brokerages would often get to know of some of the large-sized orders before they were executed, and front-run them. With the introduction of DMA, global fund managers could route their orders electronically into their broker's trading systems, and the orders would then find their way into the exchange's trading engine. The broker would get to know of the orders only after they were executed.

The advent of DMA simultaneously fuelled the growth of algorithmic trading, or programmed trading as it was commonly known in market parlance. In algo trading, a software would execute trades based on pre-assigned commands. At a basic level, the command could be to sell the futures of a stock and simultaneously buy an equivalent quantity in the cash market if the futures were quoting at a particular premium to the spot price. Conversely, it could be to sell spot and buy futures if the futures were quoting at a discount. Complex commands could interlink trading volumes, index levels and a host of other parameters to trigger a trade. DMA and algo trading went hand in hand, as the software would now take over the functions of a dealer. Earlier, if a fund manager placed an order with a dealer at a broking firm for, say, 5 lakh shares within a price range, it would be the dealer's responsibility to ensure that the order was executed in a way that the price and volume objectives were fulfilled. This meant having to execute the order in separate chunks by gauging the demand-supply situation from the screen, so as not to draw the market's attention.

With algo trading, all that would be taken care of by the software. FIIs and foreign brokerages clearly had the edge when it came to algo trading because they could afford to hire the best talent to develop proprietary software. DMA was slow to pick up initially, since the stock exchanges wanted to scrutinize the algorithms before they were allowed to run on their systems. The exchanges had a legitimate concern that algos without adequate safeguards could wreak havoc in the market. Having spent millions on their proprietary trading software, foreign players were reluctant to reveal the secret sauce of their algos. But once the stock exchanges relaxed this rule and the players did not have to reveal the specifics of their algos, DMA took off.

Domestic arbitrage firms, with their huge teams of mercenary day traders, never stood a chance in what was the equivalent of an arms race in the financial markets. For one, humans could never match the speed of programmed machines, which could spot arbitrage opportunities in a fraction of a second and execute them even before a day trader could blink. Local firms did make an attempt to fight back though, through commonly available, off-the-shelf trading software. The trouble with the generic algos was their lack of uniqueness, so that one user firm's algo trading differed little from another's. And they were no match for the high-end trading software developed by FIIs and foreign brokerages with their team of highly skilled software engineers.

There was another missing link on the road to superfast trading. Even the best of trading software would not be very effective unless the orders could be executed in the shortest possible time – measured in milliseconds – to beat competing algos. That hurdle was overcome when first NSE, and later BSE, began offering a facility known as 'co-location'. Under this, brokers could, for a fee, get to place their servers close to the exchange's trading engine. This would give the broker faster access to the buy-sell quotes streamed from the exchange and also send the executed trades back to the exchange quicker for confirmation. There was a slight lag – in milliseconds, not visible to the human eye – with which the date streamed from the exchange server reached the broker, the lag depending on the distance of the broker's server from the stock exchange's trading engine, though it was one of milliseconds. Through the co-location facility, the bigger brokers could race the small brokers in snatching the best quotes.

The smaller traders protested, since the Rs 25-odd lakh charged by NSE initially (the rates declined over a period of time) was too stiff for them, and put them at a disadvantage against foreign players for whom the amount was loose change. Local traders who played for very small spreads were hit the hardest. A software program would seize the best buy and sell quotes in the blink of an eye. Humans could never hope to match that speed. By the time a trader punched in an order after checking the prices on his screen, the software would have already snatched that trade away from him. Algos also had the ability to crowd out the smaller traders' orders by generating a large number of orders within a fraction of a second. For the small trader, it was like standing in a queue to buy tickets for a movie, only to find that the number of people ahead of him had suddenly trebled. Even assuming you were assured of tickets, you would be unlikely to get the seats of your choice. Similarly, the day trader would end up paying five paise or even more buying a stock, and get five paise (or more) less when selling a stock, simply because the algo would beat him to the best buy and sell quotes.

For a retail investor buying a stock for a longer time horizon, a five-paise or ten-paise difference did not really matter. But for the day traders, this difference was good enough to shrink their profits considerably, or even make trading itself unprofitable. The smarter among the lot changed their trading strategies and hung on, hoping for better times ahead. Instead of looking to make Rs 50 each on 100 trades, they decided to take bigger risks and attempted to make Rs 200 each on fewer numbers of trades. For some, it paid off and they were able to stay in the game. For many others, it was time to look for some other profession.

But institutional investors had other reasons to be unhappy about. Slowly but steadily, some of the privileges they had been enjoying for a long time were being taken away. It had started a couple of years ago when SEBI had asked institutions to start paying upfront margins on their cash market transactions. Until then, only non-institutional players had to pay upfront margins on cash market trades, as regulators thought it unlikely that institutions would ever default on their obligations to the stock exchanges. But the events leading to the global financial crisis punctured the aura of invincibility around financial institutions. They were now seen as entities as likely to default as a small investor or an HNI.

In May 2010, SEBI ruled that institutions would have to pay the entire application money while bidding for IPOs. So far, they had had to pay only 10 per cent of the application money while retail investors and non-institutional investors had had to pay the entire amount. As they had to pay little money upfront, institutions would bid for huge quantities. This led to a situation where heavy bidding by institutions gave an exaggerated picture of the demand for primary market offers.

High institutional interest would set off a chain reaction, as retail and other investors viewed it as an endorsement of the company's fundamentals, and felt encouraged to invest. This would also influence the listing price, which hinged on the demand for the stock during the issue process.

Understandably, both FIIs and merchant bankers were opposed to the move because it reduced their power to game the IPO process. However, SEBI refused to budge on the matter.

# 34

# Garibi Hatao, the SKS Way

There were two blockbuster public issues in 2010. I did not participate in either, but enjoyed the intellectual debates over the IPOs of SKS Microfinance, the first of two microfinance companies to hit the market in August. The size of the issue was a little over Rs 1,650 crore, consisting of a fresh issue of shares for Rs 733 crore and sale by the existing investors of the rest of the shares.

Microfinance being a new concept for the stock market, there was a lot of excitement and hype about the issue. Few understood the business model. They only knew that MFIs loaned money to the financially weakest sections of society – the poorest of the poor – who had no access to banks and other traditional sources of funds.

SKS, founded by 41-year-old Indian American Vikram Akula, drew applause, awe, and also scathing criticism for its decision to go public. The sceptics included the Nobel Prize-winning economist and pioneer of microfinance in Bangladesh, Mohammed Yunus. His contention was that the IPO would send a wrong message – that there was money to be made off poor people. After all, microfinance firms generally charged interest rates of anywhere between 30 per cent and 50 per cent to compensate for a higher risk of default by its borrowers. If an MFI's rate of loan defaults was low, it stood to make handsome returns on its investment. Supporters of the IPO were convinced that an IPO success for SKS would encourage many other microfinance firms to raise money from the stock market and scale up their operations. They said this would lead to more competition among microfinance firms and lower interest rates, thus freeing many poor borrowers from the clutches of usurious moneylenders.

The company claimed to be driven by the lofty ideal of helping the poor through credit even as it tried to revolutionize the MFI landscape in India and helped investors make money in the process. Many an investor must have likely believed there was nothing better than putting money in such an IPO, as it would be a shot at making good money while also supporting a noble cause. It was for the first time that investors were being served a potent cocktail of capitalism and altruism on Dalal Street, and everybody wanted a draught of it.

The pre-IPO investors in the company included big names like Quantum, managed by the legendary trader George Soros, and Catamaran Investments, promoted by Infosys founder N. R. Narayana Murthy.

What did not fetch as much publicity was the sale of shares held in the form of stock options by the SKS management ahead of the IPO. To me, the eagerness of a promoter to take money off the table is never a healthy sign. Founder Vikram Akula and CEO Suresh Gurumani sold a portion of their options, agreeing to lock in the rest for three years.

Investor response to the IPO was overwhelming, though many felt the shares were expensive at Rs 985 each. The track record of the company and the sound quality of its loan book were good reasons for investors to believe that its business model was scalable and that the premium valuation was justified.

SKS shares had a decent debut on the exchanges, gaining nearly 18 per cent on opening and ending the day around 10 per cent above the issue price. Its listing day performance would have been better had it not been for the weakness in the market. Still, the stock had a good run over the next month, climbing to around Rs 1,400.

But come October, and problems began cropping up for SKS, beginning with the abrupt resignation of CEO Suresh Gurumani over differences with founder Akula. The stock had been drifting lower for the past few weeks, and the power struggle within the board now put the stock under further pressure. But an even heavier blow was to fall a few days later. A spate of suicides by borrowers in Andhra Pradesh stirred the state government into issuing an ordinance to curb the activities of MFIs in the state.

The well-publicized story was that too many MFIs had sprung up in Andhra, and that agents of these firms were talking the poor into borrowing money, whether they needed it or not. These borrowers would blow up the money and later had to deal with the strong-arm tactics of the loan agents-turned-recovery agents when they failed to repay. Some killed themselves.

There was a conspiracy theory too, that SKS's growing presence had threatened the livelihood of many politicians who were thick with the moneylenders and had a vested interest in keeping the poor poor. The incidents of suicide were exaggerated to weaken the reputation of MFIs in the state. The developments hurt SKS very badly because Andhra was its biggest market in terms of its loan book. The company never recovered from that blow, and by the end of the year, the stock price was down to Rs 600, nearly 40 per cent below the IPO price.

So much for long-term investing, I thought, as I went through the chain of events. The one who had subscribed to the IPO and decided to sell out within a month would now look smarter than the one who was stilling holding the stock.

Meanwhile, as the market rose, my own bank account continued to swell steadily. The uptrend till August had been steady, but in September, the market just took off. However, the enthusiasm and excitement of the last bull run was clearly missing. It was a small group of players, mostly FIIs, who were raking in the big money.

Still, retail investors got one fair shot at making some decent returns through the Coal India IPO. Investors across all categories bid for shares of India's largest coal producer, as the issue price of Rs 245 was thought attractive. The company aimed to raise around Rs 15,200 crore through the IPO, but got bids in the region of Rs 2.3 lakh crore. The issue was oversubscribed 15 times. Strangely, institutional investors who were complaining about the new rule requiring them to pay the full application money were the most aggressive bidders. The institutional portion of the book was subscribed nearly 25 times, with Rs 1.73 lakh crore's worth of bids coming in. The institutional book in the Reliance Power IPO had attracted Rs 1.89 lakh crore's worth of bids, but there was a crucial difference. Institutions that bid in the Reliance

Power IPO had to pay just 10 per cent on application while in the Coal India IPO they had to pay 100 per cent of the application amount.

This supported my long-standing theory that you did not really have to pamper institutional investors with favourable regulations. If they smell an opportunity to make money, they will definitely invest. The retail portion of the book was subscribed two times, again underscoring the fact that if the price was right, retail investors would be as keen as their institutional counterparts to invest.

None of the investors who put money in Coal India had any cause for disappointment. The stock opened at Rs 287, and ended the day at Rs 342, at a good 40 per cent premium to the issue price of Rs 245. The Sensex topped 21,000 after a gap of more than thirty-four months, but the rally seemed a hollow one to most of us. Corporate earnings growth had begun to lose steam, and none of the brokerages were adding staff, despite the boom in stock prices.

Conventional market wisdom has it that a blockbuster IPO usually signals the peak of a bull run. This was proved right in 2008 with Reliance Power's public issue. It turned out to be true again with the Coal India IPO. I thought the success of the Coal India issue would boost sentiment and draw more investors to the market. Besides, there was no massive build-up of positions in the derivatives market, as was the case in 2008. To me, frenzied retail participation is one of the most reliable signs of a market correction. There was no sign of that either. Still, the market began to flag after the listing of Coal India shares.

# 35

# The Iron Law of Averages

A loan-for-cash scam towards the end of November undermined market sentiment further. It involved Money Matters, a Mumbai-based NBFC, senior officials at LIC Housing Finance, LIC of India, and some public sector banks.

Money Matters had suddenly shot to fame over the last year or so. Its fast-talking and ambitious founder Rajesh Sharma had begun his career in the financial market from a hole-in-the-wall office at Fort in the late 1990s. A chartered accountant by profession, Sharma's skill at finding buyers for large blocks of shares of mid- and small-sized companies was much in demand with corporations.

Sharma was well networked with important fund managers, which helped him put through some difficult deals. In 2001-02, he is said to have befriended a senior official at a retail broking house that, in a few years, would be counted among the top brokerages in the country. Talk was that this official convinced some of his high net worth clients to buy the shares that Sharma was looking to sell. That turned out to be a major break for Sharma, and from then on, the size of his deals kept getting bigger.

But Sharma was a more active player in the opaque world of bonds, where he was known for his ability to find buyers for illiquid bonds. Sharma hit the big time in equity circles in 2007, when he managed to place large blocks of shares for Bank of Rajasthan and Deccan Aviation (which subsequently became Kingfisher Airlines) with institutional investors. Despite gaining acceptance in the more glamorous world of shares, Sharma appeared to be far more at ease in the debt market, which rarely made headlines.

Sharma's business model had now evolved to the point where his firm was arranging loans for some of the top corporate houses in the country. In 2007-08, the company's annual revenue was less than Rs 10 crore and net profit Rs 4.22 crore. By the first half of 2010-11, Money Matters had made a net profit of around Rs 75 crore on revenues of Rs 224 crore, sending its stock price soaring. The company's scorching pace of growth made Sharma a force to reckon with in the financial services industry. Naturally, it also fostered jealousy and resentment among his rivals, most of whom had been left far behind in the race. One of them, an erstwhile business partner of Sharma's, is said to have snitched about Sharma's 'business model' to the investigating agencies. It turned out that Sharma was bribing officials at state-owned banks to get them to sanction loans to his clients, many of them real estate companies. In some of the cases, Sharma was able to get the banks to sanction loans to real estate companies in excess of what they were eligible for.

Sharma was arrested by the CBI, along with Ramachandran Nair, the CEO of LIC Housing Finance, and officials at LIC,

Bank of India, Central Bank of India and Punjab National Bank. Barely a month before the scam was exposed, Money Matters had raised $100 million by placing shares for Rs 625 apiece with institutional investors, who included top names like Morgan Stanley, Wellington Asset Management, GMO and Fidelity. The stock, which was quoting below Rs 100 a year ago, surged to around Rs 700 by the time of the placement. A sevenfold rise in the stock price should have prompted potential investors to do some serious homework before buying into the issue. But that is the last thing most fund managers bother to do in a booming market.

I was tipped about the stock some months before all this, and managed to make a quick buck without staying invested for too long. My friend who had told me about the stock was confident that it would touch Rs 1,000 before the year ended. I would have hung on, but for the company deciding to offer shares to institutional investors. My experience has been that much of the action in a flavour-of-the-season stock happens before a share placement. I had almost doubled my initial investment in the stock and had no qualms about cashing out. Sharma's arrest sent the stock into a nosedive, one from which it never recovered. Between 23 November and 31 December, the stock plunged from Rs 663 to Rs 130. Fund managers who had subscribed to the placement had no way of getting out, as trading in the stock would be frozen every day for lack of buyers. Over the next five months, the stock would tumble below Rs 50.

While I had made a decent profit, the regulatory glare in the wake of the scam worried me. My trade in Money Matters was not too big by my own standards but would easily figure among the sizeable trades in the stock over the last six months. I had not benefited from any insider information, and I was confident of being able to prove that. But having to disclose my trade sheets to the regulator and answer their numerous questions was something I always found distressful.

In December 2010, SEBI investigated four companies and found that their promoters had joined hands with market operator Sanjay Dangi and his associate firms to ramp up their stock prices ahead of their capital-raising through share placements to institutional investors. SEBI would later give a clean chit to most of the companies named in the report, but the promoters and market operators could no longer afford to defy the regulator with impunity.

I would have liked to end the year on a winning note, but that was not to be. To my annoyance, the loss happened in an IPO. I was never too keen on IPOs anyway but I invested because some relationships mattered more to me than money.

Even as the market was going nowhere, a company by the name of A2Z Maintenance decided to come out with an IPO. A2Z's main business was installation of power distribution lines and substations. It was also into generating power from renewable energy sources, and managed solid waste for municipalities. But the company's main calling card was a 21 per cent stake held by billionaire investor Rakesh Jhunjhunwala. He had bought the stake in 2006 for around Rs 20 crore, and now, with the company going public, planned to take some money off the table.

The success of the Coal India IPO had clearly showed that pricing mattered more than market conditions. Still, the A2Z management decided to push their luck, confident that Jhunjhunwala's brand power would help command a hefty premium, despite strong indications from fund managers that they would invest only if they felt the issue was priced reasonably. Now, the definition of what is 'reasonable' depends on the prevailing market sentiment. In a bull market, no price is too high, and in fact, investors seem to get a kick out of buying IPOs at inflated prices. But in an uncertain market, they fuss about operating ratios, earnings growth and business models.

A2Z wanted to raise Rs 675 crore through issue of fresh shares; and some of the existing investors – Rakesh included – were looking to sell a portion of their holdings in the IPO. The total size of the issue – newly issued shares and shares offered by existing investors – was around Rs 860 crore, at Rs 400 a share. At that price, Jhunjhunwala's stake in the company was worth nearly Rs 500 crore – a return of 25 times for him in less than five years. He had offered 5 lakh shares in the IPO, enough to recoup his initial investment and still be left with plenty.

The company set a price band of Rs 400-410 for the issue, and even before it opened for bidding, raised Rs 125 crore by placing a portion of the issue with anchor investors at Rs 400 a share. But other institutional investors did not show the same enthusiasm, as they felt the issue was overpriced. Even HNIs were not excited about the issue.

A couple of days before the issue opened for bidding GB rang me, calling me for a chat over beer at Geoffrey's.

'Are you trying to sell A2Z to me?' I asked him after we ordered beer.

He grinned. 'I think we know each other well enough to the point of being able to read each other's thoughts.'

'Give me the pitch,' I said, smiling back.

'Bhaiyya is convinced this is a great company in the making,' GB said.

'I guess that seals the decision. But fund managers don't seem convinced, and to be frank, neither am I. The company seems to be asking for too much,' I said.

'You put too much faith in fund managers' ability to assess a company's worth,' he said.

'They may not be the final authority on valuation, but neither are they fools. Most of them made good money in the Coal India IPO, and it is not as if we have slipped back into a bear market. Still, they are reluctant to invest, and that says something,' I said, standing my ground.

'I won't push you beyond a point, Lala. But let me put it this way: it will make me happy if you bid for a decent chunk. Besides, don't forget you have made good money off Bhaiyya's ideas in the past,' GB said, sipping his beer. His voice now seemed to have lost some of its amiability.

I could sense his displeasure and tried to make amends quickly.

'You seem to have taken offence. I never said I would not invest. I just wanted you to convince me,' I said.

'I am not offended, Lala. But I cannot help feeling that you are getting a bit carried away by your success. Else you wouldn't be lecturing me about valuations,' GB said, and took a swig at his beer.

The unsaid line here was: '. . . else you wouldn't be lecturing Bhaiyya on valuations.'

The mug covered much of his face, and for a few seconds I could see only his eyes. They seemed cold, and the piercing look gave me the jitters. I am not saying that he was trying to intimidate me, but that look did unsettle me a bit. I thought

I was arguing a business point, but GB interpreted that as a sign of arrogance.

I quickly reached across and rested my palm on his elbow as a reconciliatory gesture.

'Rest assured it is nothing like that, Govindbhai, you know that I would never refuse you,' I said.

He smiled – a signal that all was forgiven.

'Glad to know that success has not changed you at all,' he said, and we both laughed.

The issue just about sailed through, mainly on support from Rakesh's friends and business associates who had made good money from his investment tips in the past and were convinced that the Rakesh magic would work for A2Z too. The institutional and retail portions of the book were undersubscribed, while the non-institutional portion was subscribed more than three times, helping make up the shortfall.

Still, the shares had a disastrous debut, opening at a discount and never going above the issue price. Rakesh bought 5 lakh shares in the market at Rs 352 apiece, hoping his purchase would attract fresh buyers and arrest the slide in the stock price. The trade did not hurt him, considering he had sold as many shares in the IPO for Rs 400 each. The stock finally ended the day at Rs 329, a good 18 per cent below the issue price.

Promoter Amit Mittal too jumped into the fray, buying close to 9 lakh shares at Rs 336 each. But both Rakesh's and Mittal's purchases only ended up providing an exit to investors looking to jump ship. It was widely expected that the stock would fare poorly on listing. The tepid response from institutions and retail during the bidding process meant there was no demand for the stock. As soon as the shares listed, HNIs who had invested using borrowed funds started selling out, and the stock price never recovered from that wave of selling. I was not surprised by the turn of events, and accepted the market's verdict calmly since my loss was not huge.

The importance of fair pricing of an issue was proved once again in the Punjab & Sind Bank offer. The IPO, which opened for bidding a few days after the A2Z issue closed, got subscribed over 50 times because investors felt it was reasonably priced. The stock, which listed exactly a week after A2Z's disastrous debut, surged 22 per cent in opening trade. It finally closed at Rs 127, a 6 per cent premium over the issue price of Rs 120.

# 36

# New Year of Little Cheer

Year 2011 began on a sombre note for the stock market bulls. The high-profile arrests in the 2G spectrum scam soured sentiment, sending stock prices crashing. Mid-cap and small-cap shares bore the brunt of the selling fury, and it most cases, promoters were paying for their past sins.

I was approached by a few promoters to help support their stock prices, but I declined, knowing that it was going to a futile effort. Stocks in which promoters had pledged sizeable portions of their holdings were hit the hardest. I got to be hear from industry sources that JC was in his element, busy hammering such stocks. The promoters of three companies – an infrastructure firm belonging to a conglomerate, a realty firm, and a brokerage firm – wrote to the regulator saying their shares were being hammered by a bear cartel, leading to unwarranted destruction of shareholder wealth. One firm personally named JC as the mastermind behind the bear attack.

One evening as I was driving back home, I rang up JC to check what he had to say about the charges against him.

I knew he would be savouring the publicity his actions had got him.

'Promoters are screaming murder and say JC the all-powerful is running their stocks to the ground,' I said as soon as he answered the call with a gruff 'hello'.

JC chuckled, and I could visualize the pleased look on his face.

'*Arre* no, Lala, market people and the media are just exaggerating. It is true that I am short on these stocks, but my positions are not as huge as everybody is making it out to be. In fact, these promoters are trying to cover their own follies by blaming me,' he said.

I knew he was not entirely wrong. But I loved to annoy him, and decided to prod further.

'I heard one of the promoters has sworn to make you cover your positions at twice the price you have short-sold,' I said.

'Is it? Which of them? Let them try, I am waiting. *Saale* @#★★$, do you hear any of them ever complaining to SEBI whenever their stocks rise to crazy levels? They never say that bull operators are ramping up their stock prices and that retail investors could get hurt if they buy the shares at those exorbitant prices. But the moment their stock prices fall, they claim that bears are destroying shareholder wealth. Reminds me of a primary school classroom where a student says: "Teacher, this boy is beating me."

'As for the brokerage firm promoter, his behaviour is the most appalling. A couple of years ago when I was trading through his firm and hammering other companies' stocks, he never protested even once that I was destroying shareholder value. Obviously, why would he bother when he was earning good commissions from me? But when I feel his company's stock is fair game, he goes whining to SEBI.

'I tell you, Lala, I have been at the receiving end so many times when I have been short on stocks. The promoters gang up with bull operators and manipulate the prices higher. Had they not done that, the prices would have followed their natural course and I would have made good money. But do I complain to SEBI about the promoters' misdeeds? No, I don't. I take my medicine like a man, and I don't understand why they can't do the same.'

JC had a point, but the promoters too had their reasons for being furious with him. My friends in the market told me JC had a knack for identifying companies where the promoters had pledged the most shares to raise money, and then would start hammering their stocks.

---

In March 2008, shares of Chennai-based Orchid Chemicals and Pharmaceuticals plunged 39 per cent in a single trading session as two NBFCs liquidated the shares that promoter Raghavendra Rao had pledged with them. The stock first started to weaken when the US investment bank Bear Sterns, which was grappling with its own problems in the wake of the sub-prime crisis in its home country, sold Orchid shares. When the stock fell, Rao failed to meet the margin call from his lenders, who began offloading the stock in the market.

The sale of the shares resulted in Rao's stake in the company falling from 24 per cent to 14 per cent, rendering the company vulnerable to a takeover. Ranbaxy-controlled Solrex used the crash in the share price to pick up a 12 per cent stake in the company, sparking buzz of a hostile takeover. Interestingly, Religare, one of the two NBFCs that had dumped Rao's shares in the open market, was part of the Ranbaxy group.

What probably saved Orchid was Ranbaxy itself selling out to Japan-based Daiichi Sankyo in August 2008. Solrex retained its stake in Orchid for a while, but gradually exited the stock over the next couple of years.

Rao may have been lucky to retain control of his company after coming within a hair's breadth of losing it, but Vijay Kantilal Sheth of Great Offshore, an offshore oilfield services firm, was not as fortunate. In May 2009, he earned the dubious distinction of becoming the first Indian promoter in India to cede control of his company as a result of his inability to repay the loans he had taken by pledging his shares.

Sheth had pledged his entire holding of roughly 15 per cent in the company with Bharati Shipyard. With the market in a bear grip, Great Offshore crashed from around Rs 545 in September 2008 to Rs 206 by early March 2009. Bharati Shipyard asked Sheth for additional collateral or part pre-payment of the loan, both of which he could not meet, and ended up losing control of his firm.

## 37

# Fudging and Pledging

Following the Satyam Computer accounting fraud, SEBI made it mandatory for companies to disclose the quantum of shares pledged by promoters. Understandably, promoters did not want the details of their share pledges to be made public as their stocks would become vulnerable to attacks by bear operators.

And howsoever strict the disclosure norms on pledged shares, they could be circumvented by promoters to some extent. For instance, promoters routinely hold shares in *benami* accounts, which are invisible to stock exchanges, investors and regulators. These accounts are maintained for a variety of reasons. In a rising market, the promoter could make money by selling shares in bulk from these accounts to fund houses. In a falling market, the promoter could buy shares of his company and store them in this account to stabilize the stock price.

Depending on their requirements, promoters pledged their shares with financiers, usually NBFCs, but at times with overseas investors too. Sometimes, what appears on paper as equity investments by lesser-known FIIs in many mid-cap companies are, in fact, structured share-pledge deals. The promoter transfers shares from his *benami* accounts to the FII's account and gets a loan against it. The promoter pays interest to this FII, either in the domestic or overseas market, as may be the arrangement. The advantage of this arrangement is that the promoter does not have to report to the stock exchanges that he has pledged his shares.

Bears are forever sniffing around for stocks where the promoters have pledged a substantial portion of their holdings and are using the money to ramp up their stock price.

Some promoters delayed reporting the pledge transaction to the exchanges by a few days so as to keep bears guessing about the price at which the shares were pledged. But operators like JC had their own informal information network to sniff out the price. This could be through somebody at the broking firm through which the promoter operated his stock, or somebody at the NBFC from which the promoter borrowed money. Once the price was known, it became easier to smash the stock price.

Still, share prices tend to revert to their fundamental value at some point. Just as a bull operator or a bull cartel cannot keep the price of a stock permanently high, bears cannot keep the prices depressed forever. Good quality stocks quickly find buyers in the event of a steep fall. If a stock takes a long time to recover from a bear attack, it is a good indication that the original price was inflated. I must add here that when the overall mood is bearish, share prices can stay subdued for longer than usual.

The bruising decline in stock prices had taken the swagger out of many a promoter, and SEBI too was giving them cause for sleepless nights. In mid-January, Reliance ADAG chairman Anil Ambani and four directors of the group paid Rs 50 crore to SEBI under a consent deal to settle a case of violation of FII regulations and overseas debt norms. This was the highest consent fee paid by any corporate group to SEBI so far. In the course of investigating a couple of suspicious P-note transactions by two FIIs, the regulator came across evidence that the funds raised by R-ADAG firms (later merged with Reliance Power) through external commercial borrowings and foreign currency convertible bonds were being invested in the Indian stock market. Under the consent deal, R-ADAG firms Reliance Infra and Reliance Natural Resources were barred from accessing the capital market for two years.

No corporate group now seemed beyond the reach of SEBI, which in its early days had been ridiculed with uncharitable monikers such as 'paper tiger' or 'toothless watchdog'. In July, SEBI dealt another blow to the market players to keep them on the straight and narrow, this time busting the business model of many broking firms that thrived on helping clients evade income tax.

These brokers would charge 5-6 per cent commission for providing fictitious profits/losses to their clients. This was not a bad deal for tax evaders who could still save 25 per cent after paying the commission. For brokerages, this was a far more lucrative business than plain vanilla broking services, which earned them only 0.01-0.25 per cent per trade.

The brokerages used to do this by shuffling the shares between client accounts at the end of the day's trading. Sometimes, when there are too many transactions to be executed, brokers mistakenly enter orders in the wrong client's account. The stock exchanges allowed brokers to rectify such errors by shifting the shares to the correct client account. Over a period of time, brokers began to misuse this concession, shifting trades from one account to another to help clients either evade tax or launder unaccounted money.

SEBI and the tax authorities soon got wind of the game being played, and a penalty was imposed if the proportion of wrong account trades exceeded 5 per cent of the total monthly turnover of the broker. The new rule benefited many individual investors who were otherwise being short-changed by unscrupulous 'relationship managers'. Many HNIs who subscribed to portfolio management services of broking firms would grant brokers a 'power of attorney' to trade in their accounts and generate profits. The relationship manager, in connivance with the branch head, would sometimes shift some of the profitable trades to another account, and under-declare the profits to the clients. Once the new rule came into effect, the number of 'wrong' client code trades fell dramatically, and tax evaders had to look for another route to dodge the taxman. September fetched another rap on the knuckles for promoters and investors looking to game the system at the expense of small investors. SEBI pulled up seven Indian companies and a handful of 'foreign institutional investors' for trying to manipulate stock prices through GDR issues. GDRs are similar to shares, except that they can only be issued and traded in overseas markets. But the foreign investors holding GDRs can surrender them to the company and request to be issued shares of an equivalent value that can be traded in India. This process is known as 'conversion of GDRs into shares'. From the time the Indian market was thrown open to FIIs in the early 1990s, there was always a premium attached to stocks in which overseas investors had a sizeable stake. The modus operandi for stock manipulation through GDRs went like this: Shady companies would announce GDRs, which shady FIIs would subscribe to. There were operators in Dubai who specialized in such services and had dummy FII accounts, which had subscribed to the GDR issue. The money that the FIIs invested in the GDRs would belong to the promoter himself, and had been taken out of India and parked in tax havens before it was routed to the FIIs through a series of spurious transactions.

The FIIs who had subscribed to the issues would convert the GDRs into the underlying shares within a couple of months, and sell them to a group of entities related to the GDR-issuing companies. The money that the FIIs got through this sale would be transferred back to the promoters' overseas accounts through another series of deceptive transactions. The FIIs would get an 8–10 per cent commission for lending their names for the transaction.

Back in India, the front entities would artificially boost volumes in the stock, attracting retail investors. Once there was sufficient retail interest in the stock, the front entities would slowly offload their holdings. The GDR manipulation by Indian promoters came as no surprise to me since I had been hearing about such activities for a while now.

The GDR route was a good way to legitimize money stashed abroad, and to make some easy gains too in the bargain. More cases of sham GDRs would surface in the coming months. But proving the charges was the toughest part for SEBI, even if it was easy to identify instances of suspicious dealings.

In 2013, SEBI would lift the ban on the Mavi Investment Fund, saying it could not decisively establish the charge against the fund that it had aided the promoters of companies that issued sham GDRs. SEBI had tried to investigate the beneficial owners of the Mavi Investment Fund, but was unable to make much progress as the fund gave sketchy responses to SEBI's queries. Mavi's defence was that its investors were banks and financial institutions. And since these institutional investors in turn had a large number of investors who kept changing on a day-to-day basis, it was impossible to get information related to the beneficial owners.

SEBI tried to source the details from the Financial Services Commission of Mauritius where Mavi was registered. But the details provided by the FSC were not very different from what Mavi had given to SEBI. Ultimately, the Indian regulator had to back off.

Interestingly, Mavi's name had also figured in the probe into the 2G telecom spectrum scam Mavi was one of the firms through which funds were routed from Switzerland by the scam-accused to buy stakes in a company that had been allotted telecom spectrum through an opaque procedure.

# 38

# Dalal Street's Finest All-rounder

One September morning in 2011, I was glancing through the stock quotes page of a business daily when my attention was drawn to the stock price of VST (formerly Vazir Sultan Tobacco), which owns the Charminar brand of cigarettes, the third largest cigarette company in India.

It had hit a record high of Rs 1,350 the previous day. I was immediately reminded of Radhakishan Damani and his failed bid for control of the company in 2001. I checked the stock exchange website to see if Radhakishan was still holding on to the roughly 26 per cent stake in VST he had accumulated over the years. Sure enough, he was, and that stake was now worth Rs 520 crore.

That was an almost 15-fold return from the time Radhakishan first started accumulating the shares way back in 2000. Back then, the reclusive investor had stunned the market by making a hostile bid for cigarette maker VST, which had British American Tobacco (BAT) as its single largest shareholder with a 32 per cent stake. Through his investment arm Bright Star Investments, Radhakishan had accumulated a shade below 15 per cent in the company in the course of the previous year at an average price of Rs 88 per share. He was willing to pay Rs 112 per share for an additional 20 per cent in the company, at a Rs 26 premium to the market price of the stock on the day he announced the bid.

Even Radhakishan's closest associates were surprised by this act of aggression, which was completely at odds with his soft-spoken and reclusive nature. The offer document mentioned that the acquirer's (Bright Star Investments') sole intention was to increase its stake in the company. While Radhakishan may not have had any plans to run the company, his stake would have risen above that of BAT, had the open offer been successful.

Market-watchers felt Radhakishan Damani must have bet on BAT not being able to retaliate with a counter offer, as the Foreign Investment Promotion Board had twice in the past struck down BAT's application to increase its stake in VST. Strangely, it was ITC, through its investment arm Russell Credit, which jumped in with a counter-offer of Rs 115 per share. SEBI delayed clearing Bright Star's offer, as R. K. Damani was being investigated for his alleged role in the bear cartel accused of triggering the stock market crash immediately after the Union Budget of 2001.

And while ITC and BAT had sparred in the past and shared a far from harmonious relationship, BAT tacitly supported ITC's offer. Also, ITC was buying VST shares from the open market. Like Bright Star, ITC too said it wanted to own a significant stake in the company and did not have any intention of gaining management control.

A messy bidding war ensued, and it soon became evident that there were far too many obstacles, regulatory and cultural, for Radhakishan to be able to walk away with the much-coveted prize. Bright Star upped its offer price to Rs 118 per share, in response to which ITC increased its offer price to Rs 126 per share. Everybody expected Radhakishan to withdraw from the fray since he would not have been able to sustain a bidding war with a company of ITC's financial muscle.

Once again, Radhakishan surprised the market by raising the price and size of his bid to Rs 151 per share for 30 per cent of the company. Still, he failed to win over banks, insurance companies and financial institutions, which together held 22 per cent in the company.

Finally, when Bright Star's open offer did commence, VST advanced its book closure date by a day, just before the last date of the open offer. Bright Star and its investment banker ASK Raymond James cried foul, alleging that it was a deliberate move to thwart investors from buying VST shares from the open market and tendering them in the open offer.

Through the open offer, Bright Star managed to increase its stake in VST to around 20 per cent (and by another 6 per cent over the next few years), but Radhakishan's dream to own a controlling stake in VST remained just that, a dream. Some argue that there are enough stocks that have given better returns since then. That is a fair point. But here is what makes Radhakishan one of the best value investors in living memory: a back-of-the-envelope calculation shows that the acquisition cost of VST shares for Bright Star was sub-zero, considering the hefty dividend pay-outs over the last nine years. Between July 2002 and July 2011, Bright Star – the investment arm of Damani which held the VST shares –

pocketed Rs 71.36 crore through annual dividends ranging between 45 per cent and 450 per cent. This was more than the Rs 63 crore Bright Star had shelled out over the years to buy 26 per cent in VST.

I am not sure if Radhakishan got over his disappointment at being muscled out by the BAT-ITC combine. But if he were to keep his ego aside, Radhakishan had every reason to feel good about the deal. I wondered if Damani would have rolled up his sleeves and engaged himself in the day-to-day running of the tobacco firm had he got control of it.

Among all the market-men of his generation, Damani is the one I respect the most. I can think of many names on Dalal Street who are good at identifying potential multi-bagger stocks. But I cannot think of anybody else in the country who can identify a good business for investment and is also competent enough to run a business if it comes to that. Damani had already proved his entrepreneurial and managerial skills with the success of his retail chain D-Mart, which he built from scratch. A remarkable feat, considering the fierce competition from much bigger players in the sector. I knew somebody who had worked with Damani on setting up D-Mart. He told me that Damani was involved with every aspect of the venture, even personally doing the rounds of Crawford Market and Musafirkhana (in South Mumbai) for wares, scouting for variety and low prices. Damani's investment philosophy was simple: no matter how great the business, you had to buy the company at the right price to be able to get good returns.

He extended that philosophy to the running of D-Mart. He knew that customers would be looking for variety in his stores. But to build customer loyalty, he knew he would have to offer variety at a competitive price. After all, even the wealthiest of his customers loved a good deal, and they would certainly want their friends to know about the deals too. This approach paid off handsomely.

That he owned the real estate on which stood his stores helped Damani in the following years to keep a lid on operating costs. He had bought the land when it was not too expensive.

# 39

# FCCB

The volatile market trend for much of 2011 and 2012 spelled trouble for many mid-cap companies, which had binged on capital at the peak of the 2007 bull run.

These companies had raised funds through an instrument called the FCCB for capacity expansion, acquisitions, and part retirement of expensive debt. As the name suggested, the money would be raised in a foreign currency and repaid in the same currency.

The market was awash with funds at that time. The golden rule about raising funds is that you must go for it when it is available, whether you need it or not.

Promoters could have raised money by selling shares, since their stock prices were quite high. But they did not want to dilute their holdings in their companies as the stock market frenzy was expected to continue for a while.

At the same time, promoters were wary of loading their balance sheets with too much debt.

FCCBs turned out to be the answer to their prayer, as they promised the best of both worlds. FCCB or convertible, in market parlance, had features of debt as well of equity. As in the case of bonds, there was an interest charge and a fixed tenure. The key difference was that the interest would accumulate over the tenure of the bond and only had to be paid when the bonds matured. The bonds were usually of three- and five-year tenures. There was a pre-decided conversion price at which the bondholders could convert the instruments into shares at maturity. The conversion price was at a 15-20 per cent premium to the current market price of the stock.

For both the promoter and the bondholder, the preferred outcome would be the shares quoting at a premium to the conversion price when the FCCBs matured. The FCCB holder would convert the bonds into shares, and sell them in the open market and make a profit.

While going in for the FCCBs, almost all promoters assumed that the debt would not have to be repaid as the stock price would be higher than the conversion price. Also, they thought the rupee would continue to strengthen against the dollar.

Prior to announcing an FCCB issue, many promoters would join hands with market operators and jack up the stock price. This was to ensure a high conversion price (since it was at a 15-20 per cent premium to the prevailing market price at the time of the FCCB issue) and improve sentiment for the stock.

It is hard to believe that the fund managers subscribing to the FCCB issues were not aware of what the promoters were up to. Strangely, no tough questions about the companies' business models or stock valuations were asked.

But the business fundamentals of many companies and the true nature of their promoters were exposed as a result of the meltdown of 2008. And the stock prices never really recovered from the bruising sell-off. Despite the market rallying in 2009 and 2010, the stock prices of these companies were unlikely to be anywhere near the conversion price at the time of the bonds maturing.

For the first time, promoters had to think about repaying the FCCB holders as the bonds were unlikely to be converted into equity. So confident were the promoters that the bonds would never have to repaid that they did not think of making any provision for such an eventuality. By then, earnings had begun to come under pressure for a variety of reasons like high input costs and weakening demand. In quite a few cases, the companies did not have credible revenues or genuine cash flows to begin with. They were only good at inflating their stock prices by colluding with market operators. But that business model was broken. Companies would now have to refinance the FCCBs if they were to avert a default. In simple terms, they had to raise fresh money to pay off the existing debtors. Raising equity capital was out of the question, considering the battered stock prices; promoters would have to dilute much more of their stake than what they would have liked to.

And then came the final blow in the form of a nasty surprise on the currency front. During the bull market of 2007, the rupee had been steadily firming up against the dollar, and it was widely expected that the trend would continue. But as India's economic fundamentals weakened from 2011, the rupee started to weaken against the dollar, and fell by more than 20 per cent from the level seen in 2007. This spelt more trouble for the companies, as they now needed more rupees to repay the dollars.

Of course, as a desperate measure, the companies could choose to default on their obligation. But that would mean never again being able to raise capital in the international market.

Some companies offered to buy back the bonds from the holders. The deal suited the companies because the price of the bonds had fallen sharply on concerns about their repaying capacity.

Other companies tried to negotiate with the bondholders to restructure the terms of the bonds, trying to get them to settle for a lower interest rate while offering to lower the conversion price of the stock to a level not too far from the current market price.

A few companies that were struggling to convince their investors to restructure the terms of the bonds tried to play the old game of manipulating the stock price. The promoter of a mid-cap telecom firm, which had defaulted on its FCCB, took the help of a market operator to pull up the stock price so that its bondholders would agree to a revised deal.

---

By the end of 2011, a series of bad bets had left me shaken. It would be a while before I regained my confidence. I had reduced the size of my trades the last couple of months, but that was not helping much. Perhaps I was being a bit overcritical of myself. It was a tough year for almost everybody in the market, and few had made profits worth mentioning. But I suspected I was beginning to suffer a burnout. One way of fixing it would be to take a break from the market and not trade at least for a month, however strong the temptation. I decided to indulge in the small pleasures of life I had denied myself for so long and become a dispassionate observer of the market when there was time to spare. A month-long voluntary exile from the market, if you may call it that, might rejuvenate me. I was not certain if this self-medication would solve my problem, but then I had nothing to lose.

I told Bina about my plan, and she was delighted. But she was a bit sceptical too.

'I can't imagine you staying away from the market for more than a week; by the eighth day you will be suffering withdrawal symptoms and dying to get behind the trading screen,' she said with mock annoyance.

'Not this time, my dear. If nothing else, I will stick to my plan just to prove you wrong,' I said.

'But I fear the allure of your mistress will easily outweigh your desire to prove the wife wrong,' Bina persisted.

'The mistress will have to wait for a month,' I said.

'Really? I will believe it only at the end of the month,' Bina said, still not fully convinced.

I had bought a plot of land at Murbad six months ago. I wanted to spend my weekends there and grow vegetables. The turbulence in the market had kept me busy and I never got around to doing it. I finally had time on my hands to pursue my dream.

My morning walks had stopped after trading hours were advanced by an hour to 9 a.m. I used to work out on the treadmill, but that was no match to enjoying the pleasant morning air in the company of my friends in the housing society I lived in.

I also realized I had not been in touch with many of my relatives for a while now. Thanks to Facebook, I had reconnected with some of my close school friends, but had not met up with them despite promising them I would. I wanted to learn a bit of basic cooking too. For that I could not have a better tutor than Bina. And, as she managed the house so well, I had never troubled myself with the academic and personal progress of my children. I would now get to know them better as a father. Then there were the many movies I had missed last year. And suddenly, it seemed a month would be too little for the plans I had drawn up.

But even as I was busy with morning walks, movies, cooking and social calls, I kept track of the market. I got back to work in the first week of February 2012, fully refreshed from my month-long break.

Even though the economy was showing signs of slowing and the government was unable to push through any major reforms, the market continued its climb. But not for long. The mood changed for the worse towards the end of February, but the IPO of commodity bourse Multi Commodity Exchange (MCX) got an overwhelming response. MCX was the first exchange in India to go public, and given its dominant position in the commodity space, investors were excited about the issue. The plus-Rs 650-crore issue, priced at Rs 1,032 a share, the upper end of the price band for bidding, was subscribed 54 times. Notably, the retail portion of the book was subscribed 24 times, validating the theory that there would always be takers for a quality issue irrespective of general market conditions.

# 40

# The Heavy Hand of the State

It rained bad news in March, beginning with ONGC's botched offer for sale (OFS) through which the government hoped to sell a stake of 5 per cent to raise approximately Rs 12,700 crore. The issue had to be bailed out by LIC, which had to soak up almost 90 per cent of the shares on offer in the absence of demand from other institutional investors, particularly FIIs. The stock had witnessed a decent rise through January and February, leading many to believe that the issue would be a success. But it turned out that LIC had been buying the shares in the open market during that period, most likely to support the price ahead of the offer for sale. It had picked up 15.7 crore shares between 1 January and 8 February but did not disclose this to the exchanges till much later. However, FIIs would have known through their network of brokers that LIC was the buyer, and so refused to bite the bait during the OFS.

It was very likely that LIC was trying to support the ONGC stock price at the behest of the government. Nothing else could explain why the insurer chose to delay disclosure of the purchases to the stock exchanges. The episode showed both the government and the regulator in a poor light. Would SEBI have overlooked a similar violation by some other institutional investor?

Including the 37 crore shares of ONGC it picked up through the OFS, LIC had invested roughly Rs 15,000 crore in ONGC in less than three months. This was a substantial chunk of the insurer's annual kitty for investment in the stock market. Many market veterans began to wonder if LIC too would go the US-64 way, given the manner in which the government was meddling in its investment decisions.

The Union Budget in mid-March did little to cheer up the market. In fact, two proposals in the Budget made FIIs see red. One related to an amendment to the Income Tax Act allowing for taxing past transactions in which the underlying asset was in India, even if the firm controlling that asset was based abroad and the transaction had taken place outside India. The other was for the introduction of General Anti-Avoidance Rules (GAAR). GAAR empowered the Income Tax department to deny tax benefits to an FII if they had reason to believe that a transaction was carried out exclusively for the purpose of avoiding tax. Many FIIs had set up shell companies in Mauritius and were routing their investments into India through those companies, taking advantage of India's tax treaty with Mauritius to avoid paying short-term capital gains tax.

The rattled FIIs rallied under the banner of the Asian Securities Industry and Financial Markets Association (ASIFMA) and wrote a strongly worded letter to Finance Minister Pranab Mukherjee, warning that they would pull out en masse if the 'tax uncertainty' was not resolved. This was the first instance of foreign investors writing an explicitly threatening letter to the finance minister that I was aware of. India does need foreign capital, but it cannot have foreign investors dictating its financial policies.

ASIFMA had a suggestion for the minister with respect to GAAR: don't apply GAAR to 'small investments'. By 'small investments', ASIFMA meant a stake of 10 per cent or less in a listed Indian company. But that was absurd, since no FII could anyway hold more than 10 per cent in a listed Indian company. In effect, ASIFMA was saying that GAAR should not be applicable at all on stock market transactions by FIIs, whether or not some of them were abusing the Mauritius route to dodge short-term capital gains tax. To its credit, the government stood by its decisions while assuring foreign investors that the tax rules would be fairly interpreted.

# 41

# A New Entrant to the Game

After many regulatory hurdles and much legal wrangling, MCX-SX finally launched its equity trading platform in February 2013. Market conditions were far from ideal for a third stock exchange, though Jignesh Shah & Co were forever arguing that investors were getting a raw deal from incumbents BSE and NSE. Jignesh was convinced that the entry of his exchange would help grow the number of investors in the country. Not for once did I believe that theory. Not that I doubted Shah's acumen or his zeal. I mean, people don't start investing in shares just because there is a new exchange on the block. To me it appeared more likely that as the economy grew and more companies raised capital, the universe of investors would expand, benefiting stock exchanges like MCX-SX. It would not be the other way round, with a new exchange encouraging companies to go public and fire up the economy! At best, MCX-SX would be able to snatch business from rival exchanges by offering incentives to traders and investors. But that would not be the same as growing the market.

The rivals had deeper pockets and were well placed to promptly match any inducements that MCX-SX may have to offer. The broking industry was in a terrible shape because the client base had shrunk considerably after the meltdown of 2008, and brokerage firms were poaching each other's clients by offering ridiculously low rates. They still could not win client loyalty as the client would trade with whichever broker offered him the best rate. Of course, the profit margins for stock exchanges were much fatter – 35-40 per cent – than for brokerages. Some market observers were worried that it would turn out to be a race to the bottom if the stock exchanges decided to relax margin requirements to attract more members.

Given Shah's impressive track record in the commodities market, many anticipated he would rewrite the rules of the stock exchange game too. After all, he had managed to take on the powerful regulator SEBI and had emerged successful from the scrap. Shah's business sense, ambitiousness and political connections would see MCX-SX outstripping its rivals in the not-so-distant future, they thought.

For MCX-SX, the key to success lay in how soon it would be able to crack the liquidity code. More than anything else, it is the depth of the order book (liquidity, in market parlance) that is the deciding factor for a trader's or investor's choice of exchange to place his trades on. The more liquid or the more the number of buyers/sellers in a stock, the easier it is to trade large chunks of shares without impact on the price.

But creating the optimum level of liquidity is the toughest part. If an exchange is not able to do it quickly enough, it will be doomed to trail the market leader. Liquidity has the potential to perpetuate virtuous cycles as well as vicious ones. Once depth on a certain scale is achieved, it attracts more players, and this further improves the depth, which in turn attracts more players. On the downside, lack of liquidity prompts players to look elsewhere for better spreads, leading to even lower liquidity, which in turn deters even more players.

BSE's F&O segment is a classic example of how much liquidity matters. Having ceded the first-mover advantage to NSE in this space through its own blundering, BSE has not been able to catch up despite doing everything possible to attract trading members.

With MCX-SX flagging off operations, high-volume traders like me were in demand. The exchange wanted us to route a small part of our business through it. Competition in any industry is welcome, and though it would be a while before MCX-SX came anywhere close to matching the depth on NSE and BSE, quite a few traders agreed to help out the exchange. Of course, it was not purely out of charity. If MCX-SX grew in strength it would increase the bargaining powers of traders and brokers as they would now have a third exchange to choose from. Also, if the exchange did well in a couple of years' time, people like me who had supported it during its initial days could stake claim to a favour or two.

There were limits to which we could help, simply because the market had been quite volatile since the start of the year. The macroeconomic and policy environment was terrible, to say the least, and it did not look as though things would change any time soon.

Adding to the swings in the market was Fed chief Ben Bernanke's statement that the Fed was planning to cut down on the quantum of its monthly bond purchases that served as a monetary stimulus for the economy. Global markets went into a tizzy, as large dollops of liquidity resulting from the Fed's easy money policy had found their way around the globe and inflated asset prices. With the Fed calling time on its quantitative easing (QE) programme, investors were worried about a sudden drying up of an important source of global liquidity.

The dollar suddenly strengthened as foreign investors pulled out money from emerging markets – hurting their currencies – and put their money in US government bonds on which they were getting better yields. As the rupee weakened, FIIs started pulling money out of Indian equities, setting off a vicious cycle. The more heavily FIIs sold, the greater the pressure on the rupee, which in turn led to another round of selling as other FIIs tried to take out their money before the rupee weakened further.

To deter speculation in the rupee, RBI started announcing measures to make it costlier to borrow. Anybody who is bullish on the dollar, and by extension bearish on the rupee, needs to sell rupees first to buy those dollars. It is a rewarding trade as long as appreciation of the dollar more than offsets the cost of borrowing rupees. When the borrowing cost of the rupee increases, returns from this trade become unattractive.

The impact of this development was felt in the stock market. Many traders, including I, had been heavily long on private sector banks for the last many months since mid-2012. The bets had paid off handsomely, as the stocks kept climbing higher after periodic corrections. Within the banking sector, private sector players were the clear favourites of the market because of the superior quality of their books compared with those of their hapless public sector counterparts. For too long now, private sector banks had become a sort of one-way bet for traders; you had to be really unlucky to lose money on them.

It was a rude awakening for the bulls then, when RBI's measures pushed up the cost of wholesale deposits on which the private sector players were so heavily dependent. The hardest hit were the so-called new-generation private sector banks like Yes Bank, IndusInd Bank and Kotak Bank, which had much smaller savings and current account bases.

The stocks dropped off the cliff, and for many of the bulls in these stocks, a big chunk of the profits made over the last year were wiped out within a few days. The fall in these stocks was exacerbated by the leveraged positions built up in the derivatives segment, as too many bulls had piled on in the hope of making some easy money. There is never an assured-return stock in the market, and everybody is only too aware of it. But once in a while, players tend to forget this rule and it is then left to the market to harshly remind them about it.

RBI continued to put other curbs in place to bolster the rupee, such as higher duties on gold to deter imports, but the currency still continued to sink slowly. With the stock and currency markets in a tizzy, conspiracy theorists had a field day. One theory doing the rounds was that the government was holding RBI back from aggressively defending the rupee. While the RBI was announcing one measure after the other to prop up the rupee, some currency traders read between the lines to conclude that the signals from RBI suggested its heart was not in the battle.

These theorists reasoned that politicians and industrialists were looking to bring back their illicit funds stashed abroad, and the rupee was being allowed to weaken so that they could convert their dollars at the best exchange rate. And the black money was being brought back because the secrecy laws were no longer the bulletproof shield of immunity they had been in the past, said the theorists. Governments globally were putting pressure on banks in tax havens to disclose the details of customers to check for their residents suspected of flouting tax rules. The black money was being routed back to the country to also feed the politicians who would need hard cash to fight the general elections coming up in April 2014, they added.

The furore over black money in India had resulted in authorities here knocking at the doors of countries that were popular destinations for black money. Nothing came out of these expeditions, but suddenly there was nothing like a safe haven any more as far as black money account holders were concerned.

In the monetary policy review on 30 July, the RBI policy document had admitted that the country was caught in the classic 'impossible trinity' trilemma, where it was grappling with weak growth, high inflation and a weak currency. RBI said it was temporarily shifting focus away from growth and inflation to address the weakness in the currency. But just a few lines above this the document said the current policy stance was intended to address the risks to the rupee and thereby to the economy, address risks to growth, guard against inflation and ensure adequate liquidity in the system.

'That was a dead giveaway that the RBI is juggling too many balls at the same time, and would have to drop at least one of them,' my friend Sherlock said a couple of months later at one of our beer sessions. 'And that ball is most likely to be currency, despite the central bank's claim to the contrary.'

Among the factors blunting RBI's counter-attack was the steady increase in crude oil prices because of the conflict in Syria. The country could do without gold imports, but not without oil imports. Matters on the currency front climaxed on 28 August when the rupee crashed 256 paise against the dollar in a single day, the steepest fall in over eighteen years. It touched a new low of Rs 68.85 to the dollar, and many foreign banks were predicting that it would sink somewhere close to Rs 75 to the dollar by the end of the year. Stocks went into a free fall as doubts arose about the ability of the government to service its foreign debt. Companies with sizeable dollar debts were hammered on the bourses.

One of the stock market maxims is to buy when there is blood on the streets. Looking at the prices some quality stocks were going for, there could not have been a better opportunity to load up if you were willing to take a two-three-year view. I am no whiz at reading balance sheets, studying industry trends and then investing for the long term. For that I usually rely on the wisdom of some of my analyst friends, whose judgement I respect. I bought decent chunks of a few old-economy stocks, which I thought were going cheap.

But every panic seems like a different one, just as every bull market appears to be different from the previous one. There had been panic on this scale in 2008 and again in early 2009. On those occasions the problems were largely confined to stock market players and some highly dubious companies. There was nothing hugely wrong with the economy. This time, the problem was the economy itself. If the country suffered a rating downgrade and struggled to service its foreign debt, there was no saying how ugly things could get.

September saw a change of guard at RBI. Former IMF chief economist Raghuram Rajan formally took charge as RBI governor, replacing Duvvuri Subbarao, who had had a tumultuous five years in the hot seat. The announcement had already been made in August, and the market had high expectations from the new governor, whose calling card was that he had warned of the sub-prime mortgage as early as in 2005, and that too at a gathering where the US Fed chief of the time Alan Greenspan was present.

On his very first day in office, Rajan announced a bunch of proposals that helped boost confidence in the money and stock markets. Two among them stood out. One was to attract deposits from NRIs and the other was to sell dollars directly to oil marketing companies, which needed the currency for importing oil. Oil companies had to buy dollars from time to time to pay their import bills, and whenever they bought dollars from the open market, it would push up the cost of the dollars. By selling the dollars directly to oil marketing companies, RBI could ensure that the rupee did not weaken further on account of the extra demand for dollars in the market.

Neither of these measures was unconventional; in fact, RBI had deployed them in the past whenever the rupee was under pressure. In August 1998, when the rupee had weakened following the economic sanctions by the US and some other developed nations after the Pokhran tests, RBI had issued Resurgent India Bonds to attract deposits from NRIs and People of Indian Origin. The response was overwhelming, with the RBI collecting around $4.2 billion through these bonds. But Rajan brought a crucial variation to the NRI deposit scheme. NRIs were paid 3.5 per cent above the market rate for their dollars. The move turned out to be a masterstroke though Rajan much later confessed that it was not his idea and that he had initially thought of it as a stupid measure.

There were many other measures announced by Rajan, such as the promise of announcing new bank licenses shortly, debt market reforms and permission to banks to raise more foreign capital. The stock market was fired up by these announcements. It was anyway looking for some confidence-boosting signals. Rajan already had an impeccable track record, and the proposals announced on his very first day in office sent out a clear message that here was a man in a hurry.

There was no looking back for the market after that. FIIs rushed in to buy, and bears were forced to square up their short positions, mostly at a loss. From 28 August – the day the rupee fell the hardest and to its lowest level – to the third week of September, the Sensex surged an astounding 3,000 points.

You might think that I am either bragging about getting my calls on the market right most of the time, or that I am incredibly lucky. Let me assure you, it is neither. The law of averages spares nobody, however skilled or lucky a person may claim to be. The gains from the September rebound helped me make up for the bruising losses I suffered in two stocks – Financial Technologies India Limited (FTIL) and MCX – just the month before. I had trading positions as well as a small investment in each of the stocks. The returns had been average, but I was acting as a market-maker in the stocks at somebody's behest. I would buy shares when the price fell and sell them when it rose.

My losses would be compensated in cash, in case I were to incur any losses. If I made profits, I had to part with some of it. On the whole, it was a profitable transaction for me, since I was being paid to generate volumes in the stocks, and the fluctuations in prices did not hurt me much, even though they did not earn me gigantic returns.

But trouble erupted from the least expected quarter. FTIL had a subsidiary called National Spot Exchange Limited (NSEL), which had been operational since 2007. NSEL was an electronic version of the local *mandi*, meant to help commodity farmers and commodity traders find buyers from across the country for their produce at the best possible prices. As the name suggested, NSEL was to be a spot market where farmers/mill owners/traders could sell their produce directly to the buyers, collect their money and walk away. Forward dealings of any kind were banned. But in the absence of any regulatory supervision, NSEL slowly mutated into a forward market. Claiming to be a spot exchange, NSEL escaped the scanner of the Forward Markets Commission (FMC) for a long time, since FMC's mandate was to regulate forward trading in commodities.

In theory, the sellers would deposit their produce in designated warehouses, and get a warehouse receipt certifying the quality and quantity of the produce. They could sell these receipts, and the buyers could go to the warehouse with the receipts and collect the wares. The commodities that could be traded included bullion (gold, silver, platinum), agri-products (cereals, fibres, spices, paddy, sugar) and metals (steel, copper).

NSEL's first violation of the rules lay in allowing trading in products without government clearance. The second, and more damaging, violation was its introduction of 'paired contracts' to sidestep the rule banning forward contracts. NSEL was now no longer a pure spot exchange connecting sellers with buyers. It had become a platform where commodity farmers/traders could raise working capital till they managed to find a buyer for their produce at a price of their liking.

The paired contracts allowed them to borrow funds through a two-legged transaction. In the first leg, the seller would enter into a T+2 contract where he would sell his produce to the buyer at a certain price. The buyer had to pay up on the second day of the trade being put through. At the same time when this trade was being put through, the buyer would enter into a T+35 contract, selling the produce back to the commodity farmer/trader at a price slightly higher than he had bought it for. This, in effect, was the interest charge the seller was paying the buyer for the funds.

For example, a commodity seller would sell his produce to the buyer for Rs 100 in the T+2 leg and agree to buy back the produce from the buyer for Rs 101 a good 35 days later. Interestingly, the commodity seller never bought back the produce on the 35th day. The transaction would get carried forward, with the seller agreeing to pay additional interest. This cycle was repeated for months on end without the commodities ever moving out of the warehouses. The annualized rate of interest worked out to 14–15 per cent, which was much higher than traditional bank deposit rates.

The so-called 'buyers' of the commodities were no longer genuine buyers of commodities but investors looking to earn a return of 12–15 per cent on their funds. Brokerages started marketing this product as something of an assured-return scheme, where the expected returns could only be higher and never lower. The brokerages too gained from this racket, as they would lend funds to their clients at 12 per cent, which would then be invested in the paired contracts earning 15 per cent. Every month, when the contracts were rolled forward, the brokerages would deduct their interest charge and credit the rest to their clients' accounts.

The 'buyers' did not realize their counterparties were no longer genuine sellers of commodities. The 'sellers' were now mostly, or entirely, entities seeking to borrow money at 14–15 per cent to deploy it elsewhere for bigger returns. As subsequent investigations showed, there were around 13,000 investors who were lending money to twenty-five borrowers on NSEL.

It never occurred to anybody how the same stock of sugar, cumin, castor oil, paddy, raw wool and castor seed could be pledged for months on end without their quality deteriorating over time. Theoretically, if the borrower chose to default after a few months, the lender would have been in a soup because he would not have been able to recover the original value of the commodities if he were to take possession of them and sell them.

But the borrowers never defaulted on their interest payments and the investors were quite happy with that. They were only bothered about the interest rates, and certainly did not want a situation where they would have to sell the goods in the warehouses to recover their money.

Murmurs about how NSEL was a vyaj badla platform masquerading as a commodities spot exchange had begun doing the rounds. The Ministry of Consumer Affairs finally woke up – belatedly – and in July ordered NSEL to stop issue of fresh contracts and settle all outstanding contracts on their due dates instead of allowing them to be carried forward.

That triggered what was initially thought to be a 'payment crisis', but was actually the exchange's death knell, exposing the scam underlying transactions on it. The borrowers did not have the funds to repay the lenders on the due dates. At stake was around Rs 5,600 crore of investor money to be repaid. NSEL had a settlement guarantee fund (SGF), and exchange officials tried to pacify jittery investors saying the exchange would honour their trades even if the borrowers did not. But that turned out to be a false assurance. Initially, the exchange claimed that it had around Rs 840 crore in the SGF, but a few days later said there was only Rs 65 crore. This revealed that the exchange did not have a credible risk management system. The exchange then claimed there was enough collateral (commodities) in the warehouses to repay the investors.

But the full extent of the scam became clear only a few days later when the exchange began checking the warehouses for the commodities stocked in them. The majority of the receipts turned out to be fake as the quantity of the goods in the warehouses was just a fraction of what was mentioned on the receipts. In some cases, the commodities had already been pledged to banks, but receipts had still not been issued against them. Initially, NSEL CEO Anjani Sinha said he and his management were responsible for the lapses in risk management and operations that had led to the crisis. But he later retracted his statement, saying FTIL founder Jignesh Shah was fully aware of the happenings at NSEL.

Many thought it would not be too hard to recover the funds as there were only twenty-fourborrowers in all. But many of these entities had already diverted the funds they had borrowed to their group companies. In many cases the money had been invested in real estate, making it harder for the authorities to recover the funds. Anjani Sinha was arrested a couple of months after the scam surfaced, and Jignesh Shah was arrested in May the following year. Between these arrests, some of the big borrowers also got to see what a prison looks from the inside. But other than a handful of small investors, most of the investors who had put their faith in NSEL are yet to recover their money, even as investigators are trying to trace the money trail leading out of NSEL.

Initially, the government appeared to show little sympathy for the NSEL investors. It knew that ignoring 13,000 investors, most of them HNIs who had lost money investing in a complex derivatives product, was unlikely to cost it politically. When the NSEL Investors Forum approached a senior bureaucrat, he publicly rebuked the members for investing in an unregulated exchange like NSEL despite being better informed than the average investor. The chiding was not entirely undeserved, but two PSUs, PEC and MMTC, too had invested in the NSEL contracts. And what about the government's own failure to keep track of the developments at NSEL? There were adequate indications that the exchange was flouting every rule in the book. The Ministry of Consumer Affairs had even shot off a show cause notice to NSEL in October 2012. But there had been no follow-up action.

I had been hearing about trouble brewing at NSEL in June itself that year. Since the positions I had in both FTIL and MCX were not my own, I had little to worry about. But having been around in the market for so long, I also knew that matters could get out of hand quickly. I approached the person who had arranged for me to play market-maker in the stock and told him about my concerns.

'You worry unnecessarily, Lala, these things can be managed without too much trouble, as they have been so far,' he told me.

I did not press the matter further.

The stock prices of both FTIL and MCX began to slide rapidly in the third week of July after the Ministry of Consumer Affairs ordered NSEL to stop issuing fresh contracts. I once again got in touch with the person who was playing the music conductor in both stocks. I knew something was amiss and wanted to get out of my positions. But I knew that would result in my falling out of favour with some influential people in the market. Also, I hated to back out of a commitment once I had agreed to it.

But I was keen to hear what he had to say.

'Yes, things look a bit tough for now, but nothing to be alarmed about. Even otherwise, you will not be losing anything from your pocket if things take a turn for the worse,' he said. I could sense an edge of irritation in his tone.

I left it at that, though my trader's instinct told me there was a disaster looming. Despite not wanting to be proved right this time, my fears turned out to be justified. On the evening of 31 July, NSEL announced it was suspending trading in all contracts, except e-series contracts, until further notice. Delivery and settlement of all pending contracts were to be merged and deferred for fifteen ays. It was an admission that the borrowers had defaulted on their obligations.

The following day, share prices of both MCX and FTIL collapsed within minutes of the market opening. FTIL, which had closed at Rs 541 the previous day, nosedived to Rs 180, giving little time for traders to react. MCX shares crashed 20 per cent to Rs 512, and trading in it was frozen because there were only sellers in the stock. There was no way the bulls could get out.

The fall in FTIL upset me greatly because I had been told just the previous evening not to square off my long positions as it would add to the panic. I am sure the other market-makers too must have been told the same thing. But the steep erosion in price meant that I had to deposit additional margins with the stock exchange. I had expected a 10–15 per cent fall in the stock, but a 65 per cent slide was beyond my most pessimistic estimate.

I knew that if I dumped the positions, it would be a while before I could hope to be reimbursed for the losses. I called up my contact to check if the previous evening's instruction still held. I was told it did, and was asked to buy some more.

'But I will need funds for the margin,' I said.

'It will be arranged in a couple of hours' time. Let me call you back,' he said.

The call never came. I squared off my positions in FTIL, not sure if I would be paid my dues in the near future. But I was still saddled with my long positions in MCX, which crashed another 20 per cent the following day, with no buyers for the stock. The exchanges then reduced the intra-day circuit filter to 10 per cent. That only slowed the pace of decline, but did nothing to calm panicky investors who continued to head for the exit. The stock fell 10 per cent three days in a row, with still no signs of buyers, though the stock had halved over the last five trading sessions and was now quoting less than Rs 300. The exchanges then reduced the intra-day circuit filter to 5 per cent.

I and a few other traders who had fairly big long positions in the stock knew it would be some time before long-term investors considered the stock. But we also knew there would no dearth of traders looking to make a quick buck off a temporary rebound in price. On the sixth day, we got together and started buying the shares as soon as they crashed to Rs 280. As big quantities began to get traded, many sellers immediately withdrew their orders thinking the stock was poised for a short-term bounce. Many traders too jumped into the fray, hoping to sell the stock at least 10 per cent higher over the next two or three sessions. The stock began to recover, but there had to be sufficient demand for the stock so we could exit our positions without attracting too much attention. We traded among ourselves to further boost volumes and, having created an appetite for the stock, managed to sell out quietly.

We incurred a small loss on this operation in addition to the losses on the positions we had been holding. Still, we'd have lost more money had we waited. MCX fell 5 per cent on each of the following three days, again with no buyers for the stock.

By the third week of August, FTIL had fallen below Rs 150, though the selling fury had abated. The market was worried that FTIL would have to foot the Rs 5,600 crore bill owed by NSEL to its investors, since NSEL was its 100 per cent subsidiary. In its bid to assuage FTIL shareholders, the management declared that it was not liable for NSEL's dues as the two companies were separate entities. This argument may have been legally sound, but sent out the signal that FTIL was trying to disown responsibility for the events at NSEL, denting the credibility of Jignesh & Co.

MCX was on a much better wicket compared with FTIL, and the panic selling in its stock may have been overdone. But the market concern was no longer about the company's earnings prospects; it was about its corporate governance standards. The poor internal controls and lax risk management procedures at NSEL raised doubts about the systems and processes at MCX too. Also, FTIL's claim that NSEL was a separate entity led investors to believe that the parent company would not think twice before cutting them loose should a similar fate befall MCX.

Eventually, Jignesh would lose ownership of both his companies, spend three and a half months in jail, and have his assets attached as the authorities went about recovering the lenders' money.

# 42

# The Long Arm of the Regulator

The year 2014 started on a promising note. The rally that began in September 2013 was showing no signs of fatigue. With each passing day, the market seemed to be getting more confident of the BJP coming to power at the Centre. The party's prime ministerial candidate Modi promised to transform the economy in no time if his party was voted to power. Weary of endemic scams and runaway inflation, everybody was willing to believe that Modi had a magic wand to set things right. The stock market bulls were bracing for what they thought would be the return of the golden period for the economy and the mother of all bull runs. I too was one among them.

Suddenly, things started going rapidly downhill for me. I received a letter from the regulator seeking clarification about the trades I had done in a bulk drugs company a few weeks before it was acquired by a mid-sized pharma company. I will come clean on this one. I had done the trades for a well-connected investment banker who was advising the acquirer. I had taken up some positions myself, in addition to the shares I had bought for the banker. I had executed the banker's trades through some fictitious client accounts and then settled in cash. There was no way he could be linked to the trades, even though they had been done based on the information he had provided. I thought I had covered my tracks well by spreading the orders across a few brokers I could trust. Later I learnt that all of them had received letters from the regulator seeking an explanation for the trades they had done in the stock. I knew at least one of them would squeal on me to escape trouble. That would put me in a spot because I had traded quite heavily in the stock just ahead of the acquisition.

Even as I was grappling with this letter, there arrived another seeking details of my trades in a mid-cap IT stock. In this case, I had dealt for a fund manager who would later buy a huge quantity for his fund. To cut a long story short, this too was an unlawful trade.

Both trades were over a year old and I had forgotten about them. But somebody at the regulator had investigated them. I could understand their smelling out the trades in the bulk drugs firm because even the media had hinted at insider trading because of the rise in share prices ahead of the deal. But the letter relating to the trades in the IT firm could only have been the result of an anonymous tip-off to the regulator. With a good lawyer I would be able to wriggle out of it. I thought about it and finally concluded that somebody powerful was targeting me. I had no clue as to who that person could be, but it had to be somebody I had unknowingly offended. I told GB about my predicament and he promised to check if my fears were justified.

He called me a couple of days later, confirming my suspicions.

'You were right, Lala,' he said, coming to the point directly. 'You are in the bad books of Mr V. Apparently he has not forgiven you for going after his stock at a time when he had pledged his shares.'

Mr V was among the top twenty-five industrialists in the country, and I had heard stories of how he could be extremely charming but also extremely vindictive if he believed he had been slighted.

'I thought he was mature enough to understand that there was nothing personal about it,' I said.

'That is how you see it. But your raid on his stock came at a vulnerable point in his business, and he has not forgiven you for it. In fact, he had sworn to force you out of the market, and is now doing everything he can to make good his threat,' GB said.

'I am not going anywhere,' I said defiantly.

'You don't have to,' GB assured me. 'Let me see what can be done about this.'

A few days later he called again. He had nothing cheerful to say.

'The way I see it, Lala, Mr V is now in a much sounder position than he was two years ago. He now has some powerful friends in the right places. You can dig in your heels, but there will be more show cause notices coming your way. What I am more worried about is that some of the charges will be hard to shake off. Your only defence would be to name the people for whom you did the trades. But that will be bad for your reputation and business even if you get away with lighter punishment.'

I thought about it. There was no easy way out.

'What do you suggest, Govindbhai?'

'Retreat for the time being if it helps sate somebody's sense of revenge. I can call in a few favours and ensure that you don't come to harm legally. When things clear, you can always return. After all, there are no permanent friends or enemies in this market,' he said.

My exit was not on the high note I would have liked it to be. Things happened a little too quickly to allow me to plan out my next course of action. The big boys of the trade and a few close friends knew my hand had been forced. But to most acquaintances I was retiring at the top of my game, to try my hand at something more challenging.

'I envy you, Lala,' many a friend would tell me, 'it takes guts to say "I have had enough of the market".'

Through a combination of discipline and good fortune, I had ensured that money would be the least of my concerns. There was enough to last me a lifetime and more, so long as I did not crave a private beach or an island in the Caribbean. But money alone was not the answer to everything, as I always knew. Here I was, in the prime of my life at 46, with no clear idea as to what to do next. Other than guessing with a fair degree of accuracy where stock prices were heading, I had no other real skill to speak of.

A few friends suggested that I manage the portfolios of HNIs. The catch here was that I would have to do that unofficially, since I had agreed to stay away from the market. But there was no denying that I was known in the market and that there were enough people who could do with my services. A few promoters and even a couple of big names of

Dalal Street sounded me out, but I was fussy about whom I would now work with or for.

'How long do you intend to enjoy your retired life?' GB asked, when I had gone over to his place for dinner at his invitation.

I immediately sensed that he must have thought of something for me.

'Let me hear out your proposal, and I shall decide,' I told him, smiling.

GB started with surprise, then chuckled.

'Always alert, whether or not in front of the screen, Lala; that is what I like about you,' he said, and told me what he had in mind. A leading industrialist wanted me to manage the share prices of his group companies and also make money from trading in other stocks. Of course, my name would not figure anywhere officially.

"He is willing to offer 25 per cent of the profits and a free hand; I think that is good. If you make outsized profits, the share can be further negotiated,' GB said.

'Tell me that you have not already committed to him,' I said.

He grinned.

'I have not committed, but I think this deal is a good way for you to stay in the market and at the same time keep a low profile. And you don't have to be bound to him forever. Should something bigger come up, you are free to pursue it. Think about it,' GB said.

The offer made sense. I needed to stay in the game till I could figure out what to do. There were plenty of offers of a 'consultancy' nature, but this was something that would help me stay agile as a trader. Trading is something I have enjoyed and wanted to do till I felt the urge to do something else.

I began my assignment the following week. The promoter was true to his word, and I had a free run in deciding my trading strategies. He never haggled when it came to sharing profits, and I managed to meet his expectations, thanks to a fairly buoyant market riding the BJP's thumping win in the general elections.

Sometime during the year, I happened to renew contact with Dipesh, a close friend of mine from my schooldays. Dipesh, or Dipya, as we used to call him, had returned from Dubai for good two years ago and was now working for a management consultancy. During our conversation, I learnt that he had been bitten by the stock market bug after having got lucky with a few investments.

'I have been regularly trading in small stocks for nearly a year now, and have made decent money,' he said.

'Good for you, Dipya, but invest the profits from trading wisely, that is the only way to grow your wealth,' I said.

'Yes, I will. But first I need to make some more money through trading. I think I am getting a good idea of how the market works. In a few months, I should be making money on a more regular basis,' he said.

'That thinking has been the undoing of many big players in the past,' I told him as diplomatically as possible, actually meaning to tell him that he should not confuse luck for skill.

'That's okay, Lala, I am not a big player and I know where to draw my limits,' he said. 'Where I need help from you is to understand a few technical things about the market. Right now, I just fire in the direction my broker suggests. Can I call you up at least once a day?' he asked.

I told him that he was free to call me up whenever he wanted to. Over the next few months, he would regularly call me up with his doubts.

'Lala, my broker tells me the company is going to announce a stock split. Should I buy the stock?' he asked on his first call.

'Ten notes of Rs 100 each and one note of Rs 1,000 are the same,' I told him.

'Company X will announce its results the day after tomorrow, and my broker tells me that the numbers will be good. Should I buy?'

'If your broker knows the results are going to be good, many others too will know. Check how much the stock has risen over the last month. If there is a decent appreciation already, it is unlikely that you will make much money. In fact, there is a high probability of you losing money as those who have got in early will start selling out.'

'Company Y is facing labour trouble and the stock is down 5 per cent. My broker tells me it will fall further. Should I sell the shares I am holding in my portfolio?'

I recalled GB telling me that the market always seemed to delight in instant judgement before it had even ascertained all the facts.

'What stock market traders forget is that businesses are built over a period of time. Like us, businesses too have difficult phases. But if the business model is good and the promoters' intentions are fair, it will overcome the problem before long. You can't write off a company for one setback, just as you can't sack an employee for a single offence,' he had once told me when an automobile stock got hammered after a new model it introduced fetched a poor response.

'Dipya, the market tends to overreact both on good news and bad news. Unless you are a trader buying and selling by the minute, it is safer to wait till the dust settles,' I told him.

'Promoter X has been regularly buying the shares of his company. My broker says this is a definite indicator that the stock is undervalued. Should I buy?'

'A promoter buying his own stock shows his confidence in the prospects for his company. But he may be taking a two-year view. Are you willing to take a similar view?' I asked him.

'Ace investor Y has bought a big stake in a company and has been saying in the press that the company will do very well. Is it a good buy?'

'If he is going around talking up the stock, it means that he has bought the entire quantity that he was looking to buy. Again, you don't know his investment horizon. There are many companies with sound fundamentals whose shares have languished for years before the market appreciated their true worth. Their stocks have risen manifold once the market has taken notice, but you would need lots of patience to make money on them.

'I have also come across quite a few instances where the purchases by a reputed investor or fund house are actually financed by the company. On paper, the ace investor may be buying the stock, but he may be getting reimbursed by the company in some way. The company benefits because the investor's endorsement will have his followers buying the stock and boost the stock price. I am not saying this happens all the time. But it does happen.'

'Stock X will be dropped from the Nifty next month. What does it mean?'

'It means the stock has lost favour with the market, Dipya. A long period of underperformance usually precedes removal from the Sensex or Nifty. But the exclusion is not always the end of the road for these companies. Fund managers who buy only stocks that are part of the major indices may ignore these fallen stars. But if the companies do well operationally, the stocks will be back in demand and even return to the indices. For every ten stocks that fade into obscurity, there is a handful that manages to make a comeback. Hero Motocorp, Dr Reddy's, Sun Pharma and SAIL are comeback stories.'

'Company X is making a preferential allotment to institutional investors at a 10 per cent premium to the market price. Is that a good sign?'

'That new investors are willing to pay a premium is a good sign. But also check how often the company keeps raising equity capital. The corollary of equity raising is equity dilution. Value investors are not happy if a company raises equity capital often, even if new investors are willing to pay a premium.'

# Epilogue

My association with the industrialist did not last long. Non-interfering at first, he slowly began to get demanding. He did not quite like it when I refused to kowtow to his wishes. When a couple of trades went rather badly, our relations soured further.

Towards the end of 2014, we parted ways as amicably as we could. My bank balance swelled some more, but I was beginning to get disillusioned with the stock market. Close friends advised me to reinvent myself as a venture capitalist and look for potential winners in start-ups. My previous experience with start-ups had been disappointing. But the landscape had changed considerably and I did not mind trying my hand at it.

I began to take a deeper interest in my farm at Murbad and I am now also working with a non-profit organization when not meeting budding entrepreneurs. I cannot help my gut feeling that the financial markets – particularly the stock market – are so disconnected from the real world. The non-profit organization I support runs a skills training centre, and counsels and provides shelter for girls and women who have suffered abuse and violence. It was a humbling experience for me when, during a talk on the importance of saving money, a girl, perhaps eighteen, told me that she had made it a point to save at least Rs 50 every week, and hoped to own a place of her own some day.

---

I dropped by GB's office one day when I was passing that way. More than nine months had passed since my last stock market trade. I found GB in a dark mood, though he was trying his best not to let it show.

We exchanged pleasantries and reminisced about the good old times. I asked him about some of the big guns of the market, remarking that they still seemed to be in good form, going by what I had read and heard about them.

I unwittingly appeared to have touched a raw nerve.

GB did not respond immediately. He seemed to think over it, then said: 'You must have heard the Gujarati saying that if a dog walks under a moving bullock cart, you may get the impression that the dog is carrying the cart on its back. But that is an illusion. It is the bullocks who are doing the heavy work.'

'I don't get it,' I said, though I had a vague idea of what he was trying to get at.

'What I meant to say is that it is the promoter and the employees who are doing all the hard work. Just because you identify a good company to invest in, it does not make you great. The so-called legendary investor or fund manager owes his fortune to the management and the hard work of the employees. Why do you all glorify the investors so much?' GB ranted.

'But that is too extreme a view, Govindbhai. Having worked with some of the best people in the industry, I am sure you know that identifying good companies is hard work. If it was all about luck there would have been many more wealthy people in the market. And your experience will tell you that those who relied solely on luck have not lasted long,' I countered.

'Maybe . . . let us talk of something else, Lala. How are your investments shaping up?'

A few days later I met up with Monk and told him about my conversation with GB.

Monk laughed.

'Maybe one of his big-ticket clients shafted him. Or maybe he is disillusioned with life in general and the market in particular. Or maybe he recently read Taleb's *Fooled by Randomness* (a book in which Taleb argues that winning in financial markets is about chance and not skill). But don't worry; knowing him, GB will soon get over this mood. Meet him a month later and you might hear him hold forth on the stock market's contribution to the economy,' Monk said.

We chatted for a while, and Monk ordered *bhel* from the same place he had at our first meeting in his office years ago.

'Almost feels like going back in time,' I told Monk.

'Thankfully, some things never change, like this *bhelwallah* and his stuff. He has put up half a dozen stalls in Bandra and Khar, but the stall across the road remains, what shall I say, his corporate headquarters,' Monk said, grinning.

I asked Monk how his business was faring.

'The fun has gone out of this business. It has become too tough for traders and brokers. But it's not so bad for investors, though,' he said. 'Too many rules and regulations, and SEBI is now quick to pounce if it suspects something.'

A few months ago, SEBI had come down heavily on a group of listed shell companies that had been created just to help tax evaders. These companies would issue shares to investors who wanted to avoid taxes. Their share prices would be artificially inflated over a period of time. The investors would then sell the shares in the market to entities fronting for the company. These transactions were just book entries. If the investor had bought a share for Rs 10 and sold it at Rs 100 a year later, he could show Rs 90 as legitimate income from the stock market and not pay any tax on it. Not that the company was giving Rs 90 to that investor; that money would be reclaimed through a chain of bogus transactions.

Using the stock market to launder money and evade taxes had become much tougher over the last few years as the government and the regulator joined hands to plug leakages. Making money from confidential information too was no longer easy. In March 2014, L&T Finance shares fell sharply, just a day before the company issued shares to institutional investors at a sizeable discount to the market price. Somebody had leaked the pricing of the share sale, and a fund house heavily short-sold the stock. In less than two months, SEBI had hauled up the offending fund house.

I am not saying that malpractices in the market have stopped altogether. While earlier there was a 20 per cent probability of getting caught for malpractices and an 80 per cent probability of getting away, the ratio has now reversed.

A few days later I met a leading market operator of the 1990s at the wedding reception of a common friend.

'Algo has been the ruin of even the best of traders, Lala,' the operator told me as we tucked in at the food table. 'We are just no match for the smart trading software. The machines are doing to us what we did to the retail investors and day traders; they (software) pre-empt our actions and even panic us into selling out. I see a price on the screen and try to buy it, but it has already move up by 5 paise; the software has snatched it from me. I have to buy at a higher price. When I try to sell the position, the blasted software again beats me to it. I have to sell at 5 paise below what I would have liked to,' he said ruefully.

I was reminded of the days when market operators could control a stock at will once they had soaked up sufficient floating stock. They would play on the psyche of the smaller players and swing prices in such a way that at least eight times out of ten, the small fry would lose out. And now, sophisticated trading software programs were giving operators a dose of their own medicine.

'I now hand some money and shares from my portfolio to some of these FIIs that excel in algo trading; they generate a 12–14 per cent return for me annually. That is a far more peaceful way of making money than competing head on with those buggers and coming out bruised,' the operator said.

As he got up to refill his plate, I said, 'But my friends in the market tell me you can still move prices at will, as you used to back then.'

He paused, then wryly said, before walking away, 'Oh, do they? I don't want to disprove them. I can get business from promoters only if people think I am skilled at swinging prices even now.'

The rules of the game had completely changed in the last seven years. Through the late 1990s and until the early years of this century, when the market was still shallow, dealers at foreign broking houses and money managers at large fund houses were kings. And so were the market operators. All these players had access to information that mattered. But as the market grew bigger, the sphere of influence of each of these players shrank more and more. Yet, the hierarchy in the stock market food chain remained pretty much the same.

The jobbers who played for a spread of a few paise would be at the mercy of the traders who could hold their positions for an hour or two. They in turn were at the mercy of the bigger traders who could carry their positions over to the following day. Above them would be the traders (or retail investors, if you may) who had the capacity to hold positions for a month. They deferred to the market operators who could carry their positions for even longer and had crucial information at their fingertips. But the operators were no match for the FIIs, and the FIIs would be outsmarted by promoters who dabbled in their own stock. Not that promoters could sit comfortably at the top of the food chain; even they were helpless against changes in policy decided by powerful bureaucrats and ministers.

I was reminded of Amitabh Bachchan's famous dialogue in the 1990 blockbuster *Agneepath:*

*Cheenti ko bistuiya kha jaata hai, bistuiya ko mendak, mendak ko saanp nigal jaata ha, nevla saanp ko maarta hai, bhediya nevle ka khoon choos leta hai, sher bhediye ko chaba jata hai, idhar har taqatwar apne se kam ko maarkar jeeta hai.* (The lizard eats the ant, the frog the lizard, the snake swallows the frog, the mongoose kills the snake, the wolf sucks the blood of the mongoose, the lion tears the wolf apart. Out here, every strong person survives by killing those weaker than himself.)

Stockbroking is hardly a lucrative business, and even the big domestic brokerages that went public at the peak of the bull market of 2007-08 earn much of their profits from their NBFC, wealth management and financial products businesses.

The other day, I was watching a big name on Dalal Street being interviewed on a business channel. When somebody in the audience asked him to recommend a multi-bagger stock, the ace investor uttered a single line that said a lot about stock investing. 'Only posterity will tell.'

The man in the audience pressed him for a recommendation, but the investor repeated his answer. Everybody thought he was being snobbish, but he was merely speaking the truth. No value investor can say for sure that a stock he is going to buy will become a multi-bagger. He can take a calculated bet based on his reading of a few parameters. But so many things have to fall in place for that stock to eventually become a multi-bagger. Even if one or two things go wrong, the stock will never realize its true value. Conversely, even the most undeserving of stocks can briefly rise to absurd valuations for reasons that have nothing to do with the company's performance.

When the BJP swept into power in May 2014 with a comfortable majority on its own, everybody thought the market was now poised for a historic bull run. But eighteen months later, the returns have only been modest. The Indian market is struggling, like most of its emerging market peers, for reasons mostly beyond its control. That should tell you how difficult it is to make money in the stock market.

I haven't heard from my friend Dipya in a while now. Maybe the market has cured him of his delusions. Or maybe my pearls of wisdom worked and he is doing so well that he no longer needs my advice.

# A Letter to the Reader

Dear Reader,

It is an overcast afternoon in Mumbai, as I sit at my desk by the window of my study penning these thoughts. The contrast with the general mood in the stock market could not have been starker. Dalal Street – as I prefer to call it – is in the grip of a euphoria not seen in over a decade.

To a casual observer of the stock market, this may seem perverse, as people continue to die, lose jobs, see their savings wiped out by medical bills as the Covid-19 pandemic rages on.

The picture that comes to mind is of a handful of people getting rich beyond imagination in the midst of a global humanitarian crisis.

But it is not as if the Indian market is the only one celebrating; equity markets the world over are shooting skywards, and there are multiple reasons driving this trend.

Interest rates are at record lows, and returns from investments in gold and real estate have been patchy, not just in India, but in most markets globally. This is prompting money managers everywhere to reroute more money into equities, away from other asset classes. And not just fund managers, even individuals dissatisfied with paltry returns on their bank fixed deposits are turning to the stock market.

Covid has destroyed many families financially, but at the same time, a good number of families have seen a sharp rise in disposable incomes. Even those who have little or no understanding of the markets are rushing in blindly, after witnessing stock prices soar and hearing stories – often partially true – about their friends or relatives having made a killing.

This has resulted in a virtuous cycle as rising stock prices attract investors, rise higher, draw more investors and so on.

Technological advances and the rise of fintech firms offering investment management services have made it easier not just to buy and sell shares, but also to get the relevant financial numbers and ratios of a company with a few clicks of the mouse. This had led to an increase in the number of what many believe to be the 'aware and educated' retail investor, mostly youngsters in their twenties.

And retail investors who want a piece of the stock market action without straining their hearts and stomachs are putting money in equity mutual funds. A majority of them are doing so through Systematic Investment Planning (SIP), wherein they invest a fixed sum every month, irrespective of market conditions.

That is why you are seeing strong inflow into mutual fund schemes even in months when the market has fared poorly.

Many are hailing this as a new dawn for retail investors in India. Judging by the steep increase in the number of demat accounts, mutual fund folios and new trading accounts at broking firms, more retail investors dabbling in the stock market than at any time in the past. For the record, there are over 7 crore demat accounts, close to 11 crore mutual fund folios and around 2.4 crore active trading accounts at broking firms, at present. Compared to the size of our population, these numbers are still modest when adjusted for duplicate and idle accounts. Many households open multiple demat accounts so that they have a better shot at allotment when applying for an initial public offering, or simply to reduce tax liability. Likewise, multiple mutual fund folios too help in lowering tax outgo.

In the US, some hedge funds that short-sold certain stocks lost a packet when a gang of individual investors stood up to them and pushed the stock prices in the opposite direction. We are still to see a similar trend in India, mainly because the market for borrowing shares and then selling them is not developed enough. Nevertheless, retail investors are a force to reckon with today.

And yet, I am sceptical of all this talk of a 'new dawn', the 'empowered retail investor', or the 'informed retail investor'. I have seen enough such 'dawns' in the past. They began and ended in pretty much the same way. When a fresh bull market gets underway, a different set of individual investors takes the place of their fallen brethren. The surge in new demat, broking and mutual fund account openings is like the sprouting of mushrooms after rain. And when the market keeps rising, as it does in a bull phase, most newcomers feel they have mastered both the art and science of investing. Unable to differentiate between skill and luck, they keep increasing the size and number of their bets, only to lose it all when the party ends. Very few make it to the next bull market.

Before the market crash of March 2020, many individual investors were beginning to lose patience. This bunch had enthusiastically invested in stocks and mutual funds in the boom following demonetization but saw much of their gains – and in some cases, even capital – getting eroded when the rally ended abruptly sometime in 2018. The hardest hit were those who had put money in mid and small stocks or equity schemes investing in such stocks.

Following the outbreak of Covid-19, when stock markets collapsed, these investors were in a state of panic. I know many mutual fund unit holders who sold out at a loss were fearful that the net asset values of their schemes could fall even lower.

Some gritted their teeth and held on, and as soon as the NAVs reached breakeven levels or showed a small gain, they beat a hasty retreat never to mention the phrase 'stock market' again. I can only imagine their heartburn today as the market has more than doubled from the lows of March 2020.

Today, all the important financial data, disclosures and analyses of companies are easily available. But being aware of such details and reeling them off the top of one's head does not make one an astute investor. In a rising market, many retail investors like to brag about how they were able to spot a winner by a cursory glance at the financials. But nobody knows what the same investor will do when the stock stays flat for some years after the bull market ends. Blue chips like HUL, Bharti Airtel, Tata Tea, to name a few, have gone nowhere for many years at a stretch, and then suddenly made up for the lost time by delivering phenomenal returns over the next two to three years. Investors who put money in ITC a decade ago and are still holding on to the stock might be wondering if they were better off putting that money in a bank fixed deposit. The stock has been an underperformer in one of the biggest bull markets despite everything about the company's financials suggesting that its fundamentals are far superior to many of the little-known companies whose stocks have gone on to become multi-baggers. That's the stock market for you.

Of course, the tide could turn for the better tomorrow, next month, next year or three years later. But nothing about the company's financial statements can tell you when the market as a whole will change its mind and come to the conclusion that an underperformer deserves a much better valuation.

No, I am not trying to scare or discourage you from investing in the market. The point I am trying to make is that unless you stick around for some years and experience at least a couple of bull and bear phases of the market, you can never evolve as an investor.

Next, the IPOs. I feel like laughing out loud when I hear fund managers and some market gurus remark that the quality of companies coming to the market this time is much better compared to the previous bull runs. Many of these fund managers had said the same thing during the bull market of 2007–08 as well. It is a given that companies looking to go public in a bull market will demand and get exorbitant valuations because most investors are just not bothered about minor things like the company's business model, the operating environment and the promoters' credentials. They just focus on how much money they can make off the stock in the shortest possible time. A handful of these companies will reward their patient investors over time, but a vast majority will turn out to be disappointments.

Now for the pump-and-dump games. Back in the nineties and even in the noughties, the stereotype of an average market operator was a gutka-chewing, wily Gujarati or Marwari working his phones from some shady office in a Mumbai suburb or in one of the well-known cities of Gujarat or Rajasthan. Hardly anybody knew them, except for a tight-knit circle of market players. They operated from behind the scenes, hand in glove with the promoters, creating artificial volumes, ramping the stock price and then offloading the shares on unsuspecting investors drawn to the action.

Many of today's small-time operators no longer prowl in the background, waiting for gullible investors to take the bait. Instead, they smugly sit on social media platforms, position themselves as market gurus through partially true or downright fake claims of spotting winners, quote legendary investors and market wisdom, and create a buzz in the stocks they already have a position in. Some others hold online workshops promising to make market experts out of novices, and since the market has regularly been making new highs, there is no dearth of people queuing up for these courses, hoping to become the next Jhunjhunwala or Buffet.

So you see, nothing has really changed in all these years, except for the cast of characters and the setting.

My book upset a few industry people I knew well enough, Govind bhai being one of them. And he made his displeasure clear.

'*Arre* Lala, I know ours isn't the cleanest of professions, but you made it look as if the stock market is full of crooks and only those with inside information can ever hope to make money. Some of my friends and relatives said they always felt investing was a rigged game, and after reading your book, they feel vindicated,' he told me when we met at a party.

I am sorry if the book somehow gives such an impression because it was not my intention to do so. I tried to tell the story of my life and career as best as I could, and that is what the book is about: my experiences in the stock market and the people I got to know and regularly dealt with. My position in the food chain gave me a ringside view of many unsavoury practices which most people were unaware of.

In all fairness, the stock market is like any other industry with its share of corrupt people and shady practices. One could perhaps argue that the shades of grey in this line are darker compared to many other industries. A veteran broker once told me: 'This is the only industry where the raw material is money, the end product is money and the by-product, if any, is also money.'

Also, like the advertisement and entertainment businesses, investing too is driven more by perception than by reality. What else can explain investors ignoring companies with actual cash flows, but being willing to pay a ridiculous price for companies not just making losses for years, but also unlikely to become profitable in the near future.

But it is a mistake to think of the stock market as a den of gamblers where the unsuspecting investor is always preyed upon. Also, it is a misconception that only those with lots of money and inside information can succeed. It is a fact that companies are partial to big investors, and those with deep pockets can take bigger bets and hence make huge profits if they call it right. But does the so-called smart money win at every trade? Certainly not; the market is a great leveller.

Sadly, terms like 'insider information', 'insider trading' and '*andar ki khabhar*' (inside information) have become synonymous with the stock market. Quite a few times, acquaintances and relatives at parties and family functions have asked me: 'Oh, so you must be getting lots of inside information?'

Once a surgeon, whom I had been introduced to at a party, asked me the same question. Usually, I would shrug it off with a laugh and a polite answer. But on that occasion, I decided to give it back in a manner that he would never ask that question of any stock market professional in the future.

'Well, that is a misconception most people entertain,' I said, smiling. 'It is almost like saying that all doctors take kickbacks from medical reps and prescribe unwanted drugs, prolong treatment unnecessarily, and that hospitals inflate bills. I know there are doctors and hospitals like that, but I am sure you will agree not every doctor and not every hospital are the same.'

From then on, any person asking me about inside information would be politely reminded of the corrupt practices in his or her line of work and be asked if that image was accurate.

For all its inequities, the market is democratic in some ways because everybody gets a fair shot at growing their wealth as long as they take the pains to learn the rules of the game. And while I may not have written about them, I know quite a few amateur investors who managed to build a decent portfolio over many years through patience and meticulousness. Similarly, I know of quite a few analysts and fund managers who resist pressures from their bosses as well as promoters and call a stock for what it is.

A few readers, and some friends as well, griped that I did not share any of my trade secrets in the book. To that, I would say that my own techniques have constantly changed over time. And I am sure that holds true for everybody in this market. Every trader or investor may have a few basic rules which he or she will adhere to at all times, but my own experience has been that such rules are designed to protect you from getting wiped out rather than help you make extraordinary profits. Of course, if you manage to survive, then, with patience, practice and luck, you could hit payday at some point.

Here are a few things I have learnt over the course of my twenty-five-odd-year career in the stock market.

The amount of risk you are willing to take will decide the level of returns you make. But you need to see this in the context of another stock market truism: only risk what you can afford to lose. A few sleepless nights are unavoidable once you decide to play the game. But too many of them, and the fun goes out of it.

Also remember, big risks do not always guarantee big returns; you can lose big too. Know what you are getting into and why you are doing so. Start small and keep scaling up your trades/investments as your understanding of the market improves.

Gracefully accept your losses. Consider it as some kind of a tuition fee that the market demands from every player. Everybody in the market makes mistakes; even the best of investors don't have a track record of 100 per cent wins, despite their knowledge of the field and the ability to write big cheques. Sometimes the business environment can change overnight, because of a tweak in regulation or new technology, sometimes things simply don't play out the way they were expected to, or the promoter may decide to enrich himself at the expense of the shareholders.

Ask yourself whether you had failed to spot some of the warnings in time, which mistakes could have been avoided and ensure that you don't repeat them.

If you are convinced that a certain stock is a good long-term investment, don't shy away from buying it even if the price moves up 20 per cent from the time you first identified the stock. It is much costlier not to have bought that stock at all. You are never going to get any stock at a price you are most comfortable with. And even if you do get that price, you are unlikely to buy the quantity you want to. It works something like this: A stock you like is quoting at Rs 150. You feel Rs 120 is a fair price for it. But when the price comes down to Rs 120, it is only natural to wonder if it could go down further.

But relax, even the biggest of investors never buy all their quantities in one go.

Have you often heard your elders remark how cheap things were in their youth or even in middle age?

'I used to buy a kilo of really tasty apples for Rs 2 when I had started working 50 years ago. Today you get mediocre apples after paying Rs 200 a kilo.'

Well, that hasn't stopped you from buying or eating apples today, has it?

Likewise, don't focus on the absolute price of a stock. Investors are more willing to buy a stock they already own, on the way down than on the way up. If a company is doing well over time, the stock price will most likely reflect that performance and climb higher. You may have bought a stock at Rs 100 and five years later it is Rs 500. But that does not mean you should not buy more of that stock just because the price has risen fivefold.

Also, most investors prefer to buy 1,000 shares of stock available for Rs 10, than a single share quoting at Rs 10,000. But just try this out: draw up a list of stocks quoting above Rs 10,000 and see how they have fared over the last ten years, or even five years for that matter. You will be surprised.

I am not telling you to blindly buy anything that is quoting above Rs 10,000. The point I am trying to make is that don't overlook a stock just because it is quoting a high absolute price.

Once in a while, listen to your gut and take what I would call a 'write-off' bet. Meaning, put in money that you are willing to write off completely if the bet backfires. Once in a while, you do get stocks at unbelievable prices on the downside. My experience is that people who ask the least questions on such occasions often end up making the most money. Unbelievable prices on the downside usually don't last long.

Half knowledge is dangerous. There is plenty of relevant financial data easily available today. But remember, this data is available to everybody and the stock price has already factored that in. Good companies will always be expensive and the not-so-good ones will be available for less. The price-to-earnings ratio is the most widely used parameter to check if a stock is expensive, cheap or reasonably valued. But these too have to be seen in the context of many factors. If you try to use the formula in isolation, you could most likely miss out on good opportunities or end up having duds in your portfolio.

Veteran stock market investors will tell you that comfort and big returns never go hand in hand. If you are comfortable investing in a stock, it means you see the stock as a sure-shot winner. And many others too would have invested in the stock based on the same assumption. When too many people bet on the same side, I have seen that things seldom go according to the script. However good your investment idea is, there will be phases of self-doubt and regret. And that is not a bad thing. It is only when your conviction is tested that you become an investor in the true sense and a few sleepless nights are necessary to set you up for the big score.

A ninety-something broker once told me a market truism which I remember to this day. 'Trees don't grow all the way to heaven and roots don't grow all the way to hell.'

Many may not agree with me on this one, but my philosophy is that there is no harm in booking profits occasionally and spending that money well. I have heard many investors say: 'I bought xxxxx shares of that company and haven't sold a single share to date. They are now worth twenty times my original investment.'

I agree. But you can't eat shares for breakfast or dinner, right? What is the good of all that paper wealth if you are not occasionally enjoying the good things you can buy with money?

One may ask: But what about investors who don't own a big quantity of shares? Someone who has just 100 shares of a blue chip would be better off holding on to that for as long as possible to make a meaningful profit. Fair point. So here is a hack. Our elders always say that while buying a house, stretch yourself a bit financially if you can somehow manage to get a few square feet more.

I would say that applies to buying quality stocks as well. If you are able to buy 100 shares comfortably, see if you can buy 120. And if you are buying 1,000 shares, try to buy 1,200. We are all obsessed with round figures. If your call is proved right and the stock gives outsized returns sooner than you had expected, you can always book profits in the extra twenty or 200 shares you had bought. That gives you money in hand and at the same time lowers your overall cost of acquisition for the stock you are left with.

And finally, don't lose heart if you did not make as much money as you would have liked to in this bull market. The important thing is to preserve capital and wait patiently for the right opportunities. Rest assured that there will be many in the years ahead.

**Lalchand**
September 2021

# Acknowledgements

I am grateful to:

Prithvi Haldea, Bharat Shah, A. Balasubramanian, Deena Mehta, Dhirendra Kumar, Sandeep Jain, Sharad Shah, Kirti Doshi, Ashish Kumar Chauhan, BSE Ltd, Ravi Narain, Om Damani, (Late) Parag Parikh, Alarkan Mapat, R. Amarnath, Suresh K. Jajoo, Bhupen C. Dalal, Arvind Dalal, Ketan V. Parekh, Kamlesh Gandhi, Sanjay Kulkarni, Sushil Kedia, Abhishek Dalmia, Venkat Ramaswamy, Joyson Thomas, Saurabh Mukherjea, Kaushik Shah, N. Krishnan, Sachin Joneja, Bharat Iyer, Nilesh Shah, Ramesh S. Damani, Kalpraj Dharamshi, Vijay Mamgain, Sunil Nair, Mukul Agarwal, Bhavin Thakkar, Motilal Oswal, Rashesh Shah and (Late) Ramesh Makhanlal Damani.